Richard Brome
CAROLINE PLAYWRIGHT

Richard Brome

CAROLINE PLAYWRIGHT

By R. J. KAUFMANN

COLUMBIA UNIVERSITY PRESS

NEW YORK AND LONDON 1961

Library of Congress Catalog Card Number: 61–7172
Printed in Great Britain

Brome deserves to be more read than he is.
T. S. ELIOT

PREFACE

In this study of Richard Brome I have tried to utilize modern historical and critical knowledge to make Brome's work as accessible to modern readers as possible. I tried, too, to add to the factual knowledge of his life records, but despite the unfailingly thoughtful assistance of various keepers and their deputies at the British Museum, the Public Records Office, and Somerset House I found little of indisputable value. I did have better luck, with the same kindly aid from the staffs, in the British Museum, in the Folger Shakespeare Library, and in the Princeton University Library when searching for explicatory materials from English history. I wish to thank all these able and friendly librarians and archivists for their help, as I do Mr. John Russell, librarian of the University of Rochester, and his staff for many last-minute assists. I am grateful to the Modern Humanities Research Association and to the editors of *Modern Language Review* for permission to use material in Chapter IX which previously appeared under their auspices. My other obligations go further back. I owe much to Professors L. A. Landa, Alan Downer, and D. W. Robertson, Jr., all of Princeton University, for advice, useful insights, and encouragement. From Professor G. E. Bentley I have received inspiring evidence that a high degree of professional rigor can be combined with human warmth and tact. I, like many others before and since, have much to thank him for. My wife, Ruth, knows how much she has helped; the book is dedicated to her.

It remains only to say that my sympathetic account of Brome's seventeenth-century conservatism does not constitute an endorsement of that political philosophy in the twentieth century.

I have used the appropriate original quarto editions of Brome's plays for quotation.

Finally, I wish to thank Miss Anita Weiner for her very telling improvements of the text.

R. J. KAUFMANN

Rochester, New York
January, 1961

CONTENTS

Richard Brome

CAROLINE PLAYWRIGHT

I

ON BEING A CAROLINE PLAYWRIGHT

When writing about Brome it is necessary to remember that he shared the age with Spenser, Shakespeare, Milton, Donne, Jonson, and Webster, and to make one's judgments and enthusiasms answerable.[1] It is equally important to remember that Brome's plays were well received by an audience that had had the lifelong good fortune of seeing the best in the theater and that Brome was more than conventionally respected by a man as exacting as Jonson.

A close study of his extant canon of fifteen comic plays is proof that he achieved a very coherent body of work, and that this work is built out of a predictable talent for transposing an internally consistent set of moral convictions into effective dramatic statement. Brome displays the prime dramatic knack for finding the fable, the actable image, the theatrical gesture which can make his conventional social attitudes the more potent for being dramatized.

What we can be sure of is that the power Brome has as an artist derives from a close and critical relationship to the particular historical and theatrical era in which he wrote. His drama is heavily topical and is shaped by an alert sense for the shifting manners and moral attitudes of a crucial period in English history—the reign of Charles I. It was during this reign that the historical pressures working away, undermining the structure of Renaissance values, became overt and dramatic. It was during this period that the institution of British kingship, as it was understood by Chaucer, Spenser, and Shakespeare, fell never to recover, and it was then that a way of metaphorical thinking disintegrated. There is a fundamental difference between the minds,

---

[1] Previous critical work on Brome has been sparse and mainly poor in quality. A complete bibliography of Brome items is listed in this book, pp. 185–86. The standard books on Brome by Allen in 1912 and Andrews in 1913 are, respectively, an outraged diatribe against the sexual improprieties of the text and a disorganized appraisal of *einfluss* and sources. Both are sketchy and pre-modern in standards.

syntax, attitudes, literary ideals, and tone of men like Sidney, Spenser, Jonson, and Shakespeare, whose work precedes the crucial Caroline era, and those of Dryden, Pope, and Swift which follow. The Caroline period, from the historical and sociological as well as from the literary point of view, is a time of maximum stress, of breakings and severings, and of futile, make-shift, inadequate or quixotic attempts to shore up the disintegrating structure. It is a time of impractical rebels, of romantic conservatives, of strong impatient men with weak solutions —the time of Laud, Strafford, Suckling, and John Ford. It is the time, too, of literary and religious bigots. Without hyperbole, it can be called the time of birth trauma for the modern world. Elaborate analogies could be constructed between the passionately intolerant formalism of Ben Jonson and the strenuous ritualism of Laud; between the humanly insensitive, emergent absolutism of Hobbes and the over-simplified, monarch-dominated world of the heroic drama.[2]

A study of Brome's plays must work from a context larger than that of theatrical convention. It must take into consideration the continual preoccupations of the people who make up his audience, the urgent problems which are echoed and reflected (however dimly and impre-cisely) in the stage comedy of the period. Social comedy can be written about most effectively from the reconstructed vantage point of a very self-conscious and uneasy society, and Brome's plays are most interest-ing and useful when studied in this way.

The corpus of Brome's plays, neatly covering the years of Charles's personal rule (1629–41), and displaying awareness of gradually altering social attitudes, can be very useful in evaluating the basic change in values which we observe as having taken place between Shakespeare and Dryden. In short, Brome's plays form an intelligible and complex commentary on a central phase of an historical evolutionary process.

The plays *as a group* form an intelligible commentary. They are in-telligible individually under a close and thoughtful scrutiny, and, since Brome was an alert professional in the theater, his plays are frequently superior examples of the accepted variations on a few central dramatic themes that made up the inspirational repertory of the Caroline Theater. There is hardly a major type of dramatic "thinking" that he

---

[2] Mildred E. Hartsock has studied the occurrence of Hobbesian ideas in Dryden's heroic plays and has suggested the moral universe of these plays is just as constricted and selfishly arid as Hobbes' opinion of human motive and capacity would indicate. See her "Dryden's Plays: A Study in Ideas," *Seventeenth Century Studies* (2d Series: Princeton, 1937), pp. 71–176.

did not focus his attention on, either directly or through ironic or parodic commentary. Brome recapitulates and concentrates in his own work the form and scope of the non-tragic drama of his period. He was a skillful professional dramatist. He understood and could manage with admirable dexterity the available stage conventions of his time. Convention required heavy and elaborate plotting. He was a skillful plotter. Convention aroused expectations of a certain amount of good-natured bawdry. His plays have a certain amount of good-natured bawdry. Mistaken identities, exchanged babies, lost sisters, deliberate and unintentional disguises abound in his plays. They were expected. However, no central piece of action in his plays depends totally for its meaning on these mechanics of stage romance or these expedients of intrigue plotting. These elements are stylized and assimilated. They are part of what he is working with, not what he is trying to achieve.

His plays, individually and altogether, reflect and embody an attitude toward, and a criticism of, the life of his time. This attitude is a complex one presented in comic modes with conventional distortions and concessions. If social comedy derives its form from the theater, it derives its subject matter and its informing vigor from life. Its *themes* are the *preoccupations* of the times; its repeated types are modifications of (or even disguised equivalents for) its representative social classes, its pressure or splinter groups. Comedy's aim is comprehension of what is going on, and a contribution to the ordering of society along stabilizing lines of good sense, charity, and justice.

Brome's point of view is conservative. This will be a key word in the analysis. He is genuinely and deeply concerned to preserve the values of the older "Tudor culture" which is being subverted before his eyes. I have more or less coined the term "Tudor culture" to stand for that modified medieval outlook that, despite personal specializations, is equally characteristic of Jonson, Spenser, Sidney, and Shakespeare. Tudor culture erected a set of intelligible values. It saw the English nation, not a unified catholic Christendom, as the basis of political order. It was Christian with a humanistic buttressing; it was aristocratic in its belief in status, nobility, generosity, and *noblesse oblige*; it believed in learning and it believed in the gentleman. It had a distinct belief in and concern for human dignity. Its primary orientation was ethical, not theological—political, not religious.[3] The exacter

---

[3] This definition of Tudor culture is grounded in the reading of several years. Although the literature on the Renaissance in general is enormous, there is less than one would think that

judgments of this Tudor culture will emerge in the detailed consideration of the plays. It is enough to say that Brome nearly unreflectingly adhered to this traditional set of values.

A brief look at the larger historical situation may make the framing terms of the study clearer. Students of English Renaissance literature have been living unperturbed in the midst of a revolution. True, the revolution has been a gradual one—sporadic in its effects and frequently unguided in its aims, but it has been going on nonetheless. Opinions about the nature and the temporal span of the Renaissance have been slowly revised all round them, so that older assumptions are no longer tenable, without more than an occasional voice being raised by scholars of the period in England.

The Burckhardtian view of the Renaissance as a sudden efflorescence of individualism, self-consciousness, and emancipated intellectual vigor in sharp contrast to an authoritarian, intellectually sterile and ingrown, self-repetitive medieval culture, is no longer anywhere uncritically adhered to by the well informed. But that is not to say that Burckhardt's brilliantly interesting generalizations about fifteenth-century northern Italian city-state culture had not for a long time been badly overextended to apply to the rest of Europe, albeit with some modifications to allow for temporal lag in the dissemination of the "new view" of things. There is still much confusion about what constitutes "novelty" in the sixteenth and seventeenth centuries, and who is a conservative in that decisive period, and just what it is he is trying to conserve.

deals at all comprehensively or on the conceptual level with sixteenth-century England. Douglas Bush's little book, *The Renaissance and English Humanism* (Toronto, 1939), still remains the best thing available. Bush describes what I call "Tudor culture" as the "Renaissance synthesis." He says, "The broad aim of Tudor Humanism was training in virtue and good letters; the practical aim was training for the active Christian life, especially public life. For humanism was not only religious, it was both aristocratic and utilitarian . . . the writings of English humanists are chiefly on public affairs, education, and religion" (pp. 78–79). The indispensable book for beginning a study of the gradual transition from medieval modes to modern ones in the sixteenth and seventeenth centuries in England is W. K. Ferguson's, *The Renaissance in Historical Thought* (New York, 1948), especially pp. 290–385. His book is itself an extensive critical bibliography. From the growing literature on this problem, the works of Herschel Baker may be recommended: *The Dignity of Man* (Cambridge, Massachusetts, 1949), and *The Wars of Truth: Studies in the Decay of Christian Humanism in the Earlier 17th Century* (New York, 1952). Samuel L. Bethell's *The Cultural Revolution of the Seventeenth Century* (London, 1951), though brief and rather theological, is stimulating. Other available material tends to over-concentrate on the most obvious and manageable aspect of the problem, i.e., the direct effect of the "new science." Cf., for instance, Marjorie H. Nicolson, *The Breaking of the Circle* (Evanston, 1950), and Victor L. Harris, *All Coherence Gone* (Chicago, 1949). Roland H. Bainton's "Changing Ideas and Ideals in the 16th Century," *Journal of Modern History*, VIII (1936), 417–43, is wide-ranging and bibliographically full; Patrick Cruttwell in *The Shakespearean Moment* (London, 1954), writes suggestively of the concrete changes in poetry and attitude as the seventeenth century wears on.

Two leading patterns may be discerned although they are not usually collocated. The clear lines between the Middle Ages and the Renaissance have given way to shadings, have been moved about in time, or have been obliterated. Scholars have found elements of rebirth in Medieval culture and, at the same time, discovered Renaissance humanists and statesmen more conservative and traditional in their thought and aims than scholarly legend had claimed. There has even been a school which would annex the Renaissance to the Middle Ages as merely the last phase of the distintegrating "medieval synthesis." The opinions and techniques of proof are many and variously convincing. One fact is clear: The sixteenth century in northern Europe *and particularly in England* was much more clearly indebted to a continuous intellectual tradition than was once thought. The primary fact to be adduced from the pattern of reexamined history is that the shift from the medieval to the modern world was a gradual one.

Where two clear problems existed before, now there is perhaps only one. Whereas we once thought of a sharp wrench in the fifteenth and sixteenth centuries which delivered the Renaissance and a second one in the seventeenth century that produced the scientific revolution, it is now possible to think that the earlier gradual shifts and revisions were merely the ground swell preceding a genuine quake in the seventeenth century. The second major fact, then, is that the real watershed in modern history came *later* than it has been customary to believe. G. N. Clark opens his great book, *The Seventeenth Century*, with these words:

Somewhere about the middle of the seventeenth century European life was so completely transformed in many of its aspects that we commonly think of this as one of the great watersheds of modern history, comparable with the Renaissance or the Reformation or the French Revolution. For this transition, indeed, we have no single name that we can write with capital letters, but we recognize a change of atmosphere between the earlier part of the century and the later, a change accompanied by storms. The Puritan Revolution and the Civil War made the sharpest break there has ever been in the continuity of English History.[4]

It is perhaps good to reflect on these things when dealing with the drama, which finds it subject matter in human actions, its judgments in human prejudice and custom, and is special in its constitution of human beings confronting other human beings within the conventions

---

[4] *The Seventeenth Century* (Oxford, 1947), p. ix.

of art. There are innumerable ways in which this comprehensive generalization can be illustrated on the level of dramatizable material.

With the exception of London, no English community reached city size until the seventeenth century. London was relatively small until then. Furthermore, the whole conception of what a city was began to change meaning in the late sixteenth and seventeenth centuries in England and a great deal of the so-called realistic comedy of the earlier seventeenth century was born and developed in an attempt to achieve (by a process of artistic induction) an understanding of this new urban life—to establish new hierarchies of social status or stubbornly to defend old ones. The lateness of urban growth in England may well be kept in mind when pondering the assertion of a great English medieval historian speaking of an earlier era:

The majority of human beings at the Renaissance were not humanists, nor courtiers, but whether of noble or of lowly birth, still the simple children of a *patria*, like the good and lawful jurymen of a medieval assize roll, the townsmen or the members of a tithing: men and women who grew up in backgrounds of local custom and tradition, the sons and daughters of their parish Churches, which gathered up the social as well as the religious life of their districts, and were the spiritual units of the country.[5]

Professor Jacobs is speaking of the fifteenth century, but it is interesting to note that his statement is equally applicable to England through the sixteenth century and that it is only in seventeenth-century London that the common man can no longer be assumed to be of the sort described. A number of skirmishes between the court and the officials of the Municipality in London are best understood in terms of the inability of Londoners to grasp that their community was no longer a medieval town, but the capital of their nation-state and a world city. There was a great deal of civic pride, to be sure, but the growing pains are everywhere apparent and they are the kind of pains produced by the crushing of old, comfortable assumptions.

Comedy was greatly concerned with these problems though not on an abstract, analytical level. For example, in the seventeenth century the new pattern of monopolies became fixed enough to invite attack from writers of comedy. The medieval monopoly had been a town monopoly—protective, economically controlled, and made socially serviceable by traditional techniques in the guilds and customary laws of quality. In seventeenth-century England the monopolies more and more became trade monopolies on a national scale. And, these monopolies were begged, bought, or awarded from the court to courtiers or men represented at court. It was of advantage to be at the national capital or to be able to achieve social acceptability there. Brome's play, *The Court Beggar*, deals directly with monopoly beggars, as does the Duke of Newcastle's *The Country Captaine.*[6] Lipson, the famous economic historian, gives generalized forms to the problem Brome recognized. He says, "Public opinion [in 1624], still powerfully influenced by the corporate character of medieval society, sharply distinguished between the exclusive privileges bestowed on individuals and those conferred on companies."[7] Brome's attitude like that of his contemporaries, was conservative toward monopolies—an attitude which fits in well with his entire economic and social philosophy. Justice Coke summed up well the kind of conduct Brome was to attack satirically when he said in 1607, at the Norwich Assizes, that the monopolist buys patents "to annoy and hinder the whole public weal for his own private benefit." [8] A study of Brome's works shows him again and again opposing the man who is for himself only.

This single example, then, of the special complications which resulted as London became a great capital, indicates one of the many ways that change may be studied at the concrete level of dramatic representation. It also introduces us to one of the ways that the plays may be utilized as evidence for this transition. There has been a great deal of work on this complex question since modern literary scholarship has set itself the problem of surveying the road between the worlds of Jonson and Congreve. Throwing aside the facile explanation that French intervention derailed the native tradition while the court nobility was in enforced exile in France during the Interregnum, scholars have found that there is an evolutionary history from the critical humors comedy of Jonson and the satiric city comedy of Middleton to the manners comedy of Congreve and the censorious social comedy of Wycherley. In various ways many have contributed to this reconstruction project. Hotson and Harbage have repaired the bridge

---

[6] Cf. further Willian H. Price, *The English Patents of Monopoly* (Boston, 1906); Lewis Mumford, *The Culture of Cities* (London, 1946); and Ephraim Lipson, *The Economic History of England* (5th ed., London, 1948), III, 352–86.

[7] *Economic History of England*, III, 361.

[8] *Ibid.*, p. 357.

across the gulf of theatrical inactivity from 1642–60.[9] Palmer, Dobrée, Lynch, and Leech have followed the journeys of conventions, modes, and devices along the route.[10] No serious scholar any longer questions the fact that there is a line of descent from Jonson through Brome to Shadwell, or that Beaumont and Fletcher passed through the imperfect and distorting medium of the cavalier dramas of Thomas Killigrew and William Davenant on their way to the dubious eminence of the Restoration heroic stage. Etherege knew the plays of Shirley well, and Shirley recapitulated the themes and characterizations of the Elizabethan stage. These things we know.[11]

There is still a great deal of work to be done on the arrangement and evaluation of this complicated pattern of indebtedness, influence, pillaging, adaptation, and rewriting. The evidence is uneven, fragmentary, and natively biased when present—frequently absent when most necessary for the exact critical evaluation. This is the literary descent.

The job, perhaps, more permanently meaningful for an understanding of the history and literature of this period has hardly been touched. Once we have determined to our satisfaction that the literary tradition is continuous, we turn again to the harder problem. If these plays grew out of one another, they are not finally at all the same, or even very similar. The same conventions were employed in gradually adapted form to meet gradually changing specifications. Criticism first needed to log the sequential occurrence of usages. Thus we have produced studies of recurrent themes; we have established repetitive patterns of character groupings; we have observed and recorded favorite fables altered and rewritten again and again. We have, in short, established in outline the complex genealogy of this prolific and inbred family. We have yet to write its history.

To simplify the complicated task of tracing out single lines, we have

---

[9] John Leslie Hotson, *The Commonwealth and Restoration Stage* (Cambridge, Massachusetts, 1928); Alfred Harbage, *Cavalier Drama* (New York, 1936); *Sir William Davenant; Poet Venturer, 1606–1668* (Philadelphia, 1935), and "Elizabethan-Restoration Palimpsest," *Modern Language Review*, XXXV (1940), 287–319. See also Hyder E. Rollins, "A Contribution to the History of the English Commonwealth Drama," *Studies in Philology*, XVIII (1921), 267–333.

[10] John Palmer, *The Comedy of Manners* (London, 1913); Bonamy Dobrée, *Restoration Comedy* (Oxford, 1924), pp. 9–57; Kathleen M. Lynch, *The Social Mode of Restoration Comedy* (New York, 1926), pp. 1–136; and Clifford Leech, *Shakespeare's Tragedies and Other Studies in Seventeenth Century Drama* (London, 1950), pp. 159–203.

[11] Robert S. Forsythe, *Shirley's Plays in Their Relation to Elizabethan Drama* (New York, 1914).

done a thing sensible and legitimate in scientific enquiry; we have assumed the *identicality* of *similar* phenomena. This is a useful initial fiction. It expedites, nay, perhaps even makes possible, the assembling of desired data, but it is not the truth. Just because social climbers (or would-be wits) appear in both Jonson and Congreve, and just because the expedients devised to present them dramatically are clearly related in a generic way, does not at all mean that they are held up to the audience in the same way, that the audience sees them in the same way, or judges them by the same criteria. If we find lecherous old men or opportunistic and profligate young men as *type* characters throughout the period, we cannot argue that our job is finished when we have catalogued them and brought in a statistical report on frequency and locality of occurrence. These *type* characters we will find are presented with differing shadings of sympathy; their conflicts are created from different causes. There are, perhaps, historically meaningful gradations in their presentation.

To study them, and comedy generally, with proper circumspection it is wise to remember David Hume's argument that moral judgments are stretched out between the poles of approbation and disapprobation. What one approves is good; what one disapproves is bad. A citation of this extreme of moral relativism is relevant here on two counts. First, comedy is inevitably involved with some kind of arrangement of good and bad characters. This does not imply that *all* comedy is overtly moralistic, or that direct commentary on specific forms of conduct with a reformatory or approving bias is necessary or even desirable. It does mean that underlying comedy, and more or less readily discernible, there is a patterning of good and bad; there is an appeal to some set of criteria that must be understood or the drive and discretion of the humor goes limp and wanders aimlessly. Some comedy, it is clear, appeals to absolutes of moral conduct. For this comedy some forms of conduct are intrinsically foolish or vicious; they are to be understood as an abdication of reason, decency, charity, dignity, common sense, or even human nature. No one will deny that the comedy of Jonson is mainly, if not entirely, of this sort. There is always a primary orientation toward certain humanistic values—the notions of measure and balance; toward a minimum unselfishness, toward at least a partial emancipation from self-love. Brome mainly follows Jonson in his intentions and techniques, but, at the same time, the later comedy to which Brome secondarily contributes is concerned largely with manners and the excluding judgments of a small, privileged group whose approvals and disapprovals enjoy status equivalent to moral law in Jonsonian comedy. To be studied thoughtfully Brome must be placed against this evolving pattern of thought and convention both theatrical and social, for in comedy, social customs—their observance and infringement—are the center of the playwright's intention. We think of comedy as much more locally limited than tragedy, as much less involved with the big generalities of life. We think of it as concrete and particular, as geared to habits and customs. In a large measure this is true, but a misleading inference may easily be drawn from this. Insofar as comedy attempts a criticism of the social life of a community, the writer of that comedy is committed to *an abstracting process*. He must continually engage in submerged generalities about the proper role of various groups and cliques who make up the complex configuration of a society. In an altogether stable society, these generalizations are made for him; they are the received values of the community. There is some unanimity as to what is approved and what reprehended. Still, those generalizations are implicitly and extensively present in any comedy that rises above farcical horseplay. A society in flux, as seventeenth-century English society was in flux, poses a more difficult problem to its comic playwrights. New types are emerging, old types are being destroyed, most social types are being revised and modified as the society seeks a new equilibrium. In such a society it is to be expected that playwrights will form new splinter groups as their diagnoses and allegiances vary. It is to be expected, too, that they will subject the same (or to the unsympathetic eye of a modern observer they appear the same) types to repeated reexaminations. This is not an apology for repetitiousness in the Caroline drama, but rather a serious attempt to understand why a people returned regularly to the theater to see, again and again, what to us seems the same play with minor modifications.

Playwrights of the seventeenth century abstracted from their shifting milieu a repertory of standard types and scrutinized them in a number of slightly different situations. These types were not in any sense marginal eccentrics, though they might be graced with little excesses and idiosyncracies to give them stage personality. They were representatives of many hundreds of others who shared their leading beliefs, practices, obsessions, and sympathies. For example, parental authority was being questioned as new mercantile wealth created new opportunity and made it less attractive and necessary for a son to relive his father's life. With the middle class no longer uniformly committed to one set of religious practices, violent conflicts were uncovered. A middle-class son could go up or down in the social scale depending on his choices. He could exhaust his patrimony in London and end up *declassé* or he could elevate himself to the nobility by diligence or craft.[12] A whole book could be written about this subject, but here it suffices to say that the endless jokes about enforced marriages, the constant preoccupation of the playwrights with the problem of filial obedience, the cruel, stereotyped satire of the old man as father, the predictable freighting of a realistic comedy plot with specific discussion of jointures, marriage settlements, and inheritances is not padding nor does it represent a pitiable failure on the part of decadent and derivative playwrights to find new subject matter.

That the hero of innumerable comedies should acquire the audience's approbation for nothing more heroic than his ingeniously scurrilous treatment of a senile father requires for its understanding a minor sort of historical imagination. No uncritical approval of the outcome of the economic and social revolution of the seventeenth century is implied when one says that by these brash, high-schoolish, and often cruel intrigues the sons were throwing off in the only ways they knew what they considered the dead hand of the past. A telling contribution to an understanding of this very social revolution could be made by a study of the progressive irreverence of son for father through the literature of the period.

This leads us to a general point most important for understanding the role of the comic playwright. Insofar as comedy requires the power to abstract the leading forces in current social relations and to embody them in characters who will express these forces, comedy is an exercise of intellectual power. The great comic playwrights have been men of acute and powerful intellect and they have generally been rationalists— they have appealed to reason to moderate attachments to goods, fads, outmoded attitudes, and provincial prejudices. Aristophanes, Jonson, Molière, and Shaw all are drier, more abstract, less poetic, less romantic than their contemporaries. They have had the ability to abstract

---

[12] Reading books like David Mathew's *The Structure of Caroline England* (Oxford, 1948), and *The Age of Charles I* (London, 1951); and Lionel C. Knights' *Drama and Society in the Age of Jonson* (London, 1937), confirms by extensive and detailed documentation from the records those impressions of shifting realignments of class, of expanding opportunity, and dissolving loyalties, that an intelligent reading of the plays will give one.

themselves from their milieu while still caring a great deal about its problems and its controversies. It is not too much to say that they have been able to achieve a sufficient altitude to survey the large block outlines of the social patterns beneath them so as not to be misled by minor variations and all the protective coloring and verbal camouflage by which men conceal their genuine motivations and intentions from each other.

There are many theories of the comic, none of which is wholly satisfactory.[13] In critical comedy much of the best and most lasting laughter derives from the sudden access of insight into *real* as opposed to *putative* motive, into genuine desire as opposed to the conventional accepted rationalization of desire. It is a laughter of gratification and admiration. It is the pleasure of seeing clearly, in simple block outline, relationships generally obscured by the very multiplicity of shifting elements. Comedy relieves this confusion by abstracting the essential, since it does not have to witness the large and complex at too close quarters. This hypothesis about comic theory might be described by the short title "kaleidioscopic." It brings the pieces into focus and makes a pattern out of the present elements not discernible to normal vision. Even minor artists achieve this synthesis now and then.

The following primary factors are relevant to an accurate and sympathetic appraisal of the realistic comedy of Richard Brome and, by extension, of the comedy of his contemporaries: (1) that an audience brought up on the drama of Shakespeare, Webster, Jonson, Middleton, Tourneur, and Fletcher was not suddenly deprived altogether of its canons of taste; and (2) that the playwrights of the period, insofar as they were practicing professionals, sought seriously to construct plays to interest and entertain the audience.

Disruptive elements in the national life, making class lines and individual status less clear-cut, tended to break down audiences into more splinter groups and factions than Shakespeare had had to face. This undoubtedly had numerous and different effects on dramatic practice: (1) it tended to increase the importance of women in the audience; (2) it made direct appeals to class allegiances a more negotiable dramatic coin; (3) it stimulated the rise of a set of snobberies in the drama—the plays of courtly affectation, of platonic love, of honor, and exploit; (4)

[13] David H. Monro's book, *Argument of Laughter* (Melbourne, 1951), surveys critically the theories of laughter and the comic from Hobbes to Freud and Bergson. The range of opinion, the critical ingenuity, and the special pleading involved in these attempts can conveniently be traced there.

it tempted many playwrights to seek a universal solvent[14] for these internal antagonisms in his audience by separating his action from those elements most likely to divide that audience (a choice which put an unnaturally high premium on remote settings, plot as an interesting construction, and intrigue as an engaging intellectual problem to be observed for itself); and (5) it invited the playwright to examine the relationships between these very factions in his audience. He could thereby engage special interests without being forced to write what has been described as "complex hybrid plays,"[15] but which I find better described by the term "the portmanteau" or public collation drama, the kind of drama written by Thomas Killigrew or Lodovick Carlell which carries along several plots organically related neither in action, tone, nor character for the apparent purpose of providing something for everyone.[16] By studying the relationships of various social groups critically, the skilled playwright could achieve the range and variety of this kind of comprehensive drama without falling into their lax and mechanical methods.

Looking on towards Brome's own realistic comedies, we are perhaps in a position to see them more clearly in the light of the playwright's intention and the audience's expectation. Brome wrote the best straight realistic comedies of his period and only Middleton and Jonson *consistently* wrote better ones in the whole of Elizabethan drama.[17] He placed these comedies in London, wrote them largely in prose with a consistent attempt to approximate colloquial rhythm and vocabulary; and he, as did almost all of his contemporaries, used the *type* character formula without embarrassment. The plays are closely geared to the happenings of the time and at times, in their rich interlarding of topical references, seem almost to be performing the function of modern newspaper editorials. They are usually firmly located in their London setting. This increasing interest in the detailed portrayal of the physical

---

[14] Bawdry is the *nostrum* most playwrights would prescribe for an audience with divisive tendencies, though even this was increasingly denied by the influence of women.

[15] W. H. Hickerson, The Significance of James Shirley's Realistic Plays. Unpublished University of Michigan thesis: Ann Arbor, 1932.

[16] Cf., for instance, Killigrew's *The Prisoner*, a truly terrible play, structurally as primitive as anything in the early Tudor period.

[17] Shirley's best comedies, *A Witty Fair One*, *Hyde Park*, and *The Lady of Pleasure*, are superior to Brome's but they approach much more nearly to the comedy of manners. Massinger twice exceeded anything Brome achieved in his *The City Madam* and *A New Way to Pay Old Debts*. In my opinion no comedy by Fletcher matches Brome in genuine comic instinct and perception of what he was trying to achieve in comedy. It is interesting that his best realistic comedy (except *The Wild Goose Chase*), *Monsieur Thomas*, was edited for publication by Brome in 1639 and obviously had some influence upon him.

surroundings of their own London has been explored.[18] The critics treating this have, however, not correlated this interest with the over-all tendency towards self-examination inherent in the trends of Caroline realistic comedy. The movement toward a critical comedy of manners is documented by place-realism as well as by the other tendencies converging on social self-appraisal in these comedies. In a sense, place-realism is a false move towards this manners comedy; at least it is a move of uncertain efficiency.

Nothing seems clearer than this: a successful comedy of manners must await the establishment of a norm of social conduct which will be implicitly agreed upon by author and audience. It is sophisticated in the sense that all parties are "in the know" and consequently do not need to be informed as to how they should respond. If *faux pas* must be documented and explained then manners comedy loses it focus. Caroline England, and more particularly Caroline London, had not yet achieved this implicit agreement. The question of social ascendency had not been firmly established. It was to take a Civil War and a Restoration to accomplish this. The courtiers were at the top of the social scale, but they were not viewed sympathetically enough to make their manners seem to many anything but affected mannerisms. With this in mind, let us interpolate a fairly standard definition of the comedy of manners.

Any comedy of manners contains certain generally accepted elements. There must be, first of all, a clear distinction between social groups, based upon a recognition of one group who are representative of fashionable life and another group who are pretenders. These groups, to be capable of dramatic presentation, must be related by an intrigue. The action of the intrigue must take place in the midst of the fashionable life of a contemporary society definitely localized and intimately portrayed. The characters must possess a set of social attitudes which motivate their conduct and which give rise to artificial comedy either of wit or situation. The atmosphere must be more or less satirical.[19]

The central informing element of a successful manners comedy was just the thing that the Caroline playwright could not count upon. He

---

[18] Cf. Theodore Miles, "Place-Realism in a Group of Caroline Plays," *Review of English Studies*, XVIII (1942), 428–40; and Richard H. Perkinson, "Topographical Comedy in the Seventeenth Century," *English Literary History*, III (1936), 270–90. (Miles's article is far superior to that of Perkinson's studies of contemporaneous plays.) See also Marmion's *Holland's Leaguer* (1631); Shirley's *Hyde Park* (1632); Brome's *Covent-Garden Weeded* (1632?); Nabbes' *Covent Garden* (1632) and *Tottenham Court* (1633); and Brome's *Sparagus Garden* (1635).

[19] W. H. Hickerson, The Significance of James Shirley's Realistic Plays, p. 22.

could not count upon the uncontested "recognition of one group who are the representatives of fashionable life." The other terms of the formula could be met in various ways. Place-realism first of all fulfilled one requirement by narrowing the scope of the setting. The "action of the intrigue" could be "definitely localized and intimately portrayed." Besides, if there was no single normative fashion there were fashions. There were places where fashionable pursuits could be observed, so that the playwright could in effect find the same relationship of initiates and outsiders that manners comedy requires. Furthermore, by contracting "a set of social attitudes" to a few, or a single attitude toward a particular place or toward a particular kind of conduct, he could gain a temporary audience cohesion. Since any single social group lacked power to legislate its own version of manners, there were several alternatives open to the playwright: He could have identifiable groups criticize each others' manners; he could pretend, as the Cavalier dramatist repeatedly did, that there was no contest by refusing to recognize the existence of other classes; or he could condemn certain forms of excessive conduct that all could agree offered no solution. We shall see that a play like Brome's *Covent-Garden Weeded* organizes itself around a set of alternatives very much like these.

Brome's realistic comedies provide elaborate intrigue plots both for entertainment and to relate the social groups, so that they are "capable of dramatic presentation." He never achieved real comedy of manners, but he made numerous contributions toward that form in his frequently thoughtful critiques of pretense, social climbing, and coterie affectation.[20] It is arguable, for example, that satirization of the "roaring boy" clubs with their specialized codes and initiations is the lower-class parallel to satiric criticism of the equally unfruitful court coterie attempts to construct a set of manners on too narrow and exclusive a basis. It is necessary to observe that one reason for the limited achievement of Caroline comedy is that, by placing undue emphasis on the physical aspects of manners and fashions, the playwrights did not so much solve the problem of achieving a clear comic formula as thereby avoid the harder job of building a comedy comprehensive enough to explore the whole society. The plays, in attaching themselves to over-

---

[20] Kathleen M. Lynch, in *The Social Mode of Restoration Comedy* (New York, 1926), pp. 28–34, confines her discussion of Brome to this aspect of her work. Her treatment could be much expanded. Underlying all of Brome's work is the assumption that one has a *place* in society, and therefore any form of trying to rise above the received manners of one's group, place, or class is foolish and laughable.

specified settings, devote too much of their space to descriptive exercises, to exploring evanescent outcroppings of eccentricity, and to minor reformatory suggestions. One of the most interesting things about Caroline comedy is that these fads (like the place-realism one) with their misplaced emphasis were rapidly rejected. They are still in the descriptive phase of their science, but they are learning fast. The professional playwrights, despite other shortcomings, had a very well-developed, inherited sense of structure, and any fad which gained enough independent momentum to overweigh or distort the shape of plays was pruned or rejected or more generally even subsumed and assimilated in the pattern of a realistic comedy.

When we place Brome in this Caroline comic tradition we see what a combination of consistency of opinion and variety of refracting techniques he commands, just such a combination as we might expect from a highly successful man of the theater who had patterned himself intelligently after his master Jonson. Of his fifteen extant plays, all but four will be considered here. The four plays seem either to add nothing to materials better handled in other plays or to be, as it were, artistically self-evident. Two of them, *The Northern Lasse* (1629) and *The Queenes Exchange* (1629–30) are weak and immature; *The Novella* 1632) is skillful but only that; *A Mad Couple Well Match'd* (1639) is a mature, highly skilled proto-Restoration comedy which, besides witty extensions of routine Caroline obscenities, adds nothing to one's knowledge of what Brome could and did accomplish.

Brome doggedly retained a clear-headed, consistent conservatism which he employed (at times imaginatively and always competently) as an intellectual basis for selecting, organizing, and dramatically rendering his primary social protests against an emergent set of attitudes which we now recognize as the basis for the modern world. The conventions of comedy and the overworked *type* characters in the Caroline period represent in disguised, modified, and frequently almost unrecognizable forms the basic sociological, moral, and occasionally even semantic preoccupations of a time.

II

BIOGRAPHICAL ANATOMY

Three main factors distinguish Brome initially from his fellow dramatists. He was in actual fact, not by artistic persuasion, a servant protégé of Ben Jonson. He worked alone as a dramatist, with one surviving exception,[1] so there is not the confusing problem of attributions and relative contribution that must preoccupy critics of such writers as Massinger and Fletcher. Brome devoted his energies solely to comedy of the several sorts acceptable in the Caroline period. His non-dramatic work is negligible[2] and he had the taste, wit, or modesty not to essay tragedy. Because of this practice of independent authorship and because of his self-limitation to comedy, there is a helpful solidity and cohesiveness to his work. He left fifteen plays of his sole authorship and his extant work all falls within the reign of Charles I. These factors are not especially distinctive but they are nonetheless useful. There is enough to generalize about and all within the convenient (if arbitrary) measurable limits accepted by scholars in the period. In fact, the formula "Caroline period" in the English drama is in many ways less arbitrary than other designations. The interest of Charles, and more

[1] The one extant collaborative effort is *The Late Lancashire Witches* with Thomas Heywood (Stationers' Register, October 28, 1634). This collaboration has been effectively discussed by Arthur M. Clark in *Thomas Heywood: Playwright and Miscellanist* (Oxford, 1931), pp. 120–27, and by Gerald E. Bentley, *The Jacobean and Caroline Stage* (Oxford, 1941–56), I, 40–42. The latter work will hereafter be referred to as *J. and C.* Brome evidently collaborated with Heywood on at least one other occasion: A lost play *The Life and Death of Sir Martin Skink* by Brome and Heywood was entered in the Stationers' Register, April 8, 1654. Nothing is known of this play. Brome may have collaborated on a play called *Christianetta*, or *Marriage and Hanging Goe by Destiny*. The Stationers' Register entry for August 4, 1640 assigns it to Brome alone, but in Abraham Hill's seventeenth-century list of plays it was assigned to "Chapman & Brome." Cf. Joseph Q. Adams, "Hill's List of Early Plays in Manuscript," *Library*, XX (4th Series: 1939), 73 and 81.

[2] Even when necessity forced him, after the closing of the theaters, to do hack non-dramatic work he evidently felt constrained to insist that he was out of his chosen element. In his poem on the death of Henry Lord Hastings in 1645 he comments that the writing of elegies is not proper work for his muse. "For, by thy dictates, I/Never spilt Ink, except in Comedie;/Which in the thronged Theatres did appear/ All Mirth and Laughter" *Lachrymae Musarum*, London, 1649.

particularly of Henrietta Maria, in the stage had a great influence on the tone, quality, and subject matter of the drama.[3] The enthusiastic and interested (while artistically narrow and demanding) attitude of the court succeeded in influencing not merely the spectacles and plays designed for the courtier group, but also effected a sharper alignment of dramatic intention elsewhere. This court influence, partly as a cause and partly as a symptom and result of the times, pushed the playwrights into unintentional propagandizing programs by making them self-conscious members of court factions, or self-conscious opponents of its influence. Brome's work, like Shirley's and Ford's, was effectively confined to the Caroline period and it reflects, throughout, his resistance to courtier encroachment on the drama.

We cannot begin to reconstruct Brome's life with an account of his ancestry or a description of his family's or his own early environment. Brome must be a figure without a particularized and personal background. Even his birthdate is not positively known, though the traditional date of *c.* 1590 has perhaps been slightly strengthened by research.[4]

There are no sure records. The same awkwardness arises about schooling. Cibber's confident assertion that Brome went to Eton has never been confirmed.[5] It is certain that, if modern records may be trusted, he did not attend either of the Universities. It does not seem to me particularly fruitful to speculate on the extent of his learning or how he came by it in the absence of any facts whatever. That he could read and write is obvious; that he knew some Latin and a smattering of French and German may be discovered by reading his plays.[6] That he had no academic distinction in a learned age is equally apparent. Common sense would surmise that he had some primary grammar school training.[7] He does not write as a bookish poet: "his proper province was

---

[3] For arguments and evidence on this special formative influence from the Court, see Alfred Harbage, *Cavalier Drama* (New York, 1936), pp. 7–45; Kathleen M. Lynch, *The Social Mode of Restoration Comedy* (New York, 1926), pp. 43–106; *The Dramatic Records of Sir Henry Herbert*, ed. by Joseph Q. Adams (New Haven, 1917), *passim*; and L. Wallis, *Fletcher, Beaumont and Company* (NewYork, 1947), pp. 3–44.

[4] See Appendix, p. 175.

[5] According to Andrews *Richard Brome*, p. 4: "Colley Cibber, in his *List of Dramatic Authors*, boldly asserts that Brome 'had his education at Eton'."

[6] In Brome's *The City Wit*, Sarpego, the pedant, uses Latin freely. So does the curate in *The Queen and Concubine*. There is a sprinkling of French phrases in *The New Academy* and *The Sparagus Garden*. In *The Novella* there are some fragments of Dutch.

[7] Perhaps Frederick S. Boas goes too far when he dismisses the whole problem curtly: "Whatever the exact nature of his service [i.e., with Jonson] may have been, Brome was of good education" (*An Introduction to Stuart Drama* [Oxford, 1946], p. 378).

observation more than reading . . . his characters which for the most part are strongly marked, were the offspring of his own judgment and experience, and his close attention to the foibles of the human heart." [8] If we add to this a canny study of the human heart as it reacts to the antics and attitudes of the stage, a shrewd study of the drama of his predecessors, and a long-remembered training in the craft under Jonson, we will be somewhere near the truth.[9]

Whatever Brome's formal schooling might have been, by 1614 he had come into the service of Ben Jonson—then at the top of his fame. It would seem that Jonson's reference to his man Brome by name in the Induction to *Bartholomew Fair* in 1614 would have little point if Brome had not been with him long enough to have been known to the regular patrons of the theater.[10] How long it would take to build up such a familiarity in Jacobean London, if we accept such a familiarity as necessary, is impossible to say. But it is doubtful if Brome joined Jonson later than 1613. As a guess, he might have been engaged after Jonson's return, not later than June, 1613, from his trip to France as tutor to young Raleigh.[11] He would then have been about 23 years of age (if our conjectures are accurate). That Brome's formal connection with Jonson as a servant was severed around 1628 or 1629 is suggested by two recorded events. The first is the appearance, on June 30, 1628, of Brome's name in the list of the Queen of Bohemia's Players.[12] The

---

[8] *Biographia Dramatica*, ed. by David E. Baker, Isaac Reed, and Stephen Jones (London 1812), I, 68–69.

[9] For those interested in the subject of relative degrees of learning in unlearned artists, Rev. Ronald Bayne, in his article "Lesser Jacobean and Caroline Dramatists," in *Cambridge History of English Literature*, (Cambridge, 1910), VI, 252–53, and Andrews, *Richard Brome*, pp. 2–5, speculate with vim. The remarks of the former are especially well documented if a bit sanguine in opinion.

[10] Since *Bartholomew Fair* was acted at the Hope theater (October 31, 1614) by Lady Elizabeth's company rather than at the Blackfriars this might seem a poor argument. However, the play evidently was given there as a gesture by Jonson to aid his protégé Nathan Field and to start this group off well in the Hope. It could be posited, then, that Jonson expected to draw along his Blackfriar's audience by the power of his name. At least in writing his Induction he did not restrain his favorite indulgence in the intimate theatrical and topical familiarity that he was continually building up and exploiting with his audience. Cf. Edmund K. Chambers, *The Elizabethan Stage* (Oxford, 1923), II, 257–58; Bentley, *J. and C.*, I, 176; and R. Brinkley, Nathan Field, *The Actor-Playwright* (New Haven, 1928), pp. 30–31.

[11] Maurice Castelain, *Ben Jonson, L'Homme et l'Oeuvre (1572–1637)* (Paris, 1907), pp. 37–39; and Charles H. Herford and Percy Simpson, *Ben Jonson* (Oxford, 1925), I, 64–65.

[12] "A Warraunt to sweare the Queene of Bohemia's Players Groomes of his Mates Chamber in ordinary without ffee. vizt . . . Richard Broome"(from the Lord Chamberlain's Warrant books in *Malone Society Collections* [London, 1931], II, 347). This company evidently divided its time between the Red Bull and the Provinces. Cf. Bentley, *J. and C.*, I, 190. See also Alwin Thaler, "Was Richard Brome an Actor?" *Modern Language Notes*, XXXVI (1921), 89–91.

second event is that Brome seems to have set himself to writing plays for a living following the success of *The Love-sick Maid*, or *The Honour of Young Ladies*, which was licensed in February, 1629.[13] After this date we may assume that Brome was on his own. There is one further point to be related to the problem. Fleay conjectures that Ben Jonson's figure of an apprenticeship in the craft of playmaking should be taken literally when Jonson in his poetic tribute to Brome for the 1632 edition of *The Northern Lasse* congratulates Brome on joining the fellowship of playwrights "professing my old arts." He says,

> And you doe them well, with good applause,
> Which you have justly gained from the Stage,
> By observation of those Comick Lawes
> Which I, your Master, first did teach the Age.
> You learn'd it well, and for it serv'd your time
> A Prentice-ship: which few do now adays.

Fleay interprets this as meaning a literal seven years' apprenticeship running from 1623–29.[14] This may be true, but it is too uncertain to base any arguments upon it. Before going into Brome's independent career, we should turn back and recount what is known or may be inferred from the extended association between Brome and Jonson.

First, what sort of relationship was it? Was Brome a private secretary, a personal attendant, or something less? There is no direct and final evidence. Several previous commentators have tried to dodge the ugly probability that Brome was of mean origin, e.g., Bayne says, "we conjecture that the servant was not so much a valet as a secretary and amanuensis, whose duties, from the first in connection with Jonson's dramatic and literary work, required a grammar school education."[15]

[13] Adams, *Dramatic Records*, p. 32. Adams quotes from Malone's notes on Herbert's Office Book as follows: "Very good, indeed, after the ill success of Jonson's piece [*The New Inn*], the King's Company brought out at the same theatre [Blackfriars] a new play called *The Love-sick Maid, or the Honour of Young Ladies*, which was licensed by Sir Henry Herbert on the 9th of February, 1628–9, and acted with extraordinary applause. This play, which was written by Jonson's own servant, Richard Brome, was so popular, that the managers of the King's Company, on the 10th of March, presented the Master of the Revels with the sum of two pounds, 'on the good success of *The Honour of Ladies*'; the only instance I have met with of such a compliment being paid him."

[14] Frederick G. Fleay, *A Biographical Chronicle of the English Drama, 1559–1642*, I, 37.

[15] Bayne, *Cambridge History of English Literature*, VI, 225. He quotes in this connection Jonson's well-known epigram CI, "Inviting a friend to Supper": "Howsoe'er my man Shall read a piece of Virgil, Tacitus, Livy, or some better book to us," which is similar to Jonson's remark to Drummond about Nathan Field: "Nid field was his Schollar, & he had read to him the Satyres of Horace & some Epigrames of Martiall" (*Conversations with Drummond*, in *Ben Jonson*, ed. by Herford and Simpson [Oxford, 1925], I, 137). Further, as Andrews

This suggestion, even if we choose to disregard all Brome's rather speciously humble references to his own low origin, seems unconvincing. Why should Jonson, already well established as a great and influential man of letters, engage as amanuensis a man who gives no evidence whatsoever in a lifetime of literary work of any special scholarly tendencies? Jonson, it would seem, could have chosen from any number of well-trained, but moneyless, men down from the Universities and anxious to win their way in London literary circles, eager to sit at the feet of the great man. During the first decade of Brome's probable association with him (1613–23), Jonson was engaged fairly heavily in specific scholarly labors—translating, preparing his works for publication in the 1616 Folio, and working up his great masques, and hence Brome would have had a good opportunity to extend his learning, but it cannot therefore be assumed that he was specifically hired for such a task. It is more likely that the atmosphere in which he worked as a servant was so specifically scholarly that he absorbed a measure of learning from it.

It is of course possible that Brome, coming to Jonson as a valet or "man," gained new status for himself by his clever adaptability, progressively extending his duties from menial to literary tasks. Knowing the deep-set pedagogical streak in Jonson's nature, one can easily imagine that a promising young man should have been assisted to knowledge by him.

The usage, "his man, Master Broome," in the early seventeenth century would definitely suggest a domestic servant's role, especially since Jonson had no social status requiring retainers. In late life when writing verses for the Beaumont and Fletcher Folio of 1647, Brome referred to himself as one of the "Old Serving-Creatures" fit to "informe young Masters."[16] He acknowledged that he was by some "stil'd (at best) the Muses Serving-creature."[17] This poem draws its imagery from a conception of his own servile status. He says he is "Become a Waiter" in "ragged verse" to the procession of distinguished poets who have preceded him in paying honour to Fletcher's memory; he visualizes himself as a "Porter" keeping the gate against opportunists

---

observed in *Richard Brome*, Colley Cibber, whose sources of information were dubious and whose readability far outweighed his accuracy, had suggested in 1740 that Brome was an amanuensis.

[16] In his commendatory verses for the 1647 Beaumont and Fletcher Folio "To the memory of the deceased but ever-living *Author* in these his *Poems*, Mr. John Fletcher" (11. 59–60).

[17] *Ibid.*, 1. 56.

who would make the gesture of honoring Fletcher to gain prestige for themselves.[18] These controlling images, humble as they are, lose all point unless both Brome and his intended audience understood in them Brome's willingness to resume figuratively his former menial servant's role to preserve the decorum of this ritual in Fletcher's honor.

The plays of the period are most helpful here. Jonson did take a very hearty delight in the clever servingman, enough in fact to establish him as a central figure in a multitude of Jacobean and Caroline plays. There is very little harshness of discipline, or affecting of distance in the master–servant relationship that Jonson portrays. The master is the master, but his servant cooperates with him in every way and they know people in common. Brome, in his tribute for the 1647 Beaumont and Fletcher Folio, boasts that he knew Fletcher well when Jonson was his master.

> I knew him in his strength; even then, when He
> That was the Master of his Art and Me
> Most knowing Johnson (proud to call him Sonne)
> In friendly Envy swore, He had out-done
> His very selfe. I knew him till he dyed;[19]

The fact that Brome was a servant of Jonson was remarked by all the early commentators and embryo-stage historians.[20] It seems very probable that so strong an impression would have been made only if Brome's initial status was a menial one. There would not be much noteworthy in a private secretary advancing himself to independent literary status. Nor would the relatively elaborate apology by Alexander Brome in the 1659 edition of *Five New Plays* be much to the point. In what is obviously an effort to forestall snobbery, he says,

we could name famous wits who served far meaner Masters than *Ben Johnson.* For, none vers'd in Letters but know the wise *Aesop* was born and bred a wretched slave; *Lucian* a Stone-cutter; *Virgil* himself begotten by a Basket-maker, born in a ditch, and then preferred to an under Groom in the stable; nay, (to instance in our *Author's* own order) *Naevius* the Comedian a Captains mans man; *Plautus* servant to a poor Baker; *Terence* a slave as well as *Aesop*;

---

[18] *Op. cit.*, 11, 3–4, and 19–21.
[19] *Ibid.*, 11. 95–99.
[20] E.g., Edward Phillips, *Theatrum Poetarum* (London, 1675), pp. 157–58; William Winstanley, *The Lives of the Most Famous English Poets* (London, 1687), p. 144; and Gerard Langbaine, *An Account of the English Dramatic Poets* (Oxford, 1691), p. 35.

and (which for our own purpose is most of all) our Authors own *Master* handled the *Trowel* before he grew acquainted with *Seianus* or *Cataline*.[21]

This, written by Brome's first critic (commendatory verses aside), a man who knew Brome as a friend, far outweighs any genteel speculations of a later time which outrun probabilities to give a better name to a mean position. Alexander Brome would not have felt compelled to find classical analogies of slaves and manual laborers if he could have named Brome's office as that of amanuensis. Evidently what happened is this: Brome was so fortunate as to gain a servant's position with Ben Jonson while he was young enough to be formed by this relationship, and he had adequate education and intelligence to capitalize on Jonson's willingness to teach him a professional skill—playwriting—which raised Brome in the social scale.

The elements of uncertainty in discussing Brome's birthdate, schooling, and relationship with Jonson are present, if in a different form, in the question of his marriage. Rather than the usual paucity we find that records of marriages for Richard Brome are embarrassingly numerous. At least five ranging in date from 1613 to 1645 have been noted. Any one of these is within the range of credibility as a wedding date for a man born around 1590.[22]

But for our purposes it is the "marriage of effort" with Ben Jonson that we can use. A happy one it seems to have been, for this long relationship between Brome and Jonson is free of clashes or bitterness. Brome never gives evidence that his feelings were anything but warmly loyal to his old master. But shortly after their formal relationship was severed there was a difficult episode provoked by Jonson's touchiness.

When Jonson brought out the 1631 edition of *The New Inn* he appended to it an ode, superscribed:

The just indignation the author tooke at the vulgar censure of his Play, by some malicious spectator, begot the following Ode to himself.

This poem included the following stanza:

> No doubt some mouldy tale
> Like Pericles; and stale
> As the Shrieves crusts, and nasty as his fish-scraps,
> out of every dish,

---

[21] "To the Readers" in (London, 1659). *Five New Plays.*
[22] See Appendix, pp. 175–76.

Throwne forth and rack't into the common tub,
May keepe up the *Play-club*:
There, sweepings do as well
As the best order'd meale.
For, who the relish of these ghests will fit
Needs set them, but, the almes-basket of wit.

The second copy of this ode, included in the 1640 edition of Jonson's translation of the *Art of Poetry*, had an alternate reading for the 7th and 8th lines of the stanza:

Broomes [*sic*] sweeping(s) doe as well
Thear as his Masters Meale.

Gifford, mistakenly dating the 1640 revision as later in date of composition, delivered a somewhat indignant explanation which saw the old poet, Jonson, as a victim of a petty conspiracy of jealous friends (especially Randolph) to discredit Brome with his master.[23] The discovery by Tennant that the manuscript of this poem in the Bodleian confirmed the 1640 reading of "Broomes" [*sic*] led to a more plausible interpretation. Jonson had evidently written the slurring couplet about Brome in his exacerbated fury following the disgraceful failure of *The New Inn*, a fury heightened by the inferior quality of his own play which he was too acute not to recognize.[24] His anger outstripped his own sense of fair play, so that when Brome's play *The Love-sick Maid* became, immediately after the Jonson failure, an acknowledged smash hit,[25] he could not restrain himself. Although normally he would have taken pleasure and undoubtedly congratulated himself roundly at the success of his own protégé, he rather said what doubtless seemed to him only fair—that Brome had picked his brain.

Tennant went on to show that Jonson's loyal friends, who commiserated in verse to lessen the pain of the master's bruised ego, evidently saw the Brome reference in manuscript.[26] Randolph, replying to Jonson's Ode, wrote without much inspiration:

[23] William Gifford, ed., *The Works of Ben Jonson* (London, 1816), VIII, 342.
[24] For the miserable state of mind Jonson was in preceding the performance of *The New Inn* on January 29, 1629, and the apoplectic violence of his reaction to its failure, see Herford and Simpson, *Ben Jonson*, I, 94–95.
[25] See Adams, *Dramatic Records*, p. 32.
[26] Cf. *"The New Inn or The Light Heart"* by *Ben Jonson*, ed. by G. B. Tennant (New Haven, 1908), Yale Studies in English, No. 34, pp. xxi ff.

> And let those things in plush,
> Till they be taught to blush,
> Like what they will, and more contented be
> With what Broome swept from thee.[27]

While a lesser figure than Randolph remembered longer and wrote more harshly in *Jonsonus Virbius* (1638). This poetaster, R. Brideoake, wrote:

> Though the fine plush and velvets of the age
> Did oft for sixpence damn thee from the stage,
> And with their mast and acorn stomachs ran
> To the nasty sweepings of thy serving man,—[28]

Alexander Brome, in his verse tribute to Brome in the 1652 edition of *A Joviall Crew*, was probably referring to this episode (perhaps recounted to him by Brome himself) when he said

> who could go faster?
> At first to be the *Envy* of thy *Master.*

But, if the playwright remembered it to tell it to his later friends, he evidently bore Jonson no malice for it. There is no statement or suggestion which breaks the even surface of Brome's respect and gratitude toward Jonson.

That, as the 1631 revision of the lines imply, Jonson himself was not proud of their petulance, we may be fairly confident. And, it may be, too, that the good, round commendation of Brome by Jonson for the 1632 edition of *The Northern Lasse* is in part a compensation for this unjust slur.

The shadow of Jonson falls strongly over Brome. One wishes it were the only shadow a would-be biographer must contend with. The truth is from the time of well-advertised difficulties with Jonson just outlined until 1634 there is nothing really to go on.[29] Evidently Brome did some writing for the Red Bull companies; we know he did *The Northern Lasse* (1629) and *The Novella* (1632) for the King's men, and he may have done some acting, though his silence about such professional experience is not like him when later he scornfully berates the courtier dramatists who are invading his "quality." His collaboration with Thomas Heywood on the topical play, *The Late Lancashire*

---

[27] *Works of Thomas Randolph*, ed. by William C. Hazlitt (London, 1875), II, 582.
[28] *Jonsonus Virbius* (London, 1638). See also Andrews, *Richard Brome*, pp. 6–10.
[29] See Appendix II for Chronology of the plays written during these years and conjectures as to production circumstances.

Witches, in the summer of 1634 is the only firm reference we have for this period.

After Brome had completed this journalistic collaboration with Thomas Heywood on *The Late Lancashire Witches* and the play had been published during the last months of 1634,[30] he evidently turned to Red Bull for temporary employment.[31] If we are to go by the general opinion of the Red Bull as an uncouth theater catering to the sub-literate mentality of the groundlings, this would seem a definite re-gression for Brome who had written for the premier company of London. There are, however, a number of factors to be considered. There is moderately good evidence for believing that the King's company, firmly established as *the* theatrical troupe of London, was beginning to rely more and more on the solid repertory core of plays by the great triumvirate—Shakespeare, Jonson, and Beaumont and Fletcher—and that they were increasingly cultivating the production of courtier plays. It is interesting to note in support of this, that in the 1641 Lord Chamberlain's list of Kings company plays to be pro-tected there is no play in the list written later than Brome and Hey-wood's *The Late Lancashire Witches* that was neither by Massinger, by his successor Shirley, nor by one of the court dramatist group (if we include Davenant in later career as a member of that circle).[32] Further-more, Massinger, still unflaggingly productive, was in 1634 well established as King's company journeyman playwright. It is not sur-prising that Brome, unable and unwilling to write "up" to the Cavalier taste with requisite ease and knowingness, should have taken his considerable dramatic talents elsewhere. He had written more or less actively for the professional theater for at least five years; his skills were matured; and he had the confidence that at least one and perhaps several popular successes could give.[33]

More important, perhaps, in influencing Brome's decision than the limited future offered by the King's company was the fact that Prince Charles's (II) company, which had evidently just moved to the Red

[30] The play was entered in the Stationers' Register October 28, 1634 and published in the same year.

[31] Cf. Andrews, *Richard Brome*, p. 14. Of a personal letter from Professor Charles W. Wallace, who had unpublished Brome material among his notes, Andrews writes, "He [Wallace] states that Brome, previous to his contract [with Salisbury Court, July 20, 1635], was with the Red Bull Company."

[32] Cf. Bentley, *J. and C.*, I, 65–66, where this list is reproduced and placed in its proper context.

[33] *The Love-sick Maid* (1629), *The Novella* (1632), and *The Northern Lasse* (1629).

Bull, was enjoying a brief period of fame and bringing to that theater a short respite from the distaste and scorn of the better sort of theater-goer.[34]

It might be well to examine some relevant dates at this point. We know that on July 20, 1634, the King's company had petitioned the Lord Chamberlain to protect them from being "scooped" by other companies on the Lancashire Witch scandal, and that therefore the Brome–Heywood play was probably not quite finished by that date. Since the same play was entered for publication some three months later (October 28), we can assume that the play was finished by the end of August in order to give time for the rehearsals and acting of it. At almost the same time Richard Kendall, the wardrobe keeper at Salisbury Court, had talked of the London theater with Thomas Crosfield, a Fellow of Queen's College, Oxford, when the former's troupe (the King's Revels company) was in Oxford on tour. Crosfield made notes from this conversation on July 18, 1634, which include the information that "The Princes Servants [are] at ye Red-bull in St. Johns street, ye chiefe Mr. Cane a goldsmith . . ."[35] Since the Prince's company had been at the Salisbury Court theater in 1631 and 1632 (if not much longer), Kendall, from his affiliation with that theater, should speak with authority. There is reason to believe that the Prince's company brought to the Red Bull an unusual prestige. They were chosen to attend the court on the royal progress in the summer of 1634, and they presented three plays at Hampton Court in September and October, 1634, and four more at Whitehall later the same winter and the next spring.[36] A factor of interest in these records is that one Joseph Moore was included in the list of payees for these performances.[37] Joseph Moore was a fairly well-known actor for many years after his earliest appearance as one of the leaders of the Lady Elizabeth's company in 1611. He was mainly associated thereafter with provincial companies until he became affiliated with the Prince's company in 1631. He evidently had a position of authority in the company although it is difficult to determine his exact status. Bentley concludes that "There can be no doubt that he *was* a leader of the company. It is possible that, like Heminges in his later years, he was a financial agent

[34] See Bentley, *J. and C.*, I, 309–11.
[35] Cf. Bentley, *J. and C.*, II, 688; or *The Diary of Thomas Crosfield*, ed. by F. S. Boas (London, 1935), pp. 71–73.
[36] Bentley, *J. and C.*, I, 311.
[37] *Ibid.*, I, 311.

rather than an actor."[38] Since he seems to have been with the Lady Elizabeth's men during the early years of his career, it is possible that Brome had known him since the time of Jonson's *Bartholomew Fair* in 1614, for that play was given at the Hope by the Lady Elizabeth's men and we know that Brome was present at the performance and must have had access to the actors (through Jonson's allusion in the Induction to "his man, Master Broome, behind the arras.")[39] We do not need to depend on so distant and tenuous a conjecture though, for in the warrant swearing the Queen of Bohemia's Players as Grooms of the Chamber of June 30, 1628, Richard Brome stands fourth in a list headed by the name of Joseph Moore.[40] Brome, perhaps because of his humble origin, seems always to have liked a close partnership, or a father-figure to stand with.

It seems at least possible that, after the royal progress was completed late in August, 1634, and the Prince's company had returned to London to set up again at the Red Bull (this date virtually coinciding with the probable completion of *The Late Lancashire Witches* by Brome and Heywood), Moore either persuaded Brome to join them or recommended that his services be obtained. If this supposition is correct, Brome would have been associated with this company for a period of about one year until he signed his contract with Salisbury Court on July 2, 1635. It is quite reasonable to suppose that Brome may have looked upon this Red Bull connection as a temporary measure, since there would have been little point for a non-acting playwright to have become permanently associated with a company that was primarily engaged in provincial travel.[41]

It is quite certain that Brome signed a contract with the Salisbury Court theater on July 20, 1635; and it is moderately certain that it was Richard Heton, the manager of that theater, who negotiated this contract. Heton had evidently succeeded Richard Gunnell when the latter died about 1634. Bentley suggests this, saying, "It was probably Heton who induced Richard Brome to leave the company at the Red Bull and become the chief poet for the King's Revels company."[42] The ex-

---

[38] Bentley, *J. and C.*, II, 513.

[39] *Ibid.*, I, 176, and II, 512; and Edmund K. Chambers, *The Elizabethan Stage*, II, 258.

[40] Bentley, *J. and C.*, I, 188.

[41] We know that the company was on the road again at least by early spring of 1635/36 (O.S.), shortly after Brome would have left them (if our suppositions are correct), for Andrew Cane, one of the company's leaders, presented their license at Norwich on March 9 of that year (Bentley, *J. and C.*, I, 312).

[42] Bentley, *J. and C.*, I, 295.

istence of this contract has been known to scholars since 1910 when C. W. Wallace referred to it and gave some of its particulars. But since Wallace neither published his findings in full nor saw fit to reveal the documentary source, it is only from his references and from some additional information elicited by queries from a later student of Brome that we can make a partial reconstruction of the circumstances. Here is what Wallace noted:

Yet another set of documents assists here in understanding certain relations of the poet to the theater. Richard Brome, former servant to Ben Jonson and his literary disciple, in 1635 made a contract with Salisbury Court theater to write three plays a year for three years at a salary of 15s. a week, plus the first day's profits from each new play as a benefit. In 1638, it was agreed that the contract should be continued seven years longer at a salary of 20s. a week for Brome's exclusive services. But the rival theater, the Cockpit, lured him away with a better offer, and the new contract was not signed. The most interesting new items here are the limit of three plays a year and the special provision that Brome should not be allowed to publish any of his own plays without the consent of the company.[43]

Later, Wallace added further facts in correspondence with C. E. Andrews, who reports,

He states that Brome, previous to the contract, was with the Red Bull Company. The contract is dated July 20, 1635. The amount of the benefit of the first night on one occasion was estimated at £5 or upwards. Brome was to give his exclusive services to the company. One play he wrote for them, the *Sparagus Garden*, was so popular that the estimated profits to the company were £1000. In the three years during which Brome was writing for the Salisbury Court Theatre, he had written, besides numerous songs, epilogues, and revisions of scenes in revived plays, but six of the nine plays agreed on in the contract. He had also written a play or two for the Cockpit, contrary to contract.

Though Professor Wallace states in the article quoted above that the second contract was not signed, he writes me that Brome, on this new contract, which is dated August, 1638, delivered one play the following winter after Christmas, and another before Easter, 1639, which the company refused to accept. "Then he went to the Cockpit with Beeston, where he met with better favor, about which details are not given."[44]

[43] C. W. Wallace, "Shakspere and the Blackfriars," *The Century Magazine*, LXXX (1910), 751.
[44] Andrews, *Richard Brome*, pp. 14–15.

These relevant passages have been quoted at considerable length. It seems necessary since they include by far the greater part of our factual information about Brome and since, too, they must stand in the place of direct documentary evidence.[45]

The important facts in the contract are: that Brome would write only for the Salisbury Court theater, that he was to write three plays a year, and that the contract was to run for three years' time. It is interesting, too, that as the company's chief poet he would be expected to write songs, to do revisions, and to furnish prologues and epilogues. Since this last is explicitly stated, we may assume that he would write them not only for his own plays, but also for revivals as well and perhaps for new plays by other dramatists.[46] He was to be paid a regular salary, and to receive the benefits of the first day's performance. The salary itself figures out to approximately £13 per play and does not seem a very huge sum considering the steady rise in prices which characterized the reigns of the early Stuarts; but the added income from the first nights would probably swell this to a respectable figure, the sum having been estimated in one instance as about £5.[47] The suit also tells us that Brome was to publish none of his plays without the consent of the company.

Brome, by signing this contract, engaged himself to write for the King's Revels company, for whom he wrote, I think, three plays before the theaters were closed by the plague in May, 1636: *The New Academy, The Sparagus Garden,* and *The Queen and Concubine* in that order.

At this point in Brome's career, after he had completed three plays on his initial contract with Salisbury Court, there is an interruption of many months during the worst plague visitation since 1625. In about twenty months, from April, 1636 to December, 1637, more than 13,000 deaths were recorded. The theaters were closed from May, 1636 until October, 1637, with only a prematurely optimistic re-

[45] Wallace probably discovered this information among the depositions of the Court of Chancery. I made a systematic search through the Chancery depositions for the years 1635 through 1641 in hopes of finding the document or documents. My search was unsuccessful, which does not, of course, prove that the document is not still to be found there.

[46] As the seventeenth century moved along toward 1642 the play prologues become more and more like advertising copy, that is, they are not only meant to express good will or describe the wares, but also to publicize the sponsor, duel with competitors, and express the policy of the theater or acting group. This being generally true, it is fairly likely that the house poet might be called upon to write prologues for almost all the plays the theater offered.

[47] Andrews, *Richard Brome,* p. 14.

opening for a brief period in February 1636 (o.s.) to break this long stretch of time.[48] The long closing was evidently too much for the finances of the King's Revels group, so that when the theaters re-opened Brome, though still with the Salisbury Court theater, was writing for a new company—Queen Henrietta's. For this company he wrote, I think, three of his remaining extant plays, *The English Moor*, *The Antipodes*, and *The Damoiselle*, in that order.

These postplague months with Heton at Salisbury Court seem to have been shaky. On the one hand Brome wrote a play or two for his friend, William Beeston, at the Cockpit against the terms of his con-tract, and we know from his own Epilogue to *The Antipodes* published in 1640 that he had tried to give this play to Beeston and had been, evidently legally, prevented from doing so. On the other hand his re-lations with Heton were seemingly good enough to warrant a renewal of contract in August of 1638. This contract according to Wallace was never signed and hence it is possible that Brome half-heartedly complied with it until he knew what legal room he had to break with Salisbury Court and cooperate with Beeston. It is also possible that the senior Beeston's death in October, 1638, which left his son, William Beeston, in complete charge was the precipitating factor for change in a tense stalemate between Brome's legal commitments and his personal attachments.[49]

The truth is that what happened to Brome in the latter part of 1638 and the earlier part of 1639 is uncertain. Bentley states what we can be sure of with admirable concision. He says that after William Beeston organized his new company for the Cockpit theater in April, 1639, probably one of his, "first acts as manager was to secure Richard Brome as poet . . . Brome had been chief dramatist for the Salisbury Court for more than three years, and a contract to bind him to that theater for seven years more had been prepared, but his last play was written for the Salisbury Court some time before Easter 1639, and thereafter he was attached to the Cockpit." [50]

Brome was friendly with Beeston. His note to the reader at the end of the 1640 edition of *The Antipodes* where he calls Beeston "my most deserving Friend," has been mentioned, and there is a defense of Beeston against detractors whose "venemous practise" studies "nothing

---

[48] For a detailed account of the known effect of this plague period on the theaters, see Bentley, *J. and C.*, II, 661–65.
[49] Bentley, *J. and C.*, II, 370.
[50] *Ibid.*, I, 330.

more then his destruction," in the long epilogue to *The Court Beggar* in 1640. It is in every way understandable that Brome wanted to join forces with Beeston, since they were friends and "old professionals." What is not so clear (and will not be until the records of the legal squabble between Brome and the Salisbury Court management are recovered) is just how Brome managed to work free from his contractual commitments to Salisbury Court. In any case Brome came to Beeston's company after Easter, i.e., April 14, 1639.[51] Four months later, on August 10, a Lord Chamberlain's edict was issued protecting a list of plays for William Beeston:

Whereas William Beeston Gent' Gouuernor of the Kinges and Queenes young Company of Players at the Cockpitt in Drury Lane hath represented vnto his Matye that ye seuerall Playes heerafter mentioned (vizt) . . . Fathers owne sonne . . . A mad couple well mett . . . doe all & every of them properly & of right belong to the sayd House, and consequently that they are all in his propriety: And to the end that any other Companies of Actors in or about London shall not prsume to act any of them to ye preiudice of him the said William Bieston and his company: his Maty hath signifyed his royall pleasure vnto me: therby requireing mee to declare soe much to all other Companyes of Actors heerby concernable: that they are not any wayes to intermedle wth or Act any of th'above mentioned Playes . . . Given &c' Aug. 10, 1639[52]

The two plays singled out from this list of forty-five can be shown to have some relationship to Brome's affairs. The first, *Fathers Owne Sonne*, is the same as Fletcher's *Monsieur Thomas*.[53] Bentley suggests that Beeston's aim in requesting the edict was to secure "protection from the King's men, who seem to have played *Monsieur Thomas*, the *Fathers owne sonne* of this list."[54] This play was printed in 1639 (Stationers' Register, January 22) as "Acted at the Private House in Blacke Fryers," which would certainly suggest King's company rights to the play. It should be noted, however, that Richard Brome was the editor of this play, and, in his dedicatory epistle to Charles Cotton, speaks of his own personal rights to the play.

---

[51] Andrews, *Richard Brome*, p. 15, and Bentley, *J. and C.*, I, 330. Bentley there quotes a warrant (from *Malone Society Collections*, II, 389) swearing Beeston as "Gouuernor & Instructer of the Kings and Queens young Company of Actors." The warrant is dated April 5, 1639.

[52] Bentley, *J. and C.*, I, 330–31, quoted from *Malone Society Collections*, II, 389–90.

[53] Cf. *ibid.*, I, 62.

[54] *Ibid.*, p. 331.

Sir,

My directing of this piece unto you, renders me obvious to many censures, which I would willingly prevent by declaring mine own and your right thereto. Mine was the fortune to be made the unworthy preserver of it.[55]

Furthermore, in his prefatory verses, Brome speaks of the play's failure to secure rightful approbation on first hearing while suggesting that the public may have grown up to it by now. There are any number of alternative explanations of how he might have come by the manuscript. The simplest is perhaps that while he was working with the King's company in the early years of the 1630s it may have been given to him for revisions to eliminate the possibility of a repetition of its previous failure to please, and he simply kept it. The important thing is that he did claim some right to its possession. It is strange that if Brome brought the play with him to the Cockpit it should still have been known in Beeston's list by an alternative title. As a conjectural possibility, the play *Fathers Owne Sonne* might have been an earlier, rewrite version by Brome who emphasized the father–son relationship aspect of the play.

The other relevant play on the Lord Chamberlain's list, "A mad couple well meet," is almost certainly Brome's *A Mad Couple Well Match'd*. It was probably Brome's first contribution to Beeston when he joined him sometime after Easter (April 14) 1639, and a possible reason for its appearance in Beeston's list was to insure against any attempt by the Salisbury Court management to procure the play through a claim on Brome's services until he had fulfilled the contractually specified number of nine plays for them. This argument has no finality but it does correspond to the facts insofar as they are known and it has the virtue of simplicity.

Brome wrote at least two more plays for Beeston. Their collaboration, though cut short by the closing of the theaters, was a fortunate one which seems to have put a spur to Brome's aging energies. Both *The Court Beggar* (1640) and *A Joviall Crew* (1641) are plays of great purpose and vigor.

Brome is so much a man of the theater that we cannot be as much troubled by a lack of a certain death date for him as we are by the other lacunae. He lived on at least ten poverty-stricken and miserable years after 1642. During this time he did nothing accessible to us save edit

[55] From "To the Noble Honourer of the Dead Author's Works and Memory, Master Charles Cotton," in *Monsieur Thomas* (London, 1639).

the collection of elegiac verses on the death of Henry Lord Hastings, *Lachrymae Musarum* (London, 1649), known to us now only as the context for Dryden's worst poem. Brome was able to dedicate his *Joviall Crew* in the quarto edition of 1652.

He was dead in the next year when his friend, Alexander Brome, gathered *Five New Plays* to begin raising what monument posterity was to permit him.

III

UNDER THE SEAL OF BEN

Brome's association with Jonson was probably the most important and formative one of his whole life. Unfortunately, we know too little about the exact nature of their relationship—its duration, closeness, and content—to describe it with authority. It is, however, necessary for any understanding of Brome to attempt an evaluation. The phrase "the seal of Ben" is indicative.[1] The impressive power of Jonson's mind and will is everywhere apparent in his work and in the surviving testimony of his contemporaries, detractors, and admirers. It is unthinkable that one could (as Brome did) work for, and then spend one's life seeking to emulate the primary work of, such a master without feeling the impress of his aggressive attitudes and profoundly held convictions. As well as the positive impress of Jonson's opinions, Brome may well have learned some negative lessons from a master who, though great, made many mistakes. A lesser talent directly under the influence of a genius undertakes a risk about equal to the advantages he enjoys—he may be sterilized and academicized by the contact.[2]

One thing must be said bluntly at the outset. Jonson was a genius; Brome was not. Jonson was a great poet; Brome was, at best, a competent versifier. Brome was incapable of filling Jonson's role even had he been disposed to be merely an apostle of his master's gospel. They

---

[1] In the Prologue written for the revival of *The City Wit*, Brome tells his audience that the comedy "was written, when/It bore just Judgement, and the seal of Ben" (*Five New Plays*, London, 1653).

[2] Jonson's *Discoveries* contain a passage which Brome could have used to describe his attitude toward Jonson and, indeed, he might well have heard it from Jonson's own lips: "If in some things, I dissent from others, whose *Wit*, *Industry*, *Diligence*, and *Judgement* I looke up at, and admire: let me not heare presently of Ingratitude, and Rashnesse. For I thanke those, that have taught me, and will ever: but yet dare not thinke the *scope* of their labour, and enquiry, was to envy their *posterity*, what they could also adde, and find out" (*Ben Jonson*, VIII, 567). This reference, and all following references to Jonson's text, are to the standard edition edited by Charles H. Herford and Percy Simpson, 11 vols. (Oxford, 1925–52).

did, however, share a certain traditional set of values. Brome affirmed most of the values which inform Jonson's works. There is a direct spiritual affinity, a stubbornness, and a loyalty they share. Though they must be differentiated in numerous ways, nothing should be interpreted as gainsaying this fundamental harmony of attitude.

After a study of Brome's plays in the context of his times and theater, it is evident that his range, within the limits of comedy, was considerable. He could write Dekkeresque, pathetic, romantic comedy as illustrated by *The Northern Lasse*; he wrote a good London town comedy in the Middleton manner, *The City Wit*; he could, in a play like *The Novella*, follow Fletcher into intrigue comedy with a fertility in invention of situation not inferior to his; he could write something close to operetta or musical comedy as in *A Joviall Crew*; or he could control good, intellectual farce as in *The Antipodes*. His control of satire, though not so intellectually coherent and forceful as Jonson's, is better than average and neither cramped nor academic. He could make a direct attack as in *The Court Beggar*; he could satirize the absurdities of a literary genre as in *The Love-sick Court*; he could expose the vices of the town as he did in *The Covent-Garden Weeded*; or combine intrigue comedy with didactic satire as in *The Damoiselle*; and this does not exhaust his range.

In discussing the central Jonsonian influence, it is useful to take this variety into account, for a mere demonstration of direct borrowings from Jonson could be matched by parallel records of Middletonian, Fletcherian, and probably Shakespearean influence. The enquiry must be placed at a more fundamental level.

Brome's plays are far less self-repetitive than Shirley's and show more versatility in comic invention than Fletcher's. Brome is a master craftsman whose substantial gifts are delimited primarily by three characteristic practices: He was overfond of farcical horseplay; he could not intensify his language for crucial scenes; and his studies under Jonson gave him predispositions for serious satire without either Jonson's massive learning and intellect or his carefully documented moral views. As a result, to state the adverse case in its strongest form, when Brome attacks general vices or perversions there is sometimes a thin, parroting quality, a suspicion of incomplete sincerity, an uncertainty as to convictions, and a general stiffening of language. One suspects the speech or the situation has been devised for dramatic convenience. The Jonsonian mantle was too long and of too heavy fabric; Brome entangled himself and walked falteringly in it. It is not too much to say that, given to mirth-making as he was, Brome was sometimes embarrassed by the obligations he felt to thicken the texture of his plays by exhortation or serious satire.

These statements, though not inaccurate, may suggest a greater dissimilarity between Brome and Jonson than is finally valid. The noticeable dissimilarities are mainly the product of differences in endowment rather than in attitude; they are first impressions induced by Brome's very noticeable inadequacies as a poet, and by his unquestioned (but, in this context, misleadingly irrelevant) inferiority to Jonson. Because he does not always implement the Jonsonian viewpoint adequately, we may be misled into the assumption that he does not largely share it. But he does share it to a considerable extent. While taking more care than Jonson did to pack his plays with action and easy entertainment, he still manages to frame issues in terms consonant with Jonson's own moral program.

From the evidence of Brome's plays, we can infer strong and consistent likes and dislikes. He consistently ridicules popinjay courtiers and their frivolous ways; he everywhere despises fadism, pretentiousness, and fanaticism; he has a genuine, medieval contempt for the usurer and the social parasite. He has consistent, positive views correlative with these dislikes. He adhered throughout his writing career to a sense of corporate values—of status, order, the customary law, of responsible exercise of authority, of the brotherhood of men—all the things that come under a belief in the public good. These were Jonson's views and they become ever more explicit in Jonson's late plays. They were views held by a diminishing minority as the seventeenth century wore on.

Still, it must be acknowledged that, where Jonson's thinking is deeply analytical, working out from a consciously formulated and well-mediated set of moral coordinates, Brome is more the *ad hoc* troubleshooter. While Brome's thought is still traditional, his comedy runs more to correction of foibles and normative deviations which he does not view with such abiding disagreement as Jonson. The current of the century was running to greater "particularism," toward a sense of cultural relativity which made satire on a universal scale steadily more difficult. Brome did not embrace these new views, but his work was insensibly limited by them. Money worship for Jonson was a fundamental perversion—an abuse of reason. Brome understood this, but he usually conceived of it (less fundamentally) as a practice which rendered a man disagreeable, ridiculous or, at worst, a social liability. Foppery for Jonson (e.g., in *Cynthia's Revels*) was an expression of self-love and hence a negation of charity and fellow-feeling; for Brome it was a very vulnerable social vanity, a subject for mirth, a thing to be modified. These differences are considerable. But the difference is more in power of mind than in belief. Whereas Jonson could document his views and trace their logical consequences, Brome's grasp operates more on the level of the firmly held commonplaces of received assumptions, unanalyzed and, so to speak, subphilosophical.[3]

The differences between the two are ultimately traceable to the quality of conceptualizing intellect which works through local manifestation to universal principles of conduct. Jonson at his best could employ closely studied local variations of ridiculous vanity in conduct with sharp, detailed realism and yet never slip away from his framing moral principles. The characters in *The Alchemist* are Jacobean-London types; they are, even further, Blackfriar's inhabitants of the first decade of the seventeenth century. But their greedy self-seeking, their convenient rationalizations for mean, selfish conduct are explored through this vivid, evocative surface of manners. Jonson had a clear notion of what men should be. He was alternately angered and appalled by the monstrous disparity between conduct and principle. Free from any genteel repugnance for the less delicate side of life,[4] he was consistently revolted by the shameless, cowardly, mindless greed of the individual. His works are a nearly unceasing plea for rationality in conduct—the kind of rationality that is not trapped in short-term self-consideration. Jonson was fighting a rearguard action against an encroaching money economy. That it was a losing battle, we know.

---

[3] It is just because of this that in many ways Brome's plays are so valuable as subject matter for the overall study of the seventeenth century. Because he was unexceptional intellectually and subphilosophical, understanding his assumptions gives a reliable tool for establishing the presence of certain continuing views in the theater. L. C. Knights says interestingly: "The modern reassessment of the seventeenth century is largely a recognition of what was lost as well as gained by the transition to the modern world—a transition that took place not only in the spheres of practical achievement and conscious intellect but in those more subtle and more profound modes of perceiving and feeling that underlie men's conscious philosophies and explicit attitudes, and that have become so ingrained and habitual that it is only by a deliberate effort of the intelligence that we can recognize them as *not* inevitable, absolute and unchanging the permanent *donnes* of human nature: that is why they are best studied in our literature" ("Bacon and the Seventeenth Century Dissociation of Sensibility," *Explorations* [New York, 1947], p. 109).

[4] Whatever modifications this attitude underwent during his lifetime were merely convenient and superficial adaptations to Stuart paternalism. Jonson never sentimentalizes the lower classes nor does he show any precious or effeminate squeamishness about them.

Brome fought the battle, too, but with feebler weapons and with a less clear view of what constituted a compromise.

Brome was probably intimately associated with Jonson during the long years when Jonson was fighting against the disappearance of an audience who would hear and try to understand what he had to say.[5] A consecutive reading of Jonson's plays, from *Bartholomew's Fair* on to *The Magnetick Lady*, is more than a lesson in failing powers. Jonson's valiant but stiff-jointed attempts to negotiate his ideas in the current dramatic coin of the rapidly shifting times are subverted by failures to understand just how little these ideas were acceptable to audiences more and more agitated by the breakdown of values. How unconvincing attacks on the validity of the money-principle were to an audience increasingly composed of those who depended on trade, whether as genteel monopolists or as recently wealthy merchant-princelings, Jonson in his indefatigable zeal failed to see. Furthermore, as he shifts his plea to women, he does not seem to recognize that they, too, are dominated by the necessary and unquestioned dependence on money in a socially competitive coterie society centering on a court of sizeable cultural pretensions. If we leap ahead to the Restoration pattern of values, where money and what it can do forms one of the fundamental, underlying postulates of the drama, we can see how unacceptable Jonson's objects for satire were to his audience. Jonson could not be satisfied to laud prudential virtues along with Heywood and Dekker. He was, and remained to the end, a Tudor man, believing in the superiority of the aristocratic honor code of the Christian gentlemen, a code that demanded education, dignity, leisure, courage, and grace—a code that imposed obligations—the code exposited by Henry Peacham in his *Compleat Gentleman*.[6]

---

[5] The lack of recorded information about their relationship makes it impossible to state just how long they were associated. Brome had evidently been with Jonson for a while when the allusion was made to "his man, Master Broome" in the Introduction to *Bartholomew Fair* in 1614, and Brome still claimed connection with him when *The City Wit* was written (c. 1630–31). The aroused resentment of Jonson's "sons" after the nearly simultaneous failure of *The New Inn* and success of Brome's *Love-sick Maid* in 1629 would have less point unless Brome had been recently or was still fairly closely associated with Jonson at that time. Though Brome did not contribute to *Jonsonus Virbius* after Jonson's death, this can be explained by reasons other than alienation. It seems likely that Brome was associated with Jonson for at least 15 or so years (i.e., c. 1612–26) and perhaps for over 20 years. This relationship would not need to have been formal. We know that Brome was no longer a servant to Jonson in 1632 by Jonson's own use of the past tense in his verses for the 1632 edition of *The Northern Lasse*.

[6] Cf. on this general point the interesting chapters (XVI and XVIII) in Herschel Baker's *The Dignity of Man* (Cambridge, Massachusetts, 1949), entitled "Christian Humanism" and

Brome never repudiates these ideals, though the necessity he felt to ridicule and censure the new courtier-gentleman types might mislead one into thinking he was anti-aristocratic. The very reason he spent so much time criticizing court manners is because he resented the current deviation from the received norm of responsibility and dignified service which were the gentleman's obligation.

Jonson broke through the illusion of his own plays to have his characters deliver speeches in definition of these virtues. His primary concern was to drive home the lesson that these virtues of valor and love are, properly, outgoing and public in their aims. This may be seen most clearly in what must be considered his least successful play, *The New Inn* (1629). For this play, Jonson devised a plot which would provide a captive audience for the speeches of Lovel, whom Jonson described in "The Persons of the Play" as "A compleat Gentleman, A Souldier, and a Scholar."

The play has a feeble pattern of stage action which depends on mistaken identities and a final surprise revelation. This plot, superficially romantic, was handled in a perfunctory and very nearly offhand fashion by Jonson, whose intentions pointed in a different direction; it was no more important to his purposes than Wilde's creaking and ironic refurbishments of melodramatic plots were to his dramatic aims.[7] In the prefixed argument, Jonson had described the third and fourth acts as the "Epitasis, or business of the Play," and these scenes are dominated by Lovel's discourses on love and valor. The dull, romantic plot, exposited in the first two acts and concluded in the fifth, served as an excuse or foil for earnest, moral discourses. The movement of the dramatic action was slowed to a standstill in the central scenes.

Lovel is called upon to define valor before the group of travelers assembled in the New Inne. The group has organized itself into a mock feudal court and the proceedings are formalized according to the courtly code. The Host, playing the tournament herald, calls Lovel to testify:

"Sixteenth Century Ethics," respectively. See also John E. Mason, *Gentlefolk in the Making* (Philadelphia, 1935).

    [7] Brome wrote a play called *The Damoiselle*, or *The New Ordinary* about seven years after Jonson's failure. By seventeenth-century usage, Brome's subtitle is the same as Jonson's title (i.e., Inn-Ordinary). Brome's play is a very serious treatment of usury and economic vice. However, even though Brome uses the same general centering device of an inn as gathering place, he escapes completely the action-stalled results of Jonson's play by providing a subplot which crosses and recrosses the main plot.

Herebert Lovel, Thou shalt sweare vpon the testament of loue, to make answer to this question propounded to thee by the Court, *What true valour is* [italics mine]. And therein to tell the truth, the whole truth, and nothing but the truth. So help thee loue, and thy bright sword at need.

Lovel's answer is in Jonson's most serious vein:

So help me loue and my good sword at need. It is the greatest vertue, and the safety of all mankinde, the object of it is danger. A certaine meane 'twixt feare, and confidence: No inconsiderate rashness, or vaine appetite of false encountring formidable things; but a true science of distinguishing what's good or euill. It springs out of reason, and tends to perfect honesty, *the scope is alwayes honour, and the publique good:* It is no valour for a priuate cause [italics mine]. (*The New Inn* IV, iv, 32–47)

Lovel continues to answer all objections to this definition. He rejects revenge, protection of reputation (which he calls "mans Idoll, Set vp 'gainst God"), and any motive that aims for private advantage at the expense of honor. He says,

> The things true valour is exercis'd about,
> Are pouerty, restraint, captiuity,
> Banishment, losse of children, long disease:
> The least is death.
> (*Ibid.,* 105–8)

These, along with the speeches on love, formed the center of the play. The play failed and Jonson deeply resented it, as his "Ode to Himselfe" most plainly shows. That Jonson was unwilling to relinquish his conviction of the importance of the central plea in *The New Inn* is apparent from the allusions in his last completed play, *The Magnetick Lady* (1632), where he has Sir Diaphanous Silkworme, an effeminate, cowardly courtier, argue about valor with Captain Ironside, a bluff but sympathetically drawn proponent of the older more masculine virtues. Diaphanous, trying to evade the necessity of fighting a duel with Ironside who has publicly insulted him, says,

> O, you ha' read the Play there, the *New Inne,*
> Of *Ionsons,* that decries all other valour
> But what is for the publike.
> (*The Magnetick Lady,* III, vi, 92–94)

Ironside answers,

> I doe that too,
> But did not learne it there; I thinke no valour
> Lies for a private cause.
>
> (*Ibid.*, 94–96)

The implications here are double: Ironside, being of the old school, already knows these things because Jonson has merely rendered explicit the old, sound code hitherto unknown to the neo-courtier, Diaphanous; and, further, Ironside implies that ridding the commonwealth of a butterfly like Diaphanous is, after all, an act of public service.

Earlier, in *The Staple of Newes* (1625), Jonson devised a "humours" play to excoriate the fatuous overconcern with novelty and with money. In *The Magnetick Lady* he is again after the money-oriented element of society, particularly its most excessive manifestation—the usurer, Sir Moth Interest. The direction of his technique is always towards giving extra-personal significance to recognizable London types he describes as "some recent humours still, or manners of men, that went along with the times." [8] Implicit allegiance to this statement permeates Brome's plays.

Since the conventional view of Jonson is that he was the accomplished master of dramatic form (a notion which has automatically conditioned the studies made of his influence on his fellows), it is necessary to examine the difficulties, temperamental and strategic, that Jonson experienced as a dramatist in his late years. What Brome took from Jonson, how he evaluated him as an authority for practice, cannot help but have been influenced by the unresolved artistic discrepancies of Jonson's last plays.

There is a constant quest in Jonson for technical means to dramatize the essentially non-dramatic—to devise means to address his audience directly without losing their attention. There is a dangerous tendency in his late plays to circumnavigate the action itself in these attempts. As if his plots were impediments, he seems to resent them but is unable to dispense with them. Jonson used innumerable devices to achieve this end. In *The Staple of Newes* he brought the gossips on the stage to argue the intentions and success of the play in "inter-meanes" after each act. He was not satisfied with this device alone; he used "Peni-boy

---

[8] In the Indvction: or Chorus to *The Magnetick Lady*, 102–4. Shakespeare profoundly distrusted such men whom he describes in *Lear* as men who "are as the time is."

Canter" as an omniscient commentator on the motives of the other characters. As the supposedly dead father of the prodigal hero of the play, Peni-boy has the advantage of a complete disguise. He is unknown to characters and audience alike. As a beggar-fool type, he had the prerogatives of a Shakespearean bitter fool with the additional advantage that, unlike them, he has reserve powers (in his wealth and concealed paternal authority) to dictate the outcome. It is hard to go further than this in direct author-manipulation of the thesis and plot development of a play. It is not a digression to say that Jonson has strong likenesses to Shaw in his lack of faith in the power of his unaided or unsupplemented art to penetrate the public mind. Both depended excessively on extra-formal devices (such as prefaces, prologues, and direct author commentary) to direct the attention of the audience and to underscore their own aims.

For *The New Inn*, Jonson provided a synopsis of the plot in a very un-Jonsonian, pre-play narrative. The play as a piece of intelligible action is not self-contained. The occurrences on stage depend on knowledge of the prior existence of the major characters in order to have any interest whatsoever for the reader. Jonson has, it seems, gravitated toward the dramatized fable of extended duration without relaxing his dependence on the unities. The result is rather like the dramatization of the crucial chapter in a short novel. A reading of the play will prove that this peculiar combination of subject matter and technique is ineffective. The artistic conflict is basic and no amount of fulmination from Jonson can obscure the fact that he has not resolved it.

Nonetheless, the principal objection to *The New Inn* as a piece of drama is slightly different. One cannot conduct a fundamental argument with his literary medium and still procure a maximum of cooperation from it. Jonson wanted to create a situation in which the audience on the stage listening to his principal mouthpieces would become continuous with his audience in the theater. The Inne of the Light Heart in the play furnishes a transparent excuse for gathering a certain number of diverse types in an enclosed space without furnishing individual reasons for their presence.[9] Then the desire for diversion on

---

[9] The frequent allusions to Chaucer in the play suggest the Tabard Inn in the *Canterbury Tales* as the prototype for this device. In the prologue to *The Magnetick Lady*, he frankly confesses the arbitrary association of his characters for thematic-didactic discussion purposes. In the Induction, he has the audience informed that the author, continuing his lifelong study of "some recent humours still, or manners of men, that went along with the times, finding himselfe now neare the close, or shutting up of his Circle, hath phant'sied to himself, in *Idaea*, this *Magnetick Mistris*. A Lady, a brave bountifull Housekeeper, and a vertuous

the part of these persons so foregathered is used to justify a loosely integrated medley of speeches and little actions on moral themes. The form of the entire play tends toward the Boccaccio–Chaucer medley of tales with a thin substructure of correlated action. The skeleton is dimly discerned beneath the play, but (as if this were not sufficiently far from the happiest sphere for dramatic action) Jonson further divests these speeches of concrete detail. He provides a brief episode of action and then immediately has it generalized upon by one of the characters. The ratio of action to talk about that action is approximately one to four.[10] That this practice cuts a dramatist off from the cardinal advantage of the theater over other media must be clear when we realize that the power of a meaningful action in three dimensions can elicit or provoke thought in minds not normally reflective. That the integration of language spoken feelingly with all the supplementary factors of composed spectacle, gesture, business, and fable can persuade where mere unadorned, face-to-face threat or petition cannot, should be self-evident.

Jonson knew the theater well. He had long experience in utilization of its resources. So, when we find him failing so obviously to work through to his goal, we must search in another quarter for the reasons. The fashion has been to follow Dryden in calling these late plays his "dotages." It is hard to read either *The Staple of Newes* or *The Magnetick Lady* and still concur in this rather facile explanation. There is still tremendous intellectual vigor in the poetry which is nervous, flexible, and frequently of great dignity.

The offhand indictment of Jonson's intelligence and stamina just does not stand up under inspection. That Jonson failed as a social observer to realize the shifts in mores and value is, however, a different matter. It may be asserted that serious satire can be successful only when the satirist shares certain moral assumptions with an influential percentage of his audience. If he has to give an audience introductory lectures on the nature of certain virtues, he has little scope left for portraying deviations from those virtues which he desires to see corrected. That is, what Jonson perhaps thought were aberrations or temporary failures to acknowledge the moral standards he believed in were in

---

Widow; who having a young Neice, ripe for a man and marriageable, hee makes that his Center attractive, to draw thither a diversity of Guests, all persons of different humours to make up his *Perimeter*" (*Ben Jonson*, VI, 511).

[10] Cf. George B. Tennant, *The New Inn*, pp. xxxii–xxxvi, for a schematic analysis of the play as to sequences which have to do with action, or in any way forward the action, and those that do not.

reality the beginnings of a complete loss of faith in those standards. In short, Jonson, without fully realizing it, passed in the minds of his audience from the role of constructive and clear-eyed conservative to that of a reactionary vainly lauding values which no longer had any sensible value for them. Therefore, all the devices Jonson resorted to to reduce the distance between himself and his audience were desperate patchings-over of a deeper malady. Jonson was in the humiliating position of initiating laughter only to find himself laughing alone. His solution for this was to make his point more and more obvious and explicit, on the assumption that he was not being understood on a literal level. This is always the rational idealist's mistake. It is ultimately traceable to the confident, Socratic formula that knowledge is virtue. Unfortunately, no amount of annotation could modify out of existence the fundamental disagreement of belief between Jonson and his audience.

The conventional portrait of Jonson as the judicial, classically oriented man is incomplete. It is likely that Jonson's verve and spirited attack are the very things that most powerfully influenced Brome; these, and a self-consciousness about what he was doing. Brome, for all of his pretended humility, was very jealous of his "quality" and was eager to assure himself of a measure of due respect. It was this Jonson with whom Brome evidently spent most of his time. A Jonson vastly respected for his learning and his prior successes but no longer able to strike the desired tone. A Jonson rapidly becoming obsolete as a producing playwright. He was in the rather unusual position of seeing himself become a classic and yet unable to exert current influence in proportion to the accumulated esteem.

These circumstances were very likely to have influenced Brome, whose respect for his master seems never to have waned. The respect was genuine but not uncritical. Brome was too shrewd to follow Jonson blindly into repetitions of his master's failures. In the plays of Thomas Nabbes, it is all too apparent what uncritical imitation of Jonson can lead to in a playwright of lesser learning and intelligence. In Shakerley Marmion, too, the dangers of a tepid and faded academicism as the result of direct imitation are painfully recognizable. Nabbes was, as Harbage says, doctrinaire.[11] He reproduces Jonson's formal

---

[11] *Cavalier Drama*, p. 159. For representative examples of the work of Nabbes, see *Tottenham Court* (1633) and *The Bride* (1638); for Marmion, see *A Fine Companion* (1633). Marmion is a rather better poet than some of the other minor playwrights of the period, but he evidently never thought out dramatic technique for himself. Jasper Mayne's *The City Match* (1637) is perhaps an even better example of what I mean by academicism in comedy.

effects and repeats his sermon texts without either the spirit or vigor of Jonson. He observes the unities in a mechanical fashion and is morally sound in the same superficial and external manner that eighteenth-century sentimental comedy is morally sound.[12]

Brome seems to have effected a reconciliation between his loyalty to Jonson's very obvious and repeatedly declared aims, and the exigencies of pleasing a restless and diversion-hungry audience, by an avowal of mirth as his aim. By making his primary object the creation of laughter, Brome could then bargain for a certain amount of attention to more serious matters. He adopted numerous versions of the oblique (as opposed to the directly didactic) technique. This was a shrewd choice, for if Jonson, with his immense intellectual powers and his accumulated prestige, could not successfully adapt direct persuasive rhetoric to the theatrical medium, what chance did Brome have? Brome had to rely on cunning, good nature, and surprise.

[12] *Cavalier Drama*, p. 159.

IV

THE CAROLINE EDITORIAL PAGE

THIS chapter is meant to serve as a buffer between the introductory section of the book and the more fully focused critical discussion of individual plays which follow. Because the Caroline realistic comedy is artistically tentative, its playwrights are experimenting with possible ways of digesting urgently needed corrections for social abuses without losing the advantage of a matured formal structure for their plays. They wanted to be contemporary without becoming trivial. When reading the comedies of this time, one is astonished at the function the drama is performing. The plays do the work of newspapers! They report, they advertize, they protest, they deplore, they frame social questions, they editorialize. This chapter will show how Brome created "newspapers" with four of his plays. There is probably no quicker way to distinguish the intimate—almost familial—interplay of audience, playwright, and social environment which is the special earmark of Caroline drama.

The City Wit (1629–30)

The City Wit though simple, almost parabolic, in its main structure is the most promising of Brome's very early efforts. It is Brome's first direct attempt at social satire on a thematic level. Here for the first time he formulates an issue of social significance and traces it throughout his entire play, so that a single question—how the economic dishonesty generally acquiesced in is to be reconciled with personal responsibility—is the organizing principle of the action as well as of character relationships. What happens in the play happens because one of the characters, Crasy, having failed in business because he is honest, decides to investigate the advantages of deliberate deception. The play is unified in terms of the initial situation for which the remainder of the play serves as an area of logic expansion and experimentation.

Brome was fond of the tableau device on the stage,[1] that is, he translated into the dramatic medium the sort of static representation of vice and mood that one finds in the emblem books.[2] He evidently composed a number of crucial scenes in his plays with an eye to the total visual impact without regard to realistic action. Since a great deal of the more serious ethical thinking of Renaissance man was done in formalized, emblematic terms, this observation may be useful in trying to isolate the particular "flavor" of a play like *The City Wit*.[3]

The first thing one notices when re-examining *The City Wit* is how full and explicit the stage directions are for the opening scene. Crasy, recognizable only as a young man of the city, is placed at a table "with empty Money-bags, Bills, Bonds, & Bookes of accompts"; we are instructed that "He takes up the bils & papers"; then "He puts the Bills & Bonds into a Bag"; and finally that "He takes up a scroll" (I, i, 279–80). All this we are told in less than two pages and while the main spoken action is a soliloquy by Crasy on money.

> How easie a thing it is to be undone,
> When credulous Man will trust his state to others!
>
> (I, i)

We discover partly through his talk and partly through the carefully composed stage business that he is bankrupt, and the importance of his having been financially so reduced is strongly impressed on our minds.

He distinguishes himself from the numerous bankrupts of the time by taking a moral position that is not to his financial advantage. He will not sue for composition of his debts,

---

[1] He used this tableau or "living emblems" technique very fruitfully, for example, in *The Damoiselle* for placing his leading character, a usurer, at the outset and for condemning his lack of charity in the fourth act. See Chapter X in this book.

[2] This is in a sense, of course, similar to a device the morality plays must have exploited in the use of highly abstracted figures and symbolic costume and properties.

[3] This subject is too complex to pursue here. I do think that Douglas Bush's *Mythology and the Renaissance Tradition in English Poetry* (Minneapolis, 1932), and *The Renaissance and English Humanism* (Toronto, 1939); R. Tuve's *Elizabethan and Metaphysical Imagery* (Chicago, 1947), and *A Reading of George Herbert* (Chicago, 1953), as well as work by Hardin Craig, E. M. W. Tillyard, Samuel L. Bethell, L. C. Cormican, Muriel C. Bradbrook, and Lily B. Campbell, Madelaine Doran and many others have only begun to be applied really fruitfully to the ways in which drama and theater were conceived. I have never seen it suggested, for example, that the Elizabethans whom we have lauded for their acutely developed auditory sense (for listening to spoken poetry) probably also had a highly developed sense of visual form induced by habits of little reading of words and much contact with emblems, pageants, symbolic masques, conventional insignia and carving, type and class costumes, etc. Donald J. Gordon, in his studies of Jonson's masques, has demonstrated some of the subtler and more learned possibilities.

All I have is lost,
And what I have not, sought to be forc'd from me,
I must take nimble hold upon Occasion.
Or lie for ever in the Bankrupt ditch,
Where no man lends a hand to draw one out.
I will leape over it, or fall bravely in't,
Scorning the Bridge of Baseness, Composition,
Which doth infect a City like the Plague,
And teach men Knavery, that were never born to't:
Whereby the Rope-deserving Rascall gains
Purple and Furre, Trappings and golden Chains.
Base Composition, baser far then Want,
Then Beggery, Imprisonment, Slavery:
I scorn thee, though thou lov'st a Trades-man dearly
And mak'st a Chandler Lord of thousands yearly.
I will have other ayd.

                                    (I, i)

The effect of this initial situation is to create sympathy for Crasy's
financial plight at the same time as it puzzles the mind. City types on
the early seventeenth-century stage are nearly always foolish, greedy,
fanatic, crass, and underbred—all of these or any combination thereof.
Here we are presented with a city type who is alienated from the city's
assumptions. Who is he? How did he get there? Is he really a city
person? What can he do to revive himself? These questions do not
press themselves on our mind urgently, rather they arouse a reflective
interest. Most important of all, the method of presentation makes an
association in our minds between the practical question of what action
he will take—a dramatic question—and the reasons he can give for
taking it—an ethical question. In short we are made aware that Crasy
has both a problem and a conscience. Though *The City Wit* is simple,
almost rudimentary, in technique it shows in embryo form the underlying patterns which distinguish critical, thoughtful, social comedy from
theatrical and contentless entertainment. It also shows some of Brome's
major preoccupations in relatively undeveloped form. If we follow his
development of theme a little further we will see the characteristic
techniques he employs. He uses his first act to set up the problem. The
structure of the act is almost rhetorical: Crasy enters on the stage bankrupt; he scorns normal businessman expedients for redeeming himself;
he is rejected by his wife's relatives who criticize his guilelessness;
he confronts his debtors to collect money they owe him to apply

against his debts; they, in a scene faintly reminiscent of *Timon of Athens*, offer him cynically prudential advice but no money; he resolves to test their advice. In examining the terms of this sequence we see how self-consciously Brome uses the medium to make it clear that the play is an examination of this abstractly formulated problem. He is saying in effect, "If one were not honest would he be better off" or perhaps, slightly differently, "Has the new economy made honesty obsolescent?"

Crasy, soon after the opening tableau, is joined by his mother-in-law, Pyannet, and other members of the family. Pyannet, who is very talkative and self-important, berates him, whereupon he replies,

Cra. All was but my kind heart in trusting . . .
Py. Kind heart! What should Citizens do with kind hearts; or trusting in any thing but God, and ready money? . . .
Cra. . . . May not an honest man——
Py. Honest man! Who the Devill wish'd thee to be an honest man? Here's my worshipfull Husband, Mr. *Sneakup*, that from a Grasier is come to be a Justice of Peace: And, what, as an honest man? Hee grew to be able to give nine hundred pound with my daughter; and, what, by honestie? Mr. Sneakup and I are come to live i' th City, and here we have lyen these three years; and what? for honesty? Honesty! What should the City do with honesty; when 'tis enough to undoe a whole Corporation? . . .
Cra. If my uncunning Disposition be my only vice, then . . .[4]

(I, i)

and he is interrupted and Mistress Pyannet is off again. Crasy replies, firm still, "Well: If to be honest, be to be a fool, my utmost Ambition is a Coxcomb" (I, i).

Crasy then confronts his debtors one by one. The first, a courtier, laughs at his credulity for lending money without bond. The second, a pedant, offers him philosophical counsel. His brother-in-law, who is being educated as a gentleman as the Sneakups climb stealthily up the social ladder, offers him some warmed-over Epicureanism, "Desire little; covet little . . . And you shall have enough," and then adds, magnanimously, some man-of-the-world's advice, "Purchase Wit; Get wit (look you) wit . . . Prithee grow rich againe; and were good Cloaths, that we make keep our Acquaintance still." In short, he

---

[4] In this sequence I have made some cuts, but (by count) Brome reiterates the words "honesty" or "honest" fourteen (14) times in less than two pages of text—the violent underscoring of theme is evident.

tells him to exploit his wife's good looks at court as a means of rising again (I, ii). Another courtier reiterates this, "Prithee learne to have some witt. . . . Be rul'd by me, Get money, do, Get money and keep it; wouldst thrive? Be rather a knave then a Fool" (I, ii).

After more, much more, of the same "friendly" advice, Crasy is left alone.

> Is this the end of unsuspicious Freenesse?
> Are open hands of Cheerfull Pietie
> A helpfull bounty, and most easie Goodnesse,
> Rewarded thus?
> Is, to be honest, term'd to be a fool?
> Respect it Heaven. Beare up still merry heart.
> Droop not: But scorne the worlds unjust despising
> *Who through Goodnesse sinks, his fall's his Rising*
> (I, ii [italics mine])

Now, if Brome left us here we would have a concrete affirmation of the Christian principle that charity is its own reward, for that is what Crasy has been scorned for being—charitable—in both the basic sense of open-hearted sympathy and trust of one's fellow man, and in the more restricted sense of using money to alleviate others' distress. However, he does not leave it here. Crasy, understandably disenchanted, pretends a cynicism greater than he feels and advises his " 'prentice" to choose wit when given the alternatives of wit and honesty:

If ever it be in thy possible ability, wrong all Men, use thy wit, to abuse all things, that have but sense of wrong: For without mersie, all men have injur'd thy mistrustles Master . . . Cheat, chosen [*sic*, cosen?], live by thy Wits: Tis most manly, therefore most noble . . . In briefe be a knave and prosper: for honesty has beggered me.

(I, ii)

The first act is drawing to a close when Crasy advises his " 'prentice" Jeremy in this matter. They are going to put their heads together to outwit their abusers. The quality of self-conscious demonstration with which Brome is going to exploit the medium to make his points is now evident. Jeremy takes his leave, "Farewell Master, And if I put tricks upon some of them, let the end of the Comedie demonstrate." Crasy, left alone, closes the act with a direct statement of the proposition,

> The scene of our slight sports confess'd shall have,
> That any may be rich, will be a knave.
> (I, ii)

The rest of the play is a syllogistic demonstration of the truth of this proposition. Crasy, with the aid of Jeremy and innumerable disguises, proceeds through four acts to demonstrate that he is wittier than his abusers. He makes dupes and fools of them and he recovers his money and goods. He proves that his handicap was deliberate honesty not stupidity or ineffectuality. One is reminded of the story of the great Ionian philosopher, Thales of Miletus, who, tired of being told that he was a philosopher because he lacked ability to succeed in everyday affairs, cornered the market in oil presses and made a fortune which he gave away once his point was made. So Crasy after successfully mastering and embarrassing all the others, at the end takes off his disguise and enters to the assembled group "in his own habit, all hung with Chaines, Jewells, Bags of Money, &c" (V, i). He reads their advice back to them, and then after enjoying his triumph he closes the play by saying,

> My honest care being but to keep mine owne,
> What, by my slights, I got more than my due,
> I timely will restore again to you.
>
> (V, i)

Woven through the play is a series of unfavorable reflections on the self-gratifying habits of citizens and of the courtiers who live off them. The play displays no powerful insight or exceptional skill, but it is solid, coherent, unified, and, in a rather boisterous way, amusing. Its pattern of judgments illustrates Brome's characteristic beliefs. Crasy's alleged folly was not being "for himself" in the sharp, ceaseless battle of wits between men fighting for a larger personal share of goods. Brome rejects this allegation and uses comedy as his means to demonstrate his point that honesty and fair dealing are not the product of weakness but of an attitude superior to mere skill in achieving economic success which, he argues, is merely a kind of virtuosity in deception. This has been a theme of humanists in all ages—equally true and equally futile. The difference is that in the seventeenth century, before the triumph of the Hobbesian rationale for human relations, one might possibly still advocate it in the midst and not on the periphery of life. Brome's advocacy of the theme is one small strand in the pattern of his overall conservative adherence to a disappearing moral tradition.

The New Academy (1635?)

The New Academy was probably the first play that Brome wrote for the King's Revel's company after he signed his Salisbury Court contract in July, 1635. There is no title-page evidence for company or date of performance, and there are no known external references to the play. The dating must rest on internal evidence and on more general arguments about the theatrical and social milieu which surround the play. The play has a double title, both parts of which are exploited. Taking the second part first, *The New Exchange* refers to the New Exchange in the Strand as a reference in the play makes clear. Rafe Camelion, an uxorious citizen, intercepts a letter to his wife and reads the address: "To my deare daughter Mrs. *Hannah Camelion*, at her shop or house in or near The New Exchange" (II, i, 23). It would be convenient if we could say that the New Exchange was in fact new when the play was written. Actually it was built much earlier. After the stables of Durham house, facing the Strand, were pulled down,

On their site was built an exchange, called the New Exchange, which obtained some popularity. This was erected partly on the pattern of the Royal Exchange, and was opened by King James I. This, Strype tells us, "was for milliners, sempstresses, and other trades that furnish dresses." The place was opened in 1609 by James I and the queen; it was called Britain's Burse. It became fashionable after the Restoration. . . .[5]

It was simply a place where people could foregather in Brome's London. It is interesting that the brief allusion quoted is the only one in the play. But at the end of the play, Brome has his conventional double pair of lovers discover they cannot marry each other in the combinations the play has established, so they are told "they shall exchange And marry in due order." Whereupon Lafoy Junior, one of the two prospective grooms, very agreeably replies in his stage French accent, "we shall make. De exshange presently. A new exshange, De new Exshange indeed" (V, ii, 107).

The double stress here seems to be a verbal pointing at the play title, as was the not infrequent custom. There is, perhaps, a minor anomaly here which can be very readily accounted for. It has been recognized that

[5] Sir Walter Besant, *London North of the Thames* (London, 1911), pp. 316–17. He adds that Restoration plays are full of allusions to the place. The New Exchange may have begun to become fashionable before the Restoration. Regular allusions to it began to appear in the Domestic State Papers after 1635.

there was a short-lived fad of place-realism comedies on the Caroline stage.[6] Brome twice contributed to this fad in his *The Covent-Garden Weeded* (1632—33?) and his *The Sparagus Garden* (1635). The fad included Marmion's *Holland's Leaguer* late in 1631, Nabbes' *Covent Garden* (1632–33?) and *Tottenham Court* (1633), as well as Shirley's *Hyde Park* (1632). It seems quite probable that Brome added the subtitle, *The New Exchange*, to gain gratuitous appeal for his play from a fad well under way but not exhausted.[7] The false justification of the title in the last scene adds to our suspicion of a specious plan of this sort.

Further pursuing this rather tenuous line, we turn to the internal literary problem of what sort of play it is and where its emphases lie. The play is a very routine hybrid with a fairly elaborate intrigue plot built on a realistic base, although the realism is not so heavily topical as Brome's usual practice leads us to expect, so that there are no intelligible specific allusions to secure a date. Even so there are an unusual number of references to the French. Matchil, a testy merchant, in a fit of temper turns out his daughter and his charge, the daughter of a French friend, saying, "leave my house. There's *French* enough in town, that may befriend you" (I, i, 10). The play takes its title from an academy where French manners and dances are taught by "Two young *French* Gentlemen. New come ashore" (III, ii, 59) who speak either in French or in a stage accent (*ibid.*, pp. 63–65; 76–78; 85–86). Cash, Matchil's apprentice who absconds with money and dresses like a gallant, is described as "a brave gallant, one o' the Alamodes, Nothing but *French* all over" (V, i, 91).

Though there were a good many French in London all during the reign of Charles I, there was one French invasion of just the right sort to catch the theatrically alert mind which Brome shared with his master, Ben Jonson. Bentley provides the cue:

In February 1634/5 a distinguished troupe of French players came to England, and, as one might expect, attained high favour at court where the French influence was so strong in these years.[8]

---

[6] Cf. Theodore Miles, "Place-Realism in a Group of Caroline Plays," *Review of English Studies*, XVIII (1942), 428–40, and Richard H. Perkinson, "Topographical Comedy in the Seventeenth Century," *English Literary History*, III (1936), 270–90.

[7] It is possible that the scenes between the citizen Rafe Camelion and his wife might have been staged with minor props to suggest a booth at the New Exchange.

[8] *J. and C.*, I, 233. Bentley's source is Joseph Q. Adams, *Dramatic Records* (New Haven, 1917), p. 60.

The company evidently made a hit with the public. They were granted permission to use the Phoenix theater during Lent and to play "on the sermon daies, and gott two hundred pounds at least." [9] They were not content with their Phoenix successes for,

After they left the Phoenix the French players acted for a time on a special stage erected in the riding-school of M. le Febure in Drury Lane. A warrant for the erection of a stage, scaffolds, and seats in this riding academy was issued 18 April 1635, and less than three weeks later, on 5 May, a warrant was issued to the company allowing them to act in this new playing place "during pleasure." The company was evidently still in London in December 1635 ... Presumably the Frenchmen returned to Paris shortly thereafter, no doubt to the great relief of their English competitors.[10]

It seems to me the correlation between a French troupe performing in a riding academy and the stage presentation in satiric terms of an Academy where actors speaking in French stage-dialect are tutors in dance, song, manners and compliments is not too difficult to make. One wonders what sort of plays these Frenchmen could have put on for an English audience. It seems likely that to make money over a protracted period they would have had to depend on dancing and miming.

Brome's *Academy*, besides the usual emphasis on the art of compliment, features dances. They can offer,

> for Corants,—*La Miniard*,
> *La Vemide*, *Le Marquesse*, *Le Holland*,
> *La Brittaine*, *Le Roy*, *Le Prince*, *Le Montague*,
> The *Sarband*, the *Canvries*, *La Reverree*.
> For Galliards, the Sellibrand, the Dolphine,
> The new *Galliard*, the *Valette Galliard*, and *lepees*.
>
> (III, ii, 65)

This long list of offerings is commented upon and the English people present undertake to dance with the Frenchmen, saying, "I feare no *French* flashes . . . If we cannot dance 'hem of [off?] o' their legs, our wenches can, I warrant thee. Musick be ready" (*ibid.*, p. 65). The stage direction then specifies "Daunces"; so there were evidently a series of dances presented rather than the usual one.[11] This sort of

---

[9] Cf. Bentley, *J. and C.*, I, 234, quoting Sir Henry Herbert.

[10] *Ibid.*, I, 235. See *Malone Society Collections*, II, 375, 378.

[11] Earlier, Rafe Camelion says in passing, "I saw last night Your new French daunce of three, what call you it?" and his companion answers, "O the Tresboun" (III, ii, 57), They dance it (p. 50).

cataloguing of specialized French dance names and the emphasis on dancing seems indicative of an unusual design. It is most easily explained by an ephemeral excitement such as was caused by the visiting French troupe.

Evidence of a different order can be produced for a date of 1635 rather than pre-1630. It is the most difficult sort of evidence to present in a compact and persuasive form, for it rests on generic similarities between plays. By drawing the parallels between this play and the others known to date from the late thirties, the fragmentary evidence we have adduced can be strengthened.

The subplot characters, Rafe Camelion and his wife, are Brome favorites in his later plays. In fact, Rafe is a finger exercise for the later more successful character, Saleware, in *A Mad Couple Well Match'd*. Both are uxorious citizens with small merchandizing shops. Both are nearly wittols—fondly trusting their wives and virtually coercing them into adultery by refusing to suspect or dominate them. Each is given a tag line. Camelion's is "honi soit qui maly pense," and Saleware's "Sapientia mea mihi, Stultitia Tua Tibi." The tags are exploited dramatically in similar fashion and, as can be seen, are when used by the wittol type of about equivalent force. There are other parallels between these two plays. Valentine Askal in *The New Academy* is a direct prefiguration of Carelesse in *A Mad Couple Well Match'd*; both are cynical, hard-mouthed rakes of a sharper-edged sort than Brome traditionally portrays. Nathaniel Banelass, the libertine in *The English Moor*, is a transitional characterization between them. Furthermore, Strigood in *The New Academy* is exceedingly like Moneylacks in *The Sparagus Garden*, the play which immediately follows it in this interpretation of the Brome chronology.

The idea of an Academy of compliments is utilized again in *The Damoiselle* (1638).[12] These are not vague, general similarities but a specific chain of reproductions. In a period of three or four years, Brome wrote *The New Academy*, *The Sparagus Garden*, *The English Moor*, *The Damoiselle*, and *A Mad Couple Well Match'd*; for that period he evidently developed a set of personal versions of the conventions of current Caroline realistic-intrigue comedy, so that elements of one play overlap into and form the undercoating of the next.

---

[12] James Shirley used the Academy device as early as 1625 and there are numerous other examples. But I am here arguing from Brome's own career and the sort of phasal self-repetition that characterizes most minor artists.

There is not much similarity in tone, structure, and emphasis between *The New Academy* and the other known early plays—*The Northern Lasse, The City Wit, The Novella,* and *The Covent-Garden Weeded.*[13] There was a definite shift in technique with *The New Academy.* What heretofore have been assumed to be the indications of early, undeveloped craftsmanship are more accurately explained as an uncertain feeling after a new style. *The New Academy* is a mediocre play —it lacks sharpness and coherence of structure, but it prefigures substantially the much more successful achievement of *A Mad Couple Well Match'd* and through it of much Restoration comedy.

The Sparagus Garden (1635)

Probably the second play Brome wrote under his Salisbury Court contract was *The Sparagus Garden,* published in 1640 with the title page informing us that it was "Acted in the yeare 1635, by the then Company of Revels, at *Salisbury* Court."[14] The play was evidently seen through the press by Brome and contains a dedication to William, Earl of Newcastle, with whom Brome had obviously had some association, since the dedication is less impersonally flattering than a strictly conventional one. Newcastle was unique among the nobility who wrote plays, in that he admired and wrote in the vein of Jonsonian comedy and its derivatives rather than the "love and honor" mode. He evidently liked Brome's plays, for Brome says in this dedication, "My Lord! Your favourable *Construction* of my poore *Labours* commanded my *Service* to your *Honour,* and, in that, betray'd *your* worth to this Dedication."[15]

There are two sets of commendatory verses, Jonsonian scene divisions, and a careful text. Obviously Brome thought well of this

[13] Alfred Harbage in his interesting article, "Elizabethan-Restoration Palimpsest," (*Modern Language Review,* XXXV (1940), 287–319) argues that two of Dryden's plays are reworkings of lost plays by Brome, and defines a formula for Brome's comedies (pp. 304–5) that runs from the early *City Wit* and *Northern Lasse* through *Covent-Garden Weeded* and *The Sparagus Garden* right up to the late *Mad Couple, Damoiselle,* and *Court Beggar.* If his arguments were comprehensive they would be in contradiction to my contention of a change in technique around 1635. It seems to me however that Harbage refers to the persistence of minor themes and repetitions of characters standard throughout Caroline drama—rather than to matters of technique and tone which treat of what a dramatist does with such types and what kind of *attitude* he takes towards them.

[14] The play was very popular and is reported to have earned £1,000 for the company (Andrews, *Richard Brome,* p. 14). This figure is probably an exaggeration in the tradition of deposition claims, but even with great modification it gives testimony for the play's success.

[15] It seems possible to read this passage as an indication that Brome, a highly competent professional craftsman, rendered the "*Service*" to Newcastle of helping him in the construction of his plays.

play, a contention further confirmed by his proud reference to it in the
epilogue to *The Court Beggar* five years later: "And let me tell you he
has made pretty merry Jigges that ha' pleas'd a many. As (le' me see)
th'*Antipodes*, and (oh I shall never forget) *Tom Hoyden o' Tanton
Deane*." The second title alludes to a low comic rustic in *The Sparagus
Garden*[16] whose thick, Somerset dialect seems to have captivated
Brome's audience, for we have noted earlier (in quoting from the contract proceedings) that the estimated proceeds from the play were
£1,000. Whether or not this is a convenient exaggeration, the play's
popularity is attested to by the citation, not merely by the monetary
figure produced to bolster it.

   This work, like the early *The Covent-Garden Weeded* to which it
has only a general similarity, is quite full of topical reference. Since a
precise dating of the play is of some importance in establishing the correct chronological sequence of Brome's canon, we shall examine one of
his allusions closely.

   Rebecca, the demanding wife of Brittleware (a harrassed and yield-
ing husband, so favored as a type by Brome in this period), wants to
have a baby and decides to indulge her cravings as pregnant women are
permitted to do, thereby hoping to induce pregnancy as if by sympathetic magic. She expresses her craving: "I doe long to see the new
ship, and to be on top of *Pauls Steeple* when it is new built, but that
must not be yet" (II, ii, 134). Brome signed his Salisbury Court contract July 20, 1635. The allusion to the new ship would have been
meaningless for several months thereafter, for Rebecca is referring to
the ship *Charles* which is graced in the records of the period by the
name of the "great ship."[17] The ship was being built at Woolwich and
Rebecca evidently desired to be taken on a country excursion to see the
marvel for herself. As late as September, 1635, the ship was not even
begun, for there is a letter extant from the builder, Captain Pett to the
King: "If the King's pleasure were signified for beginning the work,
Pett made no doubt to have the ship finished in a year and a half."[18] A
second letter from the same man in February, 1635–36 (o.s.), indicates

---

[16] A. Harbage mistakenly thought that *Tom Hoyden o' Tanton Deane* was a separate play;
see his play list in *Cavalier Drama* (New York, 1936), p. 269, under the date 1639. He
corrected this error in his *Annals of English Drama*, 975–1700 (Philadelphia, 1940).

[17] Thomas Heywood with his alert journalist's instinct exploited popular interest in the
ship with a pamphlet, *A True description of his Majesties royal ship built at Wooll-witch* (1637).
There as throughout the *Calendar State Papers, Domestic*, for the period it is regularly called
"the great ship."

[18] *Calendar State Papers, Domestic*, Chas I (1635), VIII, p. 388.

that the ship is well under way. The necessary shipments of additional lumber should be expedited, he says, "that the works being already in great forwardness, may not be hindered."[19]

It is improbable that the building of the great ship became a favourite haunt of London sightseers until the spring of 1635–36 when such outings would have been something to see. Whether this is acceptable or not, it would seem that the allusion suggests a date late in 1635 or in early 1635–36 (o.s.).

The other allusions further substantiate what we already know— that Brome wove fresh, current material into his plays and that with a few exceptions his allusions (when they can be traced down) are to specific recent events. He cleverly exploits the newly introduced sedan chairs in devising a denouement for his plot,[20] by having the gull of the play, Tim Hoyden, conveyed onto the stage in one of these curtained litters and emerge clad as a woman. He utilizes it like a moveable inner stage for a surprising and amusing disclosure. He has Rebecca express her craving to see a play, not just any play but, a little uncertainly, she asks to see "The Knight of the burning—what dee' call't," and is answered, "The Knight of the burning Pestle." This play was evidently undergoing a successful London revival about this time, for the record of a court performance by Beeston's Queen Henrietta's company on February 28, 1635–36 (o.s.), is extant,[21] which, for a play that had previously been a failure, suggests a successful revival in public before taking it to court. In short, all identifiable topical allusions indicate that the play was probably composed several months after Brome joined the Salisbury Court theater and that in terms of our calendar it is a play of 1636 rather than 1635.

At the present time it is hard to account for the special popularity of *The Sparagus Garden*. It is a vigorous play with an abundance of Brome's special gift for natural, vigorous dialogue, and a varied and strenuous plot. Perhaps its great success lies in the lucid and amusing way in which it "literalizes in action," a metaphor underlying any number of plays in the period. The problem is that of social climbing and the ambition of the yeoman or tradesman to become a gentleman. The metaphor is the perennial one of blue blood versus the more usual variety. Brome has Tim Hoyden, the young prosperous country

[19] *Calendar State Papers, Domestic*, Chas. I (1635), VIII, p. 257.
[20] They were introduced into England only the previous year (1634), by Sir S. Duncombe (*Encyclopedia Britannica*, XXIV, 576 [11th ed., 1911]).
[21] See Bentley, *J. and C.*, I, 236, and Herbert, *Dramatic Records*, p. 56.

innocent, fall in with the theatrically flyblown crowd of cony-catchers, but if they are timeworn as stage types their device for making him into a gentleman is not. They quite literally improve his "social strain" by draining off his base blood. Brittleware and Moneylacks, the dupers, persuade him of the necessity.

Hoy. But must I bleed sir?
Mon. Yes, you must bleed: your father's blood must out. He was but a yeo-man, was he?
Hoy. As ranck a Clowne, none disprais'd, as any on *Sommersetshire.*
Mon. His foule ranke blood of Bacon and Pease-porridge must out of you to the last dram.
Hoy. You will leave me none in my body then, I shall bleed to death, and you go that way to worke.
Spr. [inge, a third coney-catcher as his name implies] Fear nothing sir: your blood shal.be taken out by degrees, and your veines replenish'd with pure blood still, as you loose the puddle.

(II, iii, 143)

The dialogue continues along these lines for a considerable time. Brome exploits the snobberies and the foolish pretensions while de-riving from the device the necessary plot stimuli. The building of a store of gentlemen's blood will require an expensive diet from which the conspirators will get their share, and eating a fashionable diet will bring the group to the "sparagus garden" which is necessary to unify the various plot elements. This blood-letting device has a dramatically effective quality that Brome mastered to an exceptional degree. It is the function of the comic dramatist to find concrete equivalents for ex-pression of current interests. Brome could find homely, easily intel-ligible ways of embodying concepts and aspirations on the stage. The blood-letting device may seem a little crude and overfarcical for modern tastes. A little historical imagination can reconstruct the terms in which the audience must have received these scenes and can re-cover at least an intellectual grasp of their immense comic possibilities.

The Sparagus Garden exploited the run of interest in place-realism so noticeable in *The Covent-Garden Weeded.* The direct exposure of the profiteering of taverners so central to the earlier play is echoed in a scene between the proprietor of the Sparagus Garden and his wife in which they discuss coldly the outrageously high prices they have ex-acted of their patrons (III, i, 154–55). The exposé of the Sparagus Garden itself is much less fully worked out, but that it is only one step above a brothel, a place of assignations and brawls, is made clear in a few tableau scenes. Finally, to account for the popularity of the play, we simply have to believe that Tom Hoyden, the socially aspiring Tim's brother, must have been a joy to the Caroline audience. Just as Brome had exploited the novelty of a north country accent in *The Northern Lasse*, adapting the pathetic character of Constance to the melodies of the accent, so in *The Sparagus Garden* he capitalized on his sharply attuned ear to introduce the best Somerset dialect in years, adapting the open, forthright, simplicity of Tom Hoyden's character to the rustic imperfection and solidity of his speech. Congreve did the same thing later with great success with Ben in *Love for Love*. A close look at *The Sparagus Garden* has indicated how intimately factual, how close to the immediate activities of the city Brome's work is.

The Antipodes (1638)

Brome's gay, imaginative, and spirited attempt to combine his instinct for theatrical pathos with a more generalized form of social satire in *The Antipodes* (1638) is not quite successful, for there is an intellectual awkwardness, a loss of proper proportion that attacks Brome whenever he becomes too abstract or intellectual. He thought in terms of actable metaphors and his discursive or choral amplification of what he perceives is usually inferior to his direct presentation of it in stage action.

Even so *The Antipodes* is Brome's most unusual play. It was published during his lifetime[22] as "Acted in the yeare 1638 by the Queenes Majesties Servants, at *Salisbury* Court in Fleet-street." The play was evidently a success, for besides speaking proudly of it in the prologue to *The Court Beggar* in 1640, Brome says in his epistle dedicating the play to William Seymour, Earl of Hertford, "If the publicke view of the *world* entertayn it with no lesse welcome, then that private one of the Stage already has given it, I shall be glad."

In a strange note appended to the text of the 1640 edition, Brome addresses the reader.

You shal find in this Booke more then was presented upon the Stage, and left out of the Presentation, for the superfluous length (as some of the Players pretended) I thoght good al should be inserted according to the allowed Original; and as it was, at first, intended for the Cock-pit Stage, in the right of my most deserving Friend Mr. William Beeston, unto whom it properly appertained;

---

[22] London, 1640.

We have noted earlier that Brome, while under contract to the Salisbury Court theater wrote a play or two for the Cockpit theater contrary to contract. Evidently he tried to submit this one to them, too, but
was legally compelled to return the play to Salisbury Court. The
opening passage of the play suggests that Brome perhaps composed this
work for the reopening of the theaters during the long months of the
plague closing. In the initial line of the play, Blaze welcomes
Joylesse back from the country.

> To me, and to the City, Sir, you are welcome,
> And so are all about you: we have long
> Suffer'd in want of such faire Company
> But now that Times calamity has given way
> (Thankes to high Providence) to your kinder visits.[23]

(I, i)

The very unforeshadowed and unexplained nature of this allusion
argues that Brome, like Jonson in his *Alchemist*, intended to make his
play immediately contemporaneous by reference to the plague and the
consequent evacuation of the city. This becomes even more likely when
further along in the play we find a reference to the absence of stage
activity in London. Discussing the preparation for the play within the
play with its setting in the Antipodes,

> it will be possible
> For him to thinke he is in the *Antipodes*
> Indeed, when he is on the Stage among us.
> When't has beene thought by some that have their wits,
> That all the Players i' th' Towne were sunke past rising.[24]

(II, ii)

It seems possible that there was a period during the long plague closing
when, after the dissolution of the King's Revels group and before the
reformation of Queen Henrietta's men, the Salisbury Court theater
had no company.[25] During that time, Brome, as a playwright contrac-

---

[23] All references are to the 1640 quarto edition.

[24] Further evidence that Brome was thinking about these things during the 1636/37 (o.s.)
plague closing is afforded by his verses for Thomas Nabbes's *Microcosmus* published in 1637.
Addressing his fellow dramatist, Brome says, "Were the restraint ta'ne off, our eares and
sight/Should fetch new shares of profit and delight/From this thy worke or World/. . . . And
friend I hope the stage agen will shine,/In part for mine owne sake as well as thine."

[25] See Bentley, *J. and C.*, I, 238–41 on the breaking up of the old and the reformation of
the new Queen Henrietta's company; and *ibid.*, I, 296 for his brief speculation on the fate of
the dissolved King's Revel group.

tually tied to the house, would have had had no outlet. He might have agreed under such circumstances to prepare a play for Beeston's opening at the Cockpit with his new company, Beeston's Boys,[26] only to be restrained from doing this by the legal opposition invoked by the Salisbury Court management. Consequenly the play, though written for a reopening which happened to fall in October, 1637,[27] could have been delayed by legal difficulties until 1638.[28] That the play was performed in 1638 is supported by allusions in the prologue to the recent courtier plays "that carry state In Scene magnificent and language high; And Cloathes worth all the rest, except the Action [i.e., the acting]." This refers almost certainly to Suckling's *Aglaura* that was acted some time during the long Christmas season of 1637/38 (i.e., December, 1637 and January, 1637–38 [o.s.]). A contemporary letter dated February 7, 1637–38 (o.s.) from George Garrard (whose job it was to keep up with current news) to the Earl of Strafford, says,

Two of the King's Servants . . . have writ each of them a Play, Sir *John Sutlin* and *Will. Barclay,* which have been acted in Court, and at the *Black Friars,* with much Applause. *Sutlin's* Play cost three or four hundred Pounds setting out, eight or ten Suits of new Cloaths he gave the Players; an unheard of Prodigality.[29]

The time sequence implication in the phrasing of the prologue, where Brome speaks of "Opinion, *which . . . has of late*" embraced these new spectacles in preference to the older style of plays, does not lead one to suppose that his prologue was written immediately after Suckling's play was performed. It is more a considered reference to the recent past. In any case, Brome's prologue asserts that he is attempting

[26] We know that Beeston had reformed his new company soon enough after his Queen Henrietta's group dissolved to act plays at court in February 1636/37 (o.s.) (Bentley, *J. and C.,* I, 324–25).

[27] *Ibid.,* II, 665.

[28] This does not conflict with the prior statement that *The English Moor* was probably the play which opened the Queen's Men's career at Salisbury Court after the plague abated in 1637. Brome had seventeen months to prepare for this reopening and doubtless did not expect the closure to persist for so long. He could easily have prepared two plays. In fact, the relative apparent effort expended on the two plays, *The Antipodes* and *The English Moor,* make it suggestively possible that the following happened: Brome carefully composed *The Antipodes* with a young company and Beeston in mind, the plague closing allowing time for careful composition. Then he tried to turn the play over to Beeston, but met legal interference by Heton, his employer at Salisbury Court; so, disappointed in this he "cobbled" together a play for the Salisbury Court reopening, hoping thereby to temporize and ultimately to avoid delivering *The Antipodes* to Heton, a plan later thwarted by legal action. This is speculative and undocumented but does offer a plausible correlation of the facts.

[29] Quoted by Bentley, *J. and C.,* I, 58 from *Strafforde's Letters,* II, 150.

in his own play, *The Antipodes*, to follow the path of the great dramatist of the past, "Who best could understand, and best devise Workes,
that must ever live upon the Stage." He will in his humble way labor to
keep true comedy alive. In asserting this, Brome comes as close as he
ever does to stating his credo and justifying his service to the stage.

> Pardon our just Ambition, yet that strive
> To keep the weakest Branch o' th' Stage alive.
> I meane the weakest in their great esteeme,
> That count all slight, that's under us, or nigh;
> And only those for worthy Subjects deeme,
> Fetch'd, or reach'd at (at least) from farre, or high:
> When low and home-bred Subjects have their use,
> As well, as those, fetch'd from on high, or farre;
> And 'tis as hard a labour for the Muse
> To mouve the Earth, as to dislodge a Starre.

When the persistence of a humble vitality in Brome's best comedies
is contrasted to the utterly sterile and embalmed quality of the most
ambitious Cavalier efforts, his resistance is mightily vindicated. Contrary to the many proclaimers of the decadence of the theater in the
Caroline period, it seems apparent that the creative high road for the
dramatists of the period coursed through the area of a spacious traditional achievement. Theatrical conservatism was healthy and potentially productive—the most radical and theatrically unrooted innovations are the major indicators of decadence.[30]

The Antipodes is conceptually a simple play, full of good fun and
homely, broad farce with a social satiric bias.[31] The device around
which the play is organized is, I believe, quite original. Perigrine, a
young, naïve country youth, has read so excessively in travel literature
that he has lost his grip on reality. His young wife, Martha, has been
totally neglected so that their marriage has never been consummated
and she has fallen ill of love melancholy. She has a neurotic fixation
on having a child. Out of this unusual postulate, Brome builds a play.

---

[30] For a contrary argument, see Alfred Harbage, *Cavalier Drama*, p. 124.

[31] *The Antipodes* has been written about slightly more often than most of Brome's plays.
In addition to standard histories of the drama see Andrews, *Richard Brome*, pp. 112–34 for
a study of sources of satire; George P. Baker's introductory essay on *The Antipodes* in the
Charles M. Gayley edition of *Representative English Comedies* (New York, 1914), III, 417–29;
and Joe L. Davis, "Richard Brome's Neglected Contribution to Comic Theory," *Studies in
Philology*, XL (1943), 520–28 which treats the play from the standpoint of comic catharsis
and therapeutic laughter. He points out quite rightly that *The Antipodes* resembles Randolph's
The Muses' Looking Glass (1630).

Letoy, "A Phantasticke Lord" with a lot of money, has the eccentric hobby of producing plays in his own house for his own entertainment.[32]

> Stage-playes, and Masques, are nightly my pastimes,
> And all within myselfe: My own men are
> My Musique, and my Actors. I keepe not
> A man or boy but is of quality:
> The worst can sing or play his part o' th' Violls,
> And act his part too in a Comedy. . . .
>
> I love the quality of Playing I, I love a Play withall
> My heart, a good one; and a Player that is
> A good one too, with all my heart: As for the Poets,
> No men love them, I thinke, and therefore
> I write all my playes my selfe, and make no doubt
> Some of the Court will follow
> Me in that too.
>
> (I, v)

Doctor Hughball, who after Corax in Ford's *The Lover's Melancholy* (1624) is, to my knowledge, the first practicing psychiatrist to appear on the English stage,[33] undertakes to cure Perigrine and through him his wife by utilizing the strange hobby of his strange friend Letoy. Together they stage a play-within-the-play which pretends the conveyance of Perigrine to the Antipodes where his abnormal appetite for incredible novelties is satisfied by the acting out of a sequence of vignettes on this topsy-turvy world. His poor wife, Martha, plays the Queen whom he woos and wins, while the inverted values of the Antipodean state are introduced as a broad satiric commentary on Brome's

---

[32] Although Mildmay Fane, Earl of Westmorland, is not known to have put on his annual entertainments at Apthorpe before 1640 (after *The Antipodes* was written), the sort of home theater diversions Brome describes are similar to what we know of Fane's theatrical projects. For an account of Fane, see Harbage, *Cavalier Drama*, pp. 198–202; and *Mildmay Fane's Raguaillo D'Oceano 1640 and Candy Restored 1641*, ed. by Clifford Leech (Louvain, 1938), pp. 7–59.

[33] Dr. Hughball anticipates by more than 300 years Sir Henry Harcourt-Reilly who performs a similar function in Eliot's *The Cocktail Party*. It is true that as early as *King Lear* state doctors prescribed some therapy for mental illness, but Ford's play and Brome's after it are the first to build a whole layer of a play on the bases of diagnosis (in systematic terms) and treatment of an illness. Ford following Burton was much more interested in what we would call psychosomatic medicine. See *The Louers Melancholy*, III, i, 11. 1249–1669, for Corax's diagnosis and treatment. See also S. Blaine Ewing, *Burtonian Melancholy in the Plays of John Ford* (Princeton, 1940), pp. 32–46. Brome had used mental illness and its treatment as a minor element in several earlier plays, notably in *The Northern Lasse* (1629) and *The Queen's Exchange* (1633/34?). Cf. Lawerence Babb, *The Elizabethan Malady* (East Lansing, 1951), pp. 123 and 167–68.

London. Of course the method effects the cure and all is blissful at the finale.

The play has an unusually small number of standard roles and a large number of small parts. It was designed quite evidently to meet the special needs of Beeston's new company with its greater than normal number of children, some of them perhaps not yet fully trained.[34] The play is fresh, original, and even today has considerable homely charm for a reader. Its satire is too dull-edged and generalized to reveal anything. It is directed against the more obvious abuses—greedy lawyers, underpayment of the artist, and monopoly begging by courtiers. Almost all the materials satirized were treated elsewhere with greater control and more intimate detail by Brome.[35]

By now what is meant by the stage as newspaper is apparent: tableau cartoons on money corruption, rehearsals of local scenes with mild corrective intent, exposure of particular vices in public servants, unwittingly parochial attempts to generalize the consequences of changes in observed behaviour. All this is familiar in theme and format, only the mode of execution is premodern. We can be sure that the demanded role of dramatist as attentive editor of popular behavior found an energetic recruit in Brome. It is everywhere in his work and undoubtedly the exact, well-researched, reportorial quality of his dramatic commentary on the increasingly complex movement of London life accounts for some of his popularity. Our preoccupation with the obviously "escapist" aspect of much Caroline drama has blinded us to just how socially engaged the better plays were. There is hardly a play in Brome's canon which makes the point more variously than *The Covent-Garden Weeded* to which we now turn.

[34] Cf. Bentley, *J. and C.*, I, 324–25, *n.* 1, for the most authoritative conjectures on the "puzzling" composition of this company. That Brome originally intended it for Beeston's company is explicitly stated in a note to the reader at the end of the 1640 edition of *The Antipodes*.

[35] The satire may be more particular than we can now understand, for Brome in the 1640 edition closes his dedication of the play to "William, Earle of Hertford," by requesting that if the play "meet with too severe Construction I hope *your* Protection."

V

PATERNALISM, PURITANISM, AND SOCIOLOGICAL COMEDY

No one, it seems to me, has written more helpfully about the post-Shakespearean drama of the early seventeenth century than L. C. Knights. His book, *Drama and Society in the Age of Jonson*, demonstrates that the dramatists of the Jacobean and Caroline era were socially deeply engaged. He says, "if this book establishes anything it should be that the reactions of a genuine poet to his environment form a criticism of society at least as important as the keenest analysis in purely economic terms; that the intelligence and perception that help to make great poetry do not function in a special 'poetic' sphere, but are immediately relevant *to all questions* of the 'good life.' "[1]

His phrase "to all questions of the 'good life'" should be stressed. Topics that are too ephemeral and local for inclusion in the serious drama of our time are included as lesser analogues or alongside large-scale but presentationally-handled socio-political issues. Both are likely to be missed by the modern reader because of (1) his certainty that a few allusions to comic convention and to type characterization can fulfill the essential critical obligations of social comedy and (2) because he looks for a conceptual and abstractly argued treatment of sociological issues. This doubly misses the point. The modern constructivist apparatus for discussing social scientific problems as such did not then exist and the playwrights would not have used it if it had, since they worked through embodiment of the issues and thought them out, as it were, in parabolic terms.

The drama of the years leading up to the Civil War in England continued the development of the Elizabethan greatness coterminously with (1) the beginnings of the newspaper; (2) the growth of

---

[1] *Drama and Society in the Age of Jonson*, p. 175 (italics mine).

increasingly serious and hardhitting political pamphleteering (a verbal *obbligato* to the physical struggle which in its urgency simplified and established modern functional English syntax for good and all); and (3) an increasing sociological pressure to take sides in the swelling argument which was finally to lead to the fracturing of communities and to bloodshed. A rather too ready notion to believe that the acting companies were docile abiders by the censorship restrictions and that the audiences of this troubled time wanted "escape theater" (which beyond doubt many did) has obscured from our critical vision the manifest content of a number of very respectable plays which deal with the serious *preoccupations* of the times at varying levels of generality and with varying degrees of disguise. Brome's play, *The Covent-Garden Weeded*, comments reportorially on events of interest, exposes specific abuses, records news, editorializes current experiences, and yet derives all these things from a dramatic fable rooted in a responsible interpretation of the good society. The play is not *propaganda* and yet it is forensic and topical. A careful reading of the play reveals something about that borderland area of socially-orientated art as well as the multiple function of Caroline social comedy.

The "minute exactness and contemporaneity' of the place-realism and the architectural allusions in the opening scene of *The Covent-Garden Weeded* were noticed and scrupulously discussed by the late Theodore Miles.[2] His work suggested to a degree how richly and intimately topical the pre-Restoration town comedies were becoming. However, since he was primarily interested in topographical references he did not explore the allusive detail with any completeness. The evidence presented in this chapter has to do with housing, licensing, soap, price-fixing, monopolies, and other items of interest to the paternalistic state. Examining this evidence will show that Mile's claims about "contemporaneity" are more richly documentable than he knew.

Crossewill, a major character, has a "humour." He has a strong and perverse will. He does the opposite of what others move him to do. His son Mihil, upon hearing of his father's presence in London, says,

Is he come up with his crosse tricks. *I* heard he was to come. And that he meanes to live here altogether. He has had an aime these dozen years to live in

---

[2] See his article "Place-Realism in a Group of Caroline Plays," *Review of English Studies*, XVIII (1942), 428–40.

town here, but never was fully bent on't until the Proclamation of restraint
spurr'd him up.   (II, i, 19)

Later in the play Crossewill himself says, in complimenting his man
Belt for discovering his sons,

And I had not sold all my land to live upon my money in Town here, out of
danger of the Statute, I would give thee a Copihold for this discovery.

(IV, i, p. 74)

The allusions are to the Royal Proclamation requiring country gentry
to resort to their own houses and to exercise their function there. It is
dated June 20, 1632.[3] This means that the play had to be composed
after the middle of 1632.

Mihil, Crossewill's son, explains to his tailor that he has "a venter in
the new soap-businesse" from which he expects money soon. The reply
is that it is an insecure business and "Besides, the women begin to
grumble against the slippery project shrewdly, and 'tis feard, will
mutinie shortly" (II, i, 19). The soap business was a particularly
troublesome Royal attempt at paternalistic control of production as a
source of revenue. The negotiations, though begun earlier, became
active in the middle of 1632.[4] That the women did in effect "mutinie"
may be inferred from a letter of 1633.

The soap business is almost at an end. The certificate is made, but not yet
published: it justifies the new soap and damns the old. Upon Monday, the
23rd [i.e., December 23, 1633] the lord mayor was sent for to court, where
his majesty and the lords rebuked him for his partial proceeding in favour of
the old soap, and disparaging the new. Their lordships sent a warrant with
four of their hands to it, the lord treasurer's being one, for to bring a poor
woman out of Southwark before them for speaking invectively against the
new soap. I think she was well chidden, and so dismissed. The new company

---

[3] *Calendar State Papers, Domestic* (hereafter called *CSP Dom.*), CCXIX, Chas I (1631–33),
357: "Proclamation commanding the gentry to keep their residence at their mansions in the
country, and forbidding them to make their habitations in London and places adjoining." See
Samuel R. Gardiner, *History of England, 1603–42* (London, 1884), VII, 240–41 for a
discussion of the intention and significance of this proclamation.

[4] *CSP Dom.*, CCXIX, Chas I (1631–33), 366 "Proclamation/concerning the well making
of soap" dated June 28, 1632, and William H. Price, *The English Patents of Monopoly*
(Cambridge, 1906), pp. 119–28. Though the venture dates from the reign of James I, "Little
was done to exploit the privilege until 1631, when it was confirmed [December 17, 1631]
and a company was incorporated for the purpose of buying up and working the patent
[January 20, 1632] . . . The company's rights were made more valuable by a proclamation"
[June 28, 1632]. (Price, *English Patents*, pp. 119–20). Since certain recalcitrant soap-makers
were commited to the Fleet by Star Chamber decree on May 10, 1633, it is probable that
Brome's allusion falls before this date.

of gentlemen soapboilers have procured Mrs. Sanderson, the queen's laundress, to subscribe to the goodness of the new soap: and the truth is, that most of those ladies that have subscribed have all of them their linen washed with Castile soap, and not with new soap.[5]

This is self-explanatory and amusing. The stamp of vain bureaucracy is upon it and the women, now coerced, assent but do not agree. Brome's prediction was evidently correct and again the date is the latter half of 1632 at the earliest.[6]

Toward the end of the play Mihil pays off a bawd named Madge who has helped him in a plot to win over his father. He gives her money, "Enough to purchase . . . a License to sell Ale, Tobaccho, and Strong-water again in Codpiece-Rowe" (V, ii, 84). This allusion would not have been likely in the original text if it had been written later than October, 1633, for on that date a royal proclamation was issued "for preventing abuses growing by the unordered retailing of tobacco . . . none of those who are permitted are allowed to keep any tavern or alehouse." [7]

How richly topical the play is is evident. That it also has a direct reforming aim is generally apparent. How directly these reforming aims are geared to current problems can be gathered from examining one central aspect. Justice Cockbrayne, in the tradition of Adam Overdoe, sets out to make the quality of the inhabitants of Covent Garden comformable to the excellence of the new architecture.

What new Plantation was ever peopled with the better sort at first; nay, commonly the lewdest blades, and naughty-packs are either necessitated to 'hem, or else do prove the most forward ventures . . . do not weeds creep up first in all Gardens? and why not then in this? which never was a Garden until now; and which will be the Garden of Gardens, I foresee't. And for the weeds in it, let me alone for the weeding of them out. And so as my reverend Ancestor *Justice Adam Overdoe* was wont to say, *In Heavens name and the Kings,* and for the good of the Common-wealth I will go about it.[8]

(I, i, 2)

---

[5] Edward Rossingham to Sir Th. Puckering, Baronet, London, December 31, 1633 in T. Birch, *The Court and Times of Charles I* (London, 1849), II, 229–30. For the official account of the investigations and solicitations of female testimony, see Thomas Rymer, *Foedera* (London 1726–35), XIX, 509–10.

[6] Since the letters quoted from are supposed to be "on top of" current developments, the inference would seem to be that the gap between the play's "prediction" and the letter's report should not be many months.

[7] *CSP Dom.*, CCXX, Chas I (1633–34), p. 244 (October 13, 1633).

[8] Miles quotes a contemporary document on the question of undesirable early occupants: "A document preserved in the *Remembrancia*, dated Oct. 1632, complains of 'the multitude

And go about it he does. His stage sleuthing in disguise is limited to the taverns where excessive prices are charged and undesirables foregather. The third act is devoted mainly to exposé, where Cockbrayne makes his first entry since the opening scene and speaks (like Overdoe) directly to the audience, "Look upon me ye Common-wealths men now, like a State-Surgeon, while I search and try The ulcerous coare of foule enormitie. These are a parcel of those venomous weeds, That ranklie pester this faire Garden-plot" (III, i, 42). In the tavern he finds the Brothers of the "Blade and Batoun" roistering in conventional Caroline stage fashion. He is tormented by them, but he does note "40. sh. for foure mens dinners, note that, yet he sayes 'tis reasonable" (*ibid.*, p. 46). He hears (along with the audience) the outrageous prices itemized as follows. The drawer, pressed by the blades about the high reckoning, blames others; "there's so much reckon'd at the bar" (*ibid.*, p. 47). Anthony, the sympathetic member of the Brothers, answers,

Ant. Nay, an't be at the bar, it stands for Law . . . A Shoulder of Mutton stuff't with Oysters, 8. sh. that cost your Master very near ten groats, a brace of Partridge 5. sh. a couple of Cocks, 4. sh. 6d. a dozen of Larks 20. d. Anchovis 6. sh. I swear but a Saucer full.
Draw. I'le be sworne they are so much reckon'd in the Kitchen.
Ant. All's law, I tell you, all's law in Tavernes. But I hope there will be a law for you one o' these dayes.

(*Ibid.*, p. 47)

Cockbrayne, quivering with excitement at his discovery, says, "indeed it is a sore abuse, another verie weed in the city. I do note that also" (*ibid.*, p. 47).

Anthony's hope was not a vain one. The sort of complaints registered in Brome's play had two closely related results. First there was a royal proclamation, dated February 1633–34 (o.s.), which fixed ceiling prices on poultry, eggs, butter, etc.[9] More directly related to the play's

---

of newly erected tenements in Westminster, the Strand, Covent Garden' . . . , which had brought great numbers of people from other parts, especially of the poorer sort" ("Place Realism in a Group of Caroline Comedies," p. 438).

[9] *CSP Dom.*, CCXX, Chas I (1633–34), p. 462 (February 12, 1633/34 [o.s.]). There we see that the tavern price in the play was double that for larks—20d. to 10d.; that two cocks should have cost about one shilling instead of 4s. 6d. In October, 1633, the council had listed in an abstract of uncompleted business "the reformation of excessive prices of all sorts of victuals" (*ibid.*, p. 266). In Thomas Rymer's *Foedera* (XIX, 477–78), one can find more detail: "We wish that Ordinaries in and about *London* may be regulated to a convenient Summ not to exceed *Two Shillings* for a Meal . . . and considering the great excess and riot that is

purpose, however, are a series of recorded proceedings against the tavern owners in the Covent Garden area.

In August, 1633, there is an official report from "Sir Henry Spiller and Lawrence Whitaker to the Council [to] Certify that they have taken a view of the taverns and victually houses within the Convent [sic] Garden, and a little lane adjoining lately called Russell Street. In Covent Garden there are 8 taverns and one building, and 15 alehouses."[10] This preliminary report is followed later in the same month by a report of the Justices of the Peace for Westminster to the Council saying that they "Have received an order to reduce the number of taverns to two and the alehouses to four in Covent Garden and Russell Street."[11] A report from a Covent Garden constable in December, 1633, shows that the suppression was under way but was being resisted by some who "Keep up their bushes and continue to sell wines."[12] Early the following year we see that the fight to maintain the proper social tone in the Covent Garden neighborhood is still being waged. A man has rented a house there and "intends to erect it into a tavern, to the great prejudice of petitioner, and other neighbours being men of eminent quality."[13]

The record could be made fuller, but the required point is made. Whether or not we maintain that the dramatic exposé of local abuses has caused state reforming action, it is almost certainly more than a coincidence that the play should have singled out a problem which was immediately acted upon by the Council. Perhaps the power of the realistic comedy is more considerable than has been conventionally assumed. Again, the extreme topicality of the play is evident.

The play also contains satire on puritanism. Crossewill's elder son, Gabriel, is presented as a fanatical puritan. His father comments on this development by saying "he has nothing but hang'd the head, as you see now, ever since Holiday sports were cried up in the Countrey.

---

occasioned by preparing and selling of Victuall in Taverns, and how the prices of sundry sorts of Viends are hereby procured; hath decreed that no Taverner or Vintner selling Wine by retaile, do hereafter sell or make ready for sale, any sort of Flesh, or Fish or other Victuall, save Bread."

[10] *CSP Dom.*, CCXX, Chas I (1633–36), p. 169, August 2, 1633.

[11] *Ibid.*, p. 195, August 29, 1633, and p. 266, October, 1633.

[12] *Ibid.*, p. 335, December 21, 1633.

[13] *Ibid.*, p. 462, February 13, 1633/34 (o.s.). The petition is answered the same day and states that these men "are required not to presume to set up any tavern there" (*ibid.*). The argument may be followed further through the State Papers—the burden of all of them is the government's prohibition of unlicensed tavern keepers, the fining of them and the petitioning of tavern keepers for enactment of the prohibition against new encroachers.

And but for that, and to talk to some of the silenc'd Pastors here in town about it, I should never have drawn him up" (I, i, 5).

Gabriel is a young man, so the allusion could not be to James I's ruling of 1618 permitting the country sports on Sunday. The allusion must be to the controversy described by Davies as "a renewed puritan attempt to suppress Sunday games—this time in Somersetshire—[which] was responsible for the reissue of the Book of Sports in 1633."[14] The King's Declaration was issued on October 10, 1633.[15] The play is probably not that late. There are contemporary accounts of the squabble leading up to the Royal Declaration. Thomas Fuller's is detailed:

Here [i.e., in Somersetshire] wakes . . . were kept on the Lord's day, with Church-ales, bid-ales, and clerks'-ales . . . The gentry of that county . . . imported Sir Thomas Richardson, Lord Chief Justice, and Baron Denham, then Judges, riding the western circuit . . . to make a severe Order for the suppressing of all ales and revels on the Lord's day . . . the aforementioned Judges made an order on the nineteenth day of March [1632–33], founded on former precedents . . . suppressing such revels . . . The Archbishop of Canterbury beheld this as a usurpation on ecclesiastical jurisdiction, and complained . . . Judge Richardson gave another strict charge against these revels . . . the archbishop sent for him, and commanded him to revoke his former Order . . . telling him it was his Majesty's pleasure he should reverse it.[16]

Reference to State documents discloses the following royal letter dated May 2, 1633, to the Justices of the Peace for Somerset.

The King understands it has been an ancient custom in that country, and in other parts, to hold feasts of dedication of churches, commonly called the 'Walkes' [wakes], and that custom has been of late interrupted. They are to certify what has been given in charge by the judges of assize who now ride that circuit, or by any others concerning the suppressing of the same, and whether any judge made an order and set it to the clergy to publish; and especially what order Lord Chief Justice Richardson made at the last assizes, for recalling a former order against those feasts, as the King's express command

---

[14] Godfrey Davies, *The Early Stuarts, 1603–1660* (Oxford, 1949), p. 74.

[15] "Once more it was announced from the throne that as soon as the Sunday afternoon service came to an end the King's 'good people' were not to 'be disturbed, letted, or discouraged from any lawful recreation, such as dancing, either men or women, archery for men, leaping, vaulting, or any other such harmless recreation, nor from having of May-games, Whit-ales and morris dances, and the setting up of maypoles, and other sports therewith used' " (Samuel H. Gardiner, *History of England, 1603–1642*, VII, 321). Cf. John Rushworth, *Historical Collections* (London, 1721), II, 193.

[16] *Church History of England*, XI, Sect. II, 34–36.

twice signified to him by the Lord Keeper was he should do. The King's intention is not to give liberty to profanation of the Lord's Day, but that the people after evening prayer may use decent and sober recreation.[17]

This episode, occurring as it did in the early months of 1633, suggests again that Brome's play is slightly later than has been generally assumed.

Summarizing the evidence brought forward, it would seem that *Covent-Garden Weeded* was composed in the late months of 1632 and early 1633 to be performed around May, 1633. Certainly the play dates after the Royal Proclamation of June 20, 1632, directing the gentry to keep to their country houses—several months later from the quality of the allusions to it. It probably antedates May 10, 1633.

Such a discussion amply demonstrates one important point. It shows how topical Brome's plays are. Doubtless dozens of allusions discernible to an alert Caroline audience are completely buried for us. It is necessary to realize how these topical allusions pile up in a play in order to grasp one of the functions realistic comedy was attempting to perform in the Caroline theater.

It is of special interest that so many of the allusions, drawn from all social activities, converge on one politico-social point—the growing economic paternalism of the Stuart government, whether it be the Council controlling soap manufacture and fixing prices, the King reaffirming customary rights, or the organized Church inhibiting puritanical interference in social life. This is not precisely propaganda. At the same time it is not completely disinterested and generalized social commentary. What it seems to be is this. Brome operated from some "philosophical" assumptions about the good society and he utilized all manner of concrete and precise contemporary detail to give substance to his critical and satirical allegations about what was happening to the good society in his time. The evidence assembled forms a suggestive beginning towards an understanding of the stage as a direct agency for social reform and adjustment.

Although *Covent-Garden Weeded* is complicated by incidental action and topical aside, the central plot of the play is quite simple in structure. It is a dramatization of the relationship of a father, Crossewill,

---

[17] *CSP Dom.*, CCXX, Chas I (1633–34), p. 41; see Hugh R. Trevor-Roper's evaluation of the incident in his fine biography of *Archbishop Laud* (London, 1940), pp. 155–59. Trevor-Roper says, "the case is in itself trivial, important only as symbolic of a far more important issue."

and his two sons, Gabriel and Mihil. Crossewill, as his name implies, is a
humorous character "self-will'd, crosse, and touchie; but suddainly re-
concil'd" (I, i, 7). He has a positive fixation on exacting obedience from
his children, and in his blind eagerness to ensure this obedience he constantly exasperates his children and drives them to subterfuge. The two
sons have, through their brushes with their father's self-will, been
driven into different excesses. Gabriel has become a puritan; in his
father's words he has grown "into a Puritanical Woodcock" (V, i,
78) Mihil, who is in London supposedly to read law and learn to be a
gentleman, has fallen in with companions who wear "long haire,"
sport gay clothes, frequent taverns and brothels, and torment honest
citizens. Gabriel is one of the *Brethren* while Mihil is one of the
Brothers of the Blade and Baton, or the Philoblathici. The structure of
the play follows the simple pattern of making two brothers become
members of two socially divergent *brotherhoods*, so that these brotherhoods can be analyzed and exposed and a reconciliation be affected between the brothers themselves and of the two of them with their father.
The play was timely and pertinent in 1633, a year of pronounced
antagonism between the puritan and court factions, and it was timely
again about 1642 when it was revived. But whatever success the play
had at its revival can more probably be attributed to its satire of the
Puritans than to the basic plea for moderation between extremes of
moral conduct which the play develops.[18]

In keeping with the central theme of the effects of Paternalism,
there will be further occasion to discuss parent–child relationships.
They were the most easily dramatized of the many difficulties accruing
between old and new attitudes—the irreconcilable fracture of one
generation from another in a period of change.[19] The question of the
power and the right of the parent to exact obedience from his child is

[18] Elbert N. S. Thompson evidently had this play mainly in mind when he wrote of the
progressive falling off in the satire of puritanism as one approaches the closing of the theaters.
"From these prominent writers of the late drama the reader may assume that the reply to the
Puritans ceased towards the end of the period. Then suddenly he comes upon Brome, Jonson's
old servant, in whose London comedies is found all of Jonson's old vehemence expressed in
the same spriit" (*The Controversy between the Puritans and the Stage* [New York, 1903],
p. 257).
[19] Elizabeth Mignon has studied a related matter in Restoration comedy in *Crabbed Age
and Youth: The Old Men and Women in the Restoration Comedy of Manners* (Durham, North
Carolina, 1947). She says: "The old men and women whom we meet in the comedy of
manners are never made comfortable for an instant of dramatic time by the young who reject
them" (p. 6). Such a statement can not be made about the Caroline comedies which preceded
the plays she is generalizing from. The conflict was still a real one and youth had not yet
won out.

the particular focus of the problem found in Caroline realistic comedy and most particularly in the plays of Brome.[20] One supposes that there has always been some conflict between the will of the old, buttressed by authority and made cautious by disenchantment, and the experimental will of the young. Certainly the argument that men are no longer what they once were is one of the irreducible constituents of comedy. In the process of tracing changes in customary social outlook and in the revision of sanctions to meet new circumstances, it is necessary to deal with shifts of emphasis in perennially recurring patterns.

In Shakespeare it is only in the frightful chaotic state in rebellion that sons turns against father, as in *Henry VI*, or in the awful world of *King Lear* that the bestial ethic of selfish ingratitude can contest the right of deference, honor, and acquiescence to the will of the old. Though Juliet and Desdemona resist the counsel and will of their parents, and with fatal results, we do see them acting with unexceptionable courtesy and respect toward them. The possibility of disobedience always exists; the attitude toward it changes.

No one can read a large body of Caroline drama without inferring that this matter of obedience was interesting in itself to the Caroline audience. It remained one of the reliable conventional ingredients of comedy throughout the period. More and more it became a thing to be laughed at and disregarded as a serious deterrant to private desire. Many a Caroline comic hero can lay no greater claim to sympathy than that he has successfully (and sometimes cruelly) duped a father—of whom it is less and less required that he be evil, meddlesome, or even unpleasant.[21]

In terms of the play, the notion of obedience is treated by Brome with a double-edged skill. The issue is at once examined and made fun

---

[20] The question of obedience to one's father and the closely related problem of enforced marriage is a virtual constant in Caroline realistic comedy. Brome utilizes one or the other in almost all his city comedies. How consciously aware of this important social problem he was is perhaps best illustrated from *The Sparagus Garden* (1635) where he makes the filial obedience theme central. Early in the play the issue is discussed abstractly by Samuel, one of the sons: "To dis-obey a father, is a crime/In any sonne unpardonable. Is this rule/So generall that it can beare noe exception?/Or is a fathers power so illimitable,/As to command his sonnes affections?/And so controule the Conquerour of all men/Even *Love* himself? no; he, that enterprizes/So great a worke, forgets he is a man;/And must in that forget he is a father,/And so if he forgoe his nature, I/By the same law may leave my Piety" (*The Sparagus Garden*, I, ii, 121).

[21] Brome explores this problem in various ways. *The Queenes Exchange* centers on a father with two sons—one loyal and obedient son, the other disloyal and self-seeking. *The Damoiselle* centers on a son's respect for his father. The miseries of enforced marriage form a standard stage version of this general problem. This is a central theme in *The Novella, The Sparagus Garden*, and *The English Moor*.

of. The contrast between the father, Crossewill, and his sons is on a comic level; for though Crossewill is perverse, he is good-naturedly so. On the other hand, there is no question about the terms of their conflict; the issue between them is whose will shall prevail, and lest this be misunderstood, Brome backs their conflict with a parallel one between Rookesbill, the Covent Garden builder, and his son, Nicholas, who are genuinely and bitterly divorced from each other.

Just before Crossewill makes his first entry, his "character" is spoken by his friend Cockbrayne who, after describing his perversity, says, "His children have all the trouble of it, that do anger him in obeying him sometimes" (I, i, 3). Whereupon Crossewill appears with his elder son and daughter and immediately speaks. "It is not enough you tell me of obedience. Or that you are obedient. But I will be obeyed in my own way" (*ibid.*, p. 3). The triple reiteration forces the thematic word on the audience's attention at the same time that the speech carries us at once into the world of comic exaggeration. As soon as greetings are exchanged and introductions made, Crossewill returns to his private passion.

I'll tell you Mr. *Cockbrayne*; never was such a father so crost in his children. They will not obey me in my way. I grant, they do things that other fathers would rejoyce at. But I will be obeyed in my own way, dee see. Here's my eldest sonne.   (*Ibid.*, p. 4)

He then berates his son in the roundest fashion. The son, Gabriel, registers the mildest protest, "Surely Sir,——" but Crossewill stifles him: "Sure you are an Asse. Hold your tongue," and Gabriel replies, "You are my father" (*ibid.*, p. 5). The droll humor of this is quickly submerged under more talk from Crossewill. Meanwhile Rookesbill, who is newly acquainted with Crossewill, tries naïvely to interest him in his own genuine trouble with his son: "I am sure there cannot be a worse, or more debauche'd reprobate then mine is living" (*ibid.*, p. 5). Crossewill turns on him for his presumption and is off again merrily. Eventually he comes aground on the problem of his daughter:

when I tell you friend, there has been so many untoward matches of Parents making, that I have sworn she shall make her own choice, though it be of one I hate. Make me her match-maker! Must I obey her, or she me, ha?
(*Ibid.*, p. 6)

His daughter meekly enquires "Wherein Sir (under correction) do I disobey you?" Crossewill answers,

In that very word, under correction, thou disobey'st me. Are you to be under correction at these years? ha! If I ha'not already taught you manners beyond the help of correction, go, seek a wiser father to mend 'hem.

(*Ibid.*, p. 6)

Brome's method now becomes obvious. Rather than follow the conventional satiric route which dictated that the child dupe the parent and make him ridiculous, thereby affirming the child's right to self-determination, Brome went one step closer to the problem. Working through character for his comic analysis and not merely through situation, he makes Crossewill the embodiment of willful caprice—amusing enough in himself but connoting something more. Obedience, the issue or question, becomes a palpable thing through the characterization of Crossewill. In his fantastically caricatured sensitivity to imagined rejections of his parental authority, he becomes a kind of symbol of private desire claiming extra-personal rights. As a comic device, it is satisfactory and as a satiric instrument, superior; for through it not only is the child's right vindicated but also the very basis of the parental claim is undercut.

Children react to this carping discipline by going underground. They react into extremes.[22] The particularly interesting trend in Crossewill's part in the play is that he himself is well balanced in his own conception of what his sons should be, but he oversteers them and consequently they lose control. Out of his immoderate humor emerges an ethic of moderation and tolerance. This is what the play is about— the issue of obedience is the instrument that Brome uses to direct his enquiry.

The question of moderation between the extremes of puritan jealous self-denial and libertine indulgence is obliquely introduced by Damaris (who is in reality Crossewill's "fallen" niece but who figures in most of the play in the disguise of a Courtesan). She is really virtuous but in a speciously cynical speech she queries the traditional morality of London.

> Why should not we in *England* use that freedome
> The famous Courtezans have in *Italy*:
> We have the art and know the Theory

[22] His daughter, later in the play, explains to a friend, "in us, *I* mean, his children, he will like nothing, no, those actions which he himself cannot deny are vertuous; he will crosse us in all we do, as if there were no other way to shew his power over our obedience . . . . Now, note the punishment that followes it. There's not a childe he has, though we all know what we do, that makes any conscience of crossing him" (III, ii, 51).

The answer she finds,

> Where's the let?
> Only in bashful coward custome, that
> Stoops i' the shoulders and submits the neck
> To bondage of Authority; to these laws,
> That men of feeble age and weaker eye-sight
> Have fram'd to bar their sons from youthful pleasures.

(I, i, 9)

As this apparently crass argument blends with the exposure of the insecure pretension to authority of the old personified in Crossewill, we uneasily ask if we are going to find the play a bald apology for amoral self-indulgence. But this is to misunderstand the play's terms. Brome is going around to show that the authority of the old is not conferred automatically and cannot apply to unreasonable propositions. Their authority accrues insofar as they embody and practice the traditional wisdom and good nature implicitly and explicitly advocated throughout the play.

Gabriel, the puritanical elder brother, refuses to follow the proper pursuits of his status as a country gentleman. Rather, "he'l run you a foot five mile another way, to meet the brethren of the separation" (I, i, 5). He is unhealthily introspective and keeps a diary: "he has a book of his own Short-writing in his pocket, of such stuffe as is fit for no mans reading indeed, but his own" (*ibid.*, p. 5). He is intolerant of others' pleasures for he has "hang'd the head . . . ever since Holiday sports were cried up in the Countrey. And but for that, and to talk with some of the silenc'd Pastors here in town about it" (*ibid.*, p. 5), he would not even appear in iniquitous London. He is constantly abstracting himself in thought from convivial gatherings. When at the tavern he withdraws into himself, he is asked, "what is hammering in your head now? Isn't not some Synodical question to put unto the brethren, concerning Whitsonales and Maygames? ha!" (II, ii, 32–33). And when he hears the music of the tavern fiddlers, he loses all control.

Such cries as these went forth before the desolation of the great City. O prophane tinkling the cymbals of Satan, that tickle the care with vanity, to lift up the mind to lewdnesse. Mine eares shall be that of the Adder against the Song of the Serpent . . . I will roare out aloud to drown your Incantations. Yes, I will set out a throat even as the beast that belloweth.

(*Ibid.*, pp. 34–35)

So he sums up neatly the intolerance, inwardness, self-suspicion, and fatuous inflexibility with which we generally associate the unsympathetically portrayed puritan.[23] Brome is not satisfied to rest here. He undertakes something that can only be described as a rudimentary psychiatric "case history." Gabriel's sister is the informant.

> My brother *Gabriel*, when he was a boy . . . was the wildest untamed thing that the countrey could possibly hold . . . he was the Ring-leader of all the youthful Frie, to Faires, to Wakes, to May-games, footbal-matches, any-thing that had but noise and tumult in it; then he was Captain of the young train-band, and exercised the youth of twenty parishes in martial discipline . . . there was not an handsom maid in an whole County could be quiet for him.[24]
>
> (III, ii, 51–52)

But since Gabriel was sexually attracted to a girl too closely related to him (though he treated her with "the civillest and best ordered affection"), his father, "fearing what youth in heat of blood might do, removes . . . *Gabriel* from home into the service of a Reverend Bishop to follow good examples" (*ibid*., p. 52). While Gabriel was thus removed from the scene, "came a Gallant into the countrey from London" and betrayed her virtue. When Gabriel heard this, he fell into discontent and "ever since he has been thus religious" (*ibid*., p. 53), and his sister thinks it happened as a resentful reaction to his "father, for sending him out of the way when the mischief was done" (*ibid*., p. 53). During this long narrative inset, a thing rare in Brome who is unusually scrupulous about his dramaturgical proportions, Katherine's auditor has expressed a healthy scepticism about the normality and sincerity of fanatical religion. She thinks "no man of his Gabriel's Religion in his wits," and will not "believe 'tis Religion in any of the gang of 'em, but mere wilful affectation"[25] (*ibid*., pp. 52 and 53). The case history recounted places a heavy blame on irresponsible paternal

---

[23] A. M. Myers, in *Representation and Misrepresentation of the Puritan in Elizabethan Drama* (Philadelphia, 1931), though he quarries the play to illustrate various preconceived classifications, does not seem to understand its methods at all. Commenting on the major satiric concentration of the play, he says, "If well acted, the part of Gabriel in act four may be a merry take-off of a drunken man, but as a picture of a Puritan it is too overdrawn to be effective" (pp. 80–81).

[24] Brome gives this a double stress by having it repeated later in the play. Gabriel's fallen cousin comments on his transformation when first she sees him again: "How cam my Cousin *Gabriel* thus translated./Out of gay clothes, long haire, and lofty spirit,/Stout and brave action, manly carriage;/Into so strict a Reformation? (IV, ii, 67).

[25] At the same time that he is reiterating the commonsense, traditional ethic of moderation, Brome is also anticipating the 18th-century attitude toward religious enthusiasm as an excess which implies madness. Readers of Swift's *A Tale of a Tub* know the attitude well.

intervention. The diagnosis is sharply relevant in relation to the circumstances of Caroline England.

Mihil, Gabriel's younger brother, with the expressed aim to "worke
out his superfluous zeale. And render him civil Christian again," leads
his brother to a tavern to exercise the simple therapy of getting him
drunk.

> I'le undertake one good fellow, that has but just as much Religion as will serve
> an honest mans turne, will bear more wine then ten of these giddy-braind
> Puritans, their heads are so full of whimseys.   (IV, ii, p. 62)

As soon as they start drinking Mihil, whose excess has been the typical
roistering profligacy of a drunken youth escaped from excessive
paternal direction, begins to question his brother about the man who
seduced and left their cousin. Gabriel heatedly takes up the subject,
saying that even if the seducer could not make suitable restitution,

> It had been good to have humbled him, though into the knowledge of his
> Transgression. And of himself for his soules good, either by course of Law, or
> else in case of necessity, where the Law promiseth no releefe, by your own right
> hand you might have smote him, smote him with great force, yea, smote him
> unto the earth, until he had prayed that the evil might be taken from him.
>   (*Ibid.*, p. 63)

This is good dialogue; it picks up the tempo as Gabriel passes from his
routine acknowledgment of the necessary first recourse to law and
passes on to his real point—righteous revenge against impurity. The
heart of the traditional resentment and fear of the Puritans, their compulsive urge to bypass society in the exercise of their duty as keeper of
their brothers' conscience, is expressed here. Mihil's answer makes the
point: "This is their way of loving enemies, to beat 'em into goodnesse"
(*ibid.*, p. 63).

Brome's satire of the Puritan mentality is now fully underway. For
Gabriel is persuaded to drink with his brother and his brother's friend,
conceding he will join them "in a cup of sincere love." When he hears
they are to be joined by women, he is shocked and wants to flee until
restrained by his brother's sharp "cannot we govern ourselves?" (*ibid.*,
p. 64).

Then in one of the funniest scenes in all of Brome, Gabriel mistakes
the *Brothers* of the Blade and Batoun (a dissolute crew of rowdies
with whom his brother Mihil has been keeping company) for his own
Puritan *Brethren* and in his confusion identifies an old bawd of their

company as a Puritan matron. Toasting her, he politely enquires after the latest gossip in dissenter circles: "this unto your welcome, hoping I shall be informed by you how the two zealous brethren thrive there? [He supposes her to come from Amsterdam] that broke in St. *Hellens*" (*ibid.*, p. 68). His brother then introduces him to their "fallen" cousin, who is masquerading as a courtesan under the name of Damaris in hopes of finding her fled seducer. Gabriel does not know her assumed name; so he is shocked when one of the gallants refers to her as "Dammy." "I dare not speak it but in thy reproof. Thou swearest Gee o Dee, Dee a m thee, as I take it" (*ibid.*, p. 69). When the offender explains, Gabriel refuses to believe him and wants to fight.

I may not forbear, I am moved for to smite him; yes, with often stripes to smite him; my zealous wrath is kindled, and he shall flee before me . . . I will pursue him in my indignation . . . And beat him into Potsheards.

(*Ibid.*, pp. 69–70)

All this is punctuated with staccato attempts at discussion as Gabriel lays about him with his sword in drunken self-righteousness. Suddenly he registers that some one of the Brothers of the Blade had referred to his quarry as "Brother." Gabriel, puzzled, stops and enquires of his brother Mihil,

Gab. Pray give me leave to ask you, do these men take part with the brethren?
Mih. Yes, and are brothers a little disguiz'd, but for some ends.
Gab. Some State-occasions.
Mih. Meer Intelligencers, to collect up such and such observations, for a great
    Separatist that is now writing a book against playing at Barlibreak,
    moulding of Cocklebread, and such like prophane exercises.
Mih. Truly, such exercises are prophane exercises, that bear the denomina-
    tions of good things ordained for mans use, as Barley, Cockles, and Bread
    are such things to be made sports and play-games? I pray you let me see
    these brethren again, to make my atonement with them.[26]

(*Ibid.*, p. 70)

[26] It seems perhaps possible that Brome, with reference to the "great Separatist" (who is writing a comprehensive work on the iniquities of various forms of play), was having some indirect fun at the expense of the notorious William Prynne whose book *Histriomastix: The Players Scourge*, appeared on January 10, 1632/33 (o.s.) cf. Harbage, *Cavalier Drama*, pp. 14–16, and Elbert N. S. Thompson, *Controversy*, pp. 159–78. The date is proper and it may even be conjectured that Prynne's monumental indiscretion formed part of the incentive to write an anti-Puritan play at this time. Shirley dedicated his *The Bird in a Cage*, written at about this time, to Prynne. Since Prynne's work was merely a larger and more aggressive summation of widespread Puritan attitudes, it is perhaps incautious to suggest this identification.

Brome works this development into effective satire of the Puritan standard of morality made famous by Jonson's devastating satire of Ananias Wholesome's rationalization of means in *The Alchemist*; for, once Gabriel is satisfied his companions are fellow Puritans, their hitherto intolerable moral obliquities become acceptable. "This done in civil sort among our selves, I hope, will prove no scandal to a brother" (*ibid.*, p. 72). Much play is made on the words "brother" and "brethren" until finally Nick, Rookesbill's son and presented as an unpleasantly immoral character in the play, sums it up:

we are brethren, sir, and as factious as you, though we differ in the Grounds; for you, sir, defie Orders, and so do we; you of the Church, we of the Civil Magistrate; many of us speak i' th' nose [i.e. are ravaged by venereal disease] as you do; you out of humility of spirit, we by the wantonnesse of the flesh; now in devotion we go beyond you, for you will not kneel to a ghostly father, and we do to a carnal Mystresse.   (*Ibid.*, p. 72)

In Caroline England of 1633, when Laud's efforts towards the identification of Church and State were beginning to intensify and arouse wide comment and resistance, such a facetious juxtaposition as this would have had special point. Both kinds of brethren would have been equally "immoral" in their orientation. In a strongly paternalistic state with an Erastian state control of ecclesiastical issues, religious enthusiasm and roistering disorder are equally disruptive to the equilibrium of society and equally an offense against the established norms of the community.

Once he accepts the company, Gabriel quickly becomes incompetently drunk. He "thirsts to do some honour to our cause. To lead forth legions to fight a battel 'gainst our malignant adversaries"[27] (ibid., pp. 72–73). But before he can grace his cause, he is overcome by drink and falls, saying, "I feare some Jesuitical fumes have invaded my Brain pan. All me thinks goes whirley, whirley, whirley" (*ibid.*, p. 73).

Enough has been presented to afford a clear notion of the amount and quality of direct satire on the Puritans in the play. Brome expended

---

[27] When Gabriel is coming out of his drunken stupor, Brome gives him a long sequence of speeches of military rant (V, ii, 87–90). It is worth observing that in a period crowded with plays featuring battle scenes and duels (Thomas Killigrew's plays are little else), Brome never staged a battle and never used a duel for serious stage business. His references to and uses of violence are almost without exception a means of rendering a character disagreeable or ridiculous. Is it too much to say that his overall moderation carried with it a correlative pacificism?

much less space and effort in portraying the alternative excess of Mihil. This was partly because he could more quickly identify Mihil's libertine transgression for an audience accustomed to the stage type which he exemplifies, and partly because Mihil is what we would call a "romantic lead" insofar as the play has one, and therefore must not be too thoroughly discredited as a sympathetic character. Brome depends on indirect means to stigmatize the life which Mihil has been leading. He stages several scenes showing the moral level at which Mihil's companions operate, but following the technique of Shakespeare in his handling of Prince Hal in the Boarshead scenes in *Henry IV*, Part I, Brome lets Mihil's companions do the dirty work while keeping Mihil well on the periphery. In one scene (IV, i) a citizen, whose sole excuse for appearing is to be a badly mauled victim, is sadistically tormented by Nick and the rest of Mihil's fellow-Brothers of the Blade. Brome is careful not to let Mihil become involved in this unpleasantness. Brome rather deftly causes the characters of the irresponsible Nick and Mihil to overlap so that he can use the former as a stalking-horse. Whereas it is clear that Crossewill considers his two sons as approaching equally undesirable extremes of conduct, Mihil never appears on the stage as an "absolute Ruffian"; this facet of his character is all reported in the comments of other characters. This can be readily illustrated. Nick acts out the excess so that Crossewill can be made to preface the illustrative scenes by saying to Nick's father of Gabriel's conduct compared to Nick's.

It is a vice, as much a vice or more, as is your sonnes, your cast-aways as you call him, that sucks no other aire, then that of Tavernes, Taphouses, Brothels, and such-like. I would like their extream qualities could meet each other at half-way, and so mingle their superfluities of humour unto a mean betwixt 'hem. It might render them both allowable subjects.   (II, ii, 30)

This prefigures the final thematic statements of the last act, when in a series of speeches the extreme dichotomy of the two sons is explicitly noted. Crossewill laments,

the affliction I suffer in my sons now. that one of them from a riotous boy, should grow into a Puritanical Woodcock; and the tother from a civil well-qualified fellow, turn'd absolute Ruffian.   (V, i, 78)

In a speech that presages the analysis of enthusiasm in Swift's *Tale of a Tub*, Crossewill sets off a nearly epic metaphor for his son Gabriel's development.

was not that dunce *Gabriel*, a most notorious wilde thing Before he steer'd a Religious course? but then he run so full a saile, that he pass'd and was beyond the line of Religion before he was aware; and as he passed it under the torrid Zone of Zeale, the Calenture took him o' the pate, that he is mad with it, and as far beyond Religion now as it is to it.

(Ibid., p. 78)

His man consoles him, saying, "Sir, there's hope that he may be fetch'd halfe way back again, by your fatherly advicement, and become a sound man."

But, we are again reminded that Gabriel's Puritan fanaticism is not the only form excess takes when Crossewill replies to his man's optimistic prediction, "And then was not *Mihil* so civil . . . And now is he flowen out as far into riot t'other way."[28] Feeling persecuted by his fortune as he does, Crossewill finally traces his sons to the tavern in time to witness Gabriel emerging from his drunken stupor in a final, wild outpouring of violent, fanatical, militaristic nonsense. He can hardly endure this latest development. "Is't possible it is thou? art thou run mad as far as hell the tother way now" (V, iii, 90). But reconsidering, he adds, "I rather thought I should have found you, sir, disputing with the Pastors, and the Elders; yet to say truth, this is the better madnesse" (*ibid.*, p. 91).

It is now plain that Brome conceived the fanatical enthusiasms of Puritanism as madness—as a crime against moderation and self-control. This is firmly substantiated by Gabriel's confession when his head finally clears.

> What *Babel* was a building in my braines?
> But now it turnes, and I can recollect
> The knowledge of a father, brother, Sister.
> And that a thousand vain imaginations,
> Like scatterings of light things upon the earth,
> Rushes, loose leaves, sprigs, straws, and dust
> Contracted by a whirlwinde, were blowen up,
> And lodg'd in the rich Seat of Contemplation,
> Usurping there the room of vertuous thoughts.
> Honour awake me from this Lethargie.

(*Ibid.*, p. 91)

Brome has completed his diagnosis of Gabriel's particular and representative malady. In his usual fashion, he has used a farcical technique

---

[28] *Ibid.*, p. 79. Erroneously numbered 97 in quarto.

to enact a serious indictment. Here he has in effect identified the spiritual drunkenness of the Puritan with physical drunkenness, so that the application of liquor to Gabriel has been homeopathically effective by exaggerating his state to the breaking point—his mental fever has broken. Peace is restored between father and sons.

It remains only to interweave the role of obedience and apply the counsel of moderation to the father. Using the images of long and short hair as the equivalents of excesses of conduct, the final judgment is made and acknowledged.

> *Cros.* I hope they'l prove my sons, and be indifferent men in time, sir, by that
>   time their haire may grow, or be reduc't to an indifferent length. . . .
> *Gab.* . . . I do you the obedience of a son, acknowledging my former formal
>   habit was more of stubbornesse then true devotion. For which I beg
>   your pardon.
> *Cros.* There's more deceit under these half Footballs, then in whole pudding-
>   bags, Well Boyes, be you indifferent sons, neither too hot nor too cold.
>   I have found a fault in myself, I confesse. I will reform it, and be an in-
>   different father.

(Ibid., pp. 94–95)

The penitent and apologetic father was in itself, something fairly new on the English stage. To have him recognize the coercing role he played in driving his sons into opposing excesses while maintaining a sympathetic character for him was something of a *tour de force* on the Caroline stage. A cautious correlation can be made between the terms of this play and the circumstances of Caroline England. Caution is required because explicit personal references and topical satire cannot be summoned for confirmation. But it is apparent to any student of the reign of Charles I and particularly of that stretch known as the "personal reign" (1629–40) leading up to the Civil War that the state suffered from an increasing paternalism. The very symbols of this excessive and domineering paternalistic state policy, Laud and Strafford, were the persons on whom public hatred centred, and they were the first great sacrifices offered to a public resistance that became increasingly willful. The undiplomatic and humorless oppression of the Puritans that Laud symbolized was just getting under way in the early years of the 1630s during his tenure as Bishop of London before he assumed the primacy of the Church of England in 1633. From this time forward, it was ever more difficult not to take sides. Without necessary explicit personal references to Laud, Brome here broaches in humorous terms the fact that one does not need to approve of puritanism—far from it—to recognize that the troublesome, stubborn excesses of the puritans might well be a reaction against excessive paternal intervention. Brome seems to be arguing that an inflexible and unintelligently restrictive policy on the part of the paternal state can induce a desperate and equally inflexible resistance. History was certainly to bear him out. It was stated at the beginning of this book that the plays present, in consciously or unconsciously disguised form, the primary social preoccupations of the age—as plays will in all ages where the comic stage is not an utterly sterile and academic thing. This is not the same thing as direct political propagandizing or detailed topical satire. It is using comedy in its most natural and fruitful fashion to detect and evaluate general social trends in terms of concrete character relationships.

The play presents ample detailed evidence that such a *submerged correlation* of stage and environmental circumstance is very possible and an intelligent member of the contemporary audience would naturally have drawn some such inference. The play is most representative of Brome's characteristic attitudes—his suspicion of excess, his dislike of coercion, his belief in good-natured tolerance—and it makes more explicit than any other play his governing belief in *measure*.

VI

PARABLE AND HAGIOGRAPHY

Richard Brome was the last representative of the conservative moral tradition in the theater at a time when the position he represented was still contemporary and not yet reactionary. Besides being a social conservative actively interested in giving dramatic expression to his beliefs as to what constituted the "good society," Brome is also one of the last masters of the art of analogical thinking—the art which enabled the dramatic construction of Shakespeare and his major contemporaries. T. S. Eliot, though an immeasurably better poet, is theatrically a direct descendent of Brome.

Brome's two basic dramatic forms were realistic comedy (with many specialized variations) and his own sly adaptations of popular tragicomedy. In *The Queen and Concubine* Brome established a pattern of social, political, and ethical views. These views are formally patterned in the play by Brome's own deliberate intention; the fabric is carefully woven. In *The Queen and Concubine* he made his most earnest (though not most successful) attempt to find artistic means for stating his convictions about the non-acquisitive sense of responsibility and the disinterested love (*Agape*) which are the informing concepts of his best work.

The Queen and Concubine was a strange play to have appeared in the middle of the Caroline period. Though it has been mistakenly described as "a rather pallid study in the school of Fletcher,"[1] and as "an interesting example of the extravagance of action and absurdity of character into which the Fletcher pattern of tragicomedy was sinking,"[2] it is only in the most superficial sense Fletcherian. It is nearer the truth that in this play "We escape from inflated sentiment and re-

---

[1] Algernon C. Swinburne, "Richard Brome," *Fortnightly Review*, LI (N.S.: 1892), 506.
[2] Thomas M. Parrott and Robert H. Ball, *A Short View of Elizabethan Drama* (New York, 1943), p. 174.

turn to a simplicity of moral feeling which belongs to the earlier days of the drama," [3] for far from being a bootless attempt at a current theatrical fad, the play is primarily a contribution, in dramatic form, to the extensive marriage literature of the period,[4] and its superficial terms of presentation—a selection of tragicomic conventions—are due in part to theatrical strategy and in part to an attempt to dignify the presentation by extending concern for the outcome beyond the purely domestic sphere. To put the issue in concrete and temporarily reckless terms, the play moves in an area somewhere between *Othello* and Dekker's *Patient Grissil*—at an infinite distance, poetically and artistically, from the former but concerned to make some of the same affirmations. It is an essential *comedy*, in that, for the mature English stage tradition comedy is circumscribed by the marriage problem. At its most serious, as in *Volpone*, *The Tempest*, *The Cocktail Party*, *Love for Love*, English comedy has scrutinized love's corruption or love's redemption, just as the lighter comedies have had cuckoldry, adultery, the love-game debate, or the comic vicissitudes of the marital state itself as their subject matter. It might be said that the way to reorient English comedy is to do what Eliot or Congreve or the Shaw of *Candida* did, that is, break with the automatic assumptions about love and marriage which determine the comic theater of one's time.

Study of the play is given initial impetus by an accidental fact. The primary source of the play is known, which is true for no other Brome play. Koeppel long ago established that Brome drew his central fable from Greene's *Penelope's Web* (1587).[5] It is a naïve, overtly didactic tale told to illustrate one of the virtues "necessary to be incident in every vertuous woman," namely obedience. The tale, told without subtlety or humor, makes its heroine a paragon of every virtue and particularly of that submissive, resigned, long-suffering quality that medieval man called obedience. The story is amply weighted with

[3] Ronald Bayne, "Lesser Jacobean and Caroline Dramatists," *Cambridge History of English Literature*, VI (1910), 231.

[4] For an account of the tradition of non-dramatic marriage literature to which the play is related, see Chilton L. Powell, *English Domestic Relations 1487–1653* (New York, 1917); Louis B. Wright, *Middle-Class Culture in Elizabethan England* (Chapel Hill, 1935), pp. 121–69 and 201–27. And for a quite successful instance of the use of this literature in critical explication of Shakespeare, see Roland M. Frye's unpublished Princeton University thesis, The Accepted Ethics and Theology of Shakespeare's Audience (Princeton, 1952), particularly pp. 146–98 and 319–32. See also Peter Ure, "Marriage and the Domestic Drama in Heywood and Ford," *English Studies*, XXXII (1951), 200–16.

[5] "Brome's *Queen and Concubine*," *Quellen und Forschungen*, LXXXII (Strassburg, 1897), 209–18.

Greene's very vocal piety and is altogether a most unlikely source for a Caroline tragicomedy. Most important is its direct, almost propagandistically moralized nature.

Brome transposed Greene's Egyptian setting into Sicily, the shopworn locale for tragicomedy, substituted Italian for Greek Romance names, and generally conventionalized the new materials of the plot to meet routine Caroline stage standards for tragicomedy. He spent nearly his whole first act elaborating a plot sequence which plays no part at all in his source. This is a contest between two generals, Sforza, the father of the concubine, and Petrucchio, whom the former has superseded in the King's favor. It is typically Fletcherian. Beyond the obvious need to provide some subordinate characters to swell the small number of major actors in Greene's simple narrative (giving normal stage complexity to the fable), and the corollary necessity of providing some motivating patterns to fill the fairy tale vacuum of totally implied or ignored motive in the source, Brome provided this court-faction contest between rival generals as a specious, external concession to the tragicomic mode. It plays no important part in the main action of his plot, gathers no interest, and merely provides occasions for some interpolated scenes on honor and duty and the insecurity of royal favor.[6] This aspect of the play is mainly at the level of exposition, that is, the conflicts are stated and described but not developed; almost all dialogue they elicit is rhetorical declaration and not dramatically functional. Yet, since the concentration of this material is in the early action, it gives a superficial Fletcherian coloration to the play.

Brome takes from Greene a brief statement of which the narrative possibilities were not developed, and expands it into a substantial portion of his play. Greene's tale and Brome's play are fundamentally simple. An old, lustful King falls in love with a young, ambitious girl, and in order to make her his concubine he must reject and exile his virtuous wife and Queen. The unadorned point of Greene's story, and the elaborated theme of Brome's play, is the admirable and orthodox patience and obedience of the Queen under the adversities she suffers. Greene simply says that, after the exile of the Queen,

The *Souldan* [i.e. the King] not satisfied with this injurie, caused presently Proclamation to be made, that the Princesse [Queen] should have no reliefe,

---

[6] See for example, II, vi–viii, where Petrucchio, the restored court general, visits Sforza in prison for a brief colloquy on honor and princely policy.

but what she earned with her hands, . . . and her maintenance, no other then her owne indevour could provide.[7]

Greene makes only the most minor use of this harsh condition; to guarantee that the poor Queen's deprivation is clearly evident to the reader and to give occasion for a passing contrast (in his reflexive, pastoral vein) between the healthy simplicity of country life and the corrupt and worrisome atmosphere of the court.[8]

Proportionately, Brome expands this section tremendously; indeed, after the exposition is complete and Eulalia, the good Queen, has been banished to the country, the play centers on her relations with the rustics. The court is referred back to for occasional scenes rather than the other way round. Brome trebles the stress on the court–country contrast and relates it integrally with his main theme. In these country scenes, he introduces a loyal fool, Andrea, who (along with a loyal counselor) follows Eulalia into exile in an obvious reminiscence of the Fool and Kent in *King Lear*.[9] This gives opportunity for extended comic scenes between Andrea and the sympathetically portrayed rustics, and between the rustics themselves. These scenes well illustrate the complete alteration in technique and tone Brome effected in dramatizing his source without deviating from the central theme of female virtue or the didactic stress of Greene's original.

The technique of the play presents a study in contrasts. By constructing a pyramiding set of oppositions in theme, character, and situation, Brome argues his case for old-fashioned and substantial virtues. The contrasts are interlocked, each adding meaning to the others. There are contrasts of lust and love, of reason versus passion, timeserving versus true loyalty, obedience versus ambition, belief in providence versus malicious intrigue, true kingship versus tyranny, dotage versus wisdom, court versus country, and, covering and subserving many of these, appearance versus reality.

The Queen and Concubine has a definite technical affinity to *The Tempest*. *The Tempest*, of all Shakespeare's plays, is the one which

---

[7] *The Life and Complete Works of Robert Greene*, ed. by Alexander B. Grosart (1881–83), V, 176 (The Huth Library edition).

[8] *Ibid.*, p. 185, where the Queen tells her successor "Madame, although I want an imperiall Crowne, and other Crownes also: this lacke I find frees me from care, and I sleepe more in the Cottage, then ever I slumbred in the Court."

[9] Emil Koeppel, *Quellen und Forschungen*, LXXXII, 218, noted the fool's derivation: "Bei Andrea, dem treuen Narren der Königin Eulalia, welcher der geliebten Herrin in's Eland folgt, denken wir an Lear's Narren."

approaches most nearly the "moral masque." The characters, though not morality figures, are further by one remove from the human experience of the reader than is usual in Shakespeare. It is loose and inexact to call them allegorical figures—they do not denote with precision abstract values. But, it is incontestable that the characters have a definite extra-personal significance and that there is meant to be a constant cross reference between the presented action and the moral values which underlie it. The play at times approaches direct statement and the characters are more impersonally motivated than is usual in drama. This is generally known. However, with the current abuse of the word "symbolic" and with the evident difficulty we moderns have with symbolic or emblematic conceptions, such things need to be said. The problem of the didactically inclined dramatist is just how to gain some of the control and coherence of the morality play without dehumanizing the characters and petrifying the action. Direct statement has no reverberations—it cannot persuade the unpersuaded. Strict morality is a ritual form, since the conflicts have already been resolved, evaluated, and stylized into accepted generalities. Shakespeare partly resolved this problem in *The Tempest* by evoking a fairy tale mood in an isolated and detached setting with the agency of magical power to control and subjugate improbabilities. Brome, always remembering the insuperable disparity in ability, follows Shakespeare's path in *The Queen and Concubine*. In fact, there are times when the play moves nearly into the realm of hagiography—instead of an account of a virtuous wife, he seems to be writing the life of St. Eulalia, Queen of a mythical Sicily, a realm where divine Providence becomes observably functional and the extremes of unexplained virtue and unmotivated vice gain a new kind of detached and distant acceptability.

The saintly Queen in rustic exile teaches the little country girls to sing,

> What if a Day, or a moneth, or a year
> Crown thy Delights
> With a thousand wish'd contentings?
> May not the chance of a Night or an Hour
> Cross thy Delights
> With as many sad Tormentings?
> Fortune, Honour, Beautie, Birth,
> Are but blossomes dying.
> Wanton Pleasures, doating Mirth,
> Are but Shadows flying.

> All our Joys
> Are but Toys,
> Idle thoughts deceiving:
> None hath power
> Of an Hour
> In our lifes bereaving.[10]

This song, with its clear accents on the illusory and transient nature of things, is the theme song of the play. It is proper that the Queen, who embodies the *unshadowed* side of the theme, should have taught her innocent country charges to sing it. Various elements in the play converge on and in the song.

At the beginning of the third act, when he has completed the necessary exposition of his fable and has drawn the terms of the factional struggle in the court, Brome turns to the real burden of his play. He presents Queen Eulalia in soliloquy. In a very long speech she appraises her wretched situation—alone, exiled, without the promise of normal charitable succour. The poetry is intrinsically mediocre:

> What's my loss?
> What was the State and glory of a Court,
> But stars and lights through dangerous Ambition,
> To ends beyond our selves, in whose achievements,
> We make our selves but nothing to our selves.

Continuing, she draws a fundamental distinction in the imagistic terms of the play,

> They do but sleep, that live in highest Pompe;
> And all their happiness is but a dream,
> When mine is reall:
>
> (III, i, 44)

Their rich show is "Made to please their eyes" (*ibid.*, p. 44). The images are simple enough, but the appearance–reality contrast is capable of great extension, and its affinity to "the baseless fabric of this vision" is immediately apparent.

Her speech continues and birds chirp in the background as she develops (with inadequate pastoral lyricism) the contrast of court and

---

[10] IV, iii, 88, but also quoted facing p. 1 of the quarto edition of the play. The song is attributed to Campion and appeared in Richard Alison's, *An Hour's Recreation in Music*, (1606). There are numerous non-crucial variants between that text and the one printed with Brome's play. This occurrence of the song is not noted in Percival Vivian's chronicle of its extraordinary vogue "in the manuscripts and printed books of the sixteenth and seventeenth centuries" (cf. his edition of *Campion's Works* [Oxford, 1909], pp. 377–78).

country life in favor of the latter. She falls asleep and a "Genius" enters on the line "Sleep in thy Sainted Innocence." Against the background of muted musical strains and the dumb-show spectacle of the
continuing intrigue of the court she has left behind, the "Genius" be-
stows upon her magical superhuman powers,

> I thy Brain inspire
> With a Divine Prophetick Fire;
> Thou shalt be able to Fore-doom
> The ends of many things to come.
>   (III, ii, 47)

To this he adds miraculous powers of healing and teaching:

> Many diseas'd by Grief and Pain,
> Of thee shall Health and Strength obtain.
> . . . Handy-Works and Literature,
>   (*Ibid.*, p. 47)

and she shall teach those rustics she has come among "how to improve
Their Wealths by Neighbour-hood and Love":
The "Genius" departs and Eulalia awakens

> to live, for others Good.
> Who live but for themselves, are but for show,
> And stand like barren Trees, where good might grow.
>   (*Ibid.*, p. 47)

The thematic strands of selfishness versus disinterested devotion to the
public interest and the general contrast of appearance and reality are
brought together here.

The court and country are now separated not only in rhetorical
contrasts but in the physical stage action. Lodovico and Andrea, the
two loyal and selfless followers of the exiled Queen, the one an aged
counselor, the other a fool (described later as "*Senex & Ineptus,*" p. 59),
appear in the country to seek their Mistress.

> Farewel, thou foolish Pomp, and Pride of Court,
> Whose shine is but an *Ignis fatuus.*
> That leads fond Mortals from the path of Vertue,
> And Tracts of real Comforts: thus I shake
> Thy wanton Dust from off my Feet, to tread

> The wayes of Truth and Innocence: this Air
> Breaths Health upon me, Peace, and perfect Pleasure.
> Where the swoln Courts sophisticated Breath
> Did but disease my Blood, and taint my Senses.
>
> (III, iii, 48)

When the three are rejoined, their reunion makes thematically an identification of true loyalty, reality, sunlight, health and the country. Immediately after they are reunited rustics enter crying "O misery! O Desolation! . . . O Calamity." Affliction has fallen heavily upon their province though they have

> been held obedient to the Church,
> True Subjects to the King, and friendliest Neighbours
> Among our selves, all Sicily could boast of:
> This part of it, or Province, being call'd
> *The Paradice of Love.*
>
> (III, iv, 51–52)

Brome uses several speeches to underscore the significance of the Province's name before he proceeds to the cause of dismay. He makes it clear that these people lived in a kind of small utopia of neighborliness and charity (cf. *ibid.*, p. 52). It is then revealed that the onset of their torments coincided with the moment of the King's rejection of the good Queen and the common acceptance of his accusation of the Queen as an adulteress. They attribute their miseries to the Queen's sin. But the Queen says, "Might you not judge as well, it was th' injustice and the wrongs the innocent Queen hath suffer'd, that has brought sense of her injuries upon her Province?" (*ibid.*, p. 54), And Lodovico, who acts the familiar role in Brome of the "plain-dealer," adds less gently, " 'Tis plain, your fowl mistrust is the infection that rages in you" (*ibid.*, p. 54).

We are not dealing with realistic techniques in this play. Rendering Brome's pattern here into prose discourse, we find that the most innocent, even paradisical, area of the state has been corrupted by the naïve acceptance of the ethic of the court and for the loss of faith in virtue (i.e., the Queen). The people must suffer vicariously for the Queen. The Queen coming among them raises them up to faith in her (i.e., in virtue) through the agency of miraculous powers supernaturally granted to her. In a much cruder form is seen the same undisassociated pattern of sensibilities which controls Shakespeare's *The Tempest.*

Her gifts, for stage purposes, are magical, but at the same time she acts as a providential instrument and as the embodiment of an abstraction as well as being literally the deposed Queen of the narrative.

She modestly cures the ailing and distressed as a chosen agent, saying, "Bless'd Providence assist me whilst with Prayers [note, not by magic] I use the gift thou gav'st me for the cure of these afflicted People" (*ibid.*, p. 54), When the cured exclaim, "O sure you are some Heavenly Saint or Goddess" (*ibid.*, p. 54), she warns them, "Beware Idolatry, and onely send All praise to th' power whose mercy hath no end" (*ibid.*, p. 54). But Lodovico, the author character, is unwilling to accept this modest valuation of the miraculous, and tells her,

> O happy woman, now no more a Queen,
> But Holy Saint: I see how Providence
> Means to advance thy injur'd innocence.
>
> (*Ibid.*, p. 55)

Against this country pattern of loyalty, love, neighborhood, and grateful exercise of Providential powers, Brome works point by point contrasts of the court equivalents. To the Kent-like loyalty of Lodovico, he opposes the sycophantic opportunism of the evil minion, Flavello, who, hoping to rise by his services to the Concubine, Alinda, worships her in idolatrous terms, calling her "my bounteous Goddess" and "sacred Deitie," to which Alinda (rather than correcting him) replies, "O most Celestial sound!," and "Oh Divine," and urges him to prove his faith and devotion by killing Eulalia (III, viii, 63–64). The spectator has just watched the Queen rejecting such extravagant praise from those who have far more reason for gratitude. The two attitudes towards idolatry (itself a confusion of immediate appearance with underlying reality) are so sharply contrasted as to be unmistakable.

In another stylized contrast, Brome opposes the understated loyalty of the fool, Andrea (who covers his devotion with buffoonery) to the time-serving, self-congratulatory loyalty of the courtier Horatio, whose character is given as

> . . . the onely man
> That does the King that service, just to love
> Or hate as the King does, so much and so long,
> Just to a scruple or a minute.
>
> (I, iv, 10)

Horatio is constantly chewing the pleasant cud of his own loyalty: "A right old Courtier I, still true to th' Crown,"[11] while he lives in a private moral universe vacant of all values save this one "loyalty."

The dramatic exploitation of the court–country opposition must be enlarged, for the central moral contrast—that of Eulalia's obedience to the ambition of the Concubine—is intimately related to it. When the King first feels his lustful attraction to Alinda, her father is present. Her father censures her for responding with an impudent flirtatiousness to the King's advances, and, blaming her condition on the court atmosphere, orders her into the country.

> Ile try
> If Countrey-Air and Diet can restore you
> To your forgotten modestie and Duty.
>   (I, vi, 13)

She scoffs at his moralizations and tells him that what he wrongly calls impudence is "Courtship."

> What Courtier sits down satisfied with the first
> Office or Honour is confer'd upon him?
> If he does so, he leaves to be a Courtier.
>   (*Ibid.*, p. 14)

All her fathers arguments are canceled by her ambition, for disobedience and contempt of her father are an outgrowth of her desire to rise, as he finally recognizes when unbelievingly he says, half in question, half in discovery, "Do you dream of being a Queen?" (*ibid.*, p. 15).

Though the relation of ambition to disobedience is not complicated, it emphasizes the sharply stylized quality of the contrast between the two title roles. Ambition, in a hierarchical society, is a threat to the established order. Its connotation was shifting during this period. For Nashe, writing at the end of the sixteenth century, the word had a necessarily disagreeable significance: "Ambition is any puft vp greedy humour of honour or preferment," and Shakespeare, in *Henry VIII*, merely has to mention that "By that sinne fell the Angels." In Brome's play, when the two women exchange roles, one by the virtue of obedience accepts and makes the best of her plight, thereby transcending fortune. The other, plagued by restless ambition which generates its own

---

[11] This is a tag-line repeated over and over in the play. Brome, like Fielding and Dickens, was very partial to this device.

discontent, cannot even enjoy her new found good fortune. Brome uses ambition as a charged word and concept in the old-fashioned sense.

The Queen, who is deposed as a result of the conjunction of the King's lust and the Concubine's ambition, states her intention to reside in her "due Obedience" and,

> still retain the duty of a wife,
> Which though it be rejected, shall not throw
> Me from the path a Subject ought to go.
>
> (I, vii, 17)

Properly she resigns herself to the sovereignty of him who is both her husband and her King, only reserving the inner right to "a higher Judge [to] refer my Cause" (I, viii, 19). Obedience here is a willing acceptance of one's proper status and this implies the acceptance of the direction of others in a still higher one. It implies further the practice of the virtue patience, the opposite of ambition. Conversely, ambition may be defined as aggressive dissatisfaction with one's status and the willingness to make morals expendable in achieving a higher eminence. Immediately after the Queen has accepted her plight with impeccably orthodox patience, Alinda enters alone and passionately orates,

> Mount, mount, my thoughts, above the earthy pitch
> Of Vassal minds, whilst strength of womans wit
> Props my Ambition up.
>
> (I, ix, 19)

Scorning the "base and abject mindes" who are pleased with "servile Bondage," she aspires to nothing less than "the top of Soveraignty" (*ibid.*, pp. 19–20).

Brome's treatment of the relationship between the doting King and his ambitious Concubine is almost exclusively devoted to displaying, in various ways, her gaining of sovereignty over him, a process by which she completely inverts the rightful order. When the King announces to his assembled Parliament that he is replacing Eulalia with the Concubine, he says,

> [know] . . . that I your King,
> Am *Subject* to this all-deserving Lady.
>
> (II, ii, 25 [italics mine])

The courtiers, talking of his act, call it "Tyrannie" and fear "the ruine of the State" that must result from "the King's dotage" (i.e., subjecting himself to his Concubine), and they recognize that unless they do something to alleviate the situation they "shall seem born more for our selves than Countrey" (II, iii, 28–30).[12] But even as they are talking, attention is called to the minion of the Concubine surrounded by petitioners: "Oh! he [her minion, Flavello] engrosses all the Suits, and commends them to the White Hand, whose disposing will make the whole Kingdom black in Mourning" (ibid., p. 31).

This one small scene dramatizes sharply the potentially disastrous subjection of the King. A contemporary commentator on wifely duties makes the point clearly:

[if the husband does not rule] . . . it cometh to passe, that more petitions and suites are made to the wives of Magistrates in the cases of justice then to the Magistrates themselves: and the favour of their wives is more esteemed then their owne: so as the power of governing, and the maine stroke in determining matters is from their wives; they are but the mouthes and instruments of their Wives, in so much as among the common people the title of their places and offices is given to their wives.[13]

Alinda's control over the King grows steadily until she is merely asking things of him in order to test his love and subservience. At the height of her unresisted influence over him, she demands the executive murders of his exiled Queen and their son. She poses arguments about the problem of the succession. Whereupon the King, persuaded, is made to answer, with heavy dramatic irony, "Thy wisdom [has] inspir'd me: all shall be/(Be thou but my *Alinda*) rul'd by thee" (III, xi, 75), Alinda, gratified, answers in the repetitive image of the play, "My glories were *eclips'd*, but now they *shine*' (*ibid.*, italics mine). The

[12] It cannot be stressed too strongly how closely Brome tags the various moral positions assumed by his characters. In this play the nobles exactly describe their responsibility according to traditional morality. Henry Peacham, in his conservative *Compleat Gentleman*, written at almost exactly the same time, says in defining nobility, "For since all Vertue consisteth in Action, and no man is borne for himselfe, we adde, beneficiall and vsefull to his Country; for hardly they are to be admitted for Noble, who (though of never so excellent parts) consume their light, as in a darke Lanthorne . . ." (ed. by Gordon, p. 2). This belief in stewardship and *noblesse oblige* is one of the foundation stones of Shakespeare's ethic (cf. especially the Sonnets and the "Problem" plays) and of Jonson's mature position for which *The New Inn* is the *locus classicus*.

[13] Quoted by Roland M. Frye, "The Accepted Ethics and Theology of Shakespeare's Audience," p. 276 (from William Gouge, *Of domesticall duties* [1622] p. 359). Iago evilly insinuates the same dotage in *Othello* when he calls Desdemona "Our Captain's Captain." That the ambitious Concubine is up-ending the proper order of things could be documented from a dozen sources in marriage and sermon literature. The poem "A Happy Husband," (2d ed., 1622), by the poetaster, Patrick Hannay, is a serviceable example of nearly the same date. It is useful because he is not a divine and because his mind is so utterly pedestrian and middle-of-the-road. He says, "*Obedience* first. *thy* will to his must fit,/(He is the *Pylot* that must gouerne it)/It *man* condemnes of inabilitie,/When *Women* rule, that are borne to obey" [italics mine].

Concubine's ambition finally rises to such a height that any reservation or temporizing on the part of the doting King is taken by her as an intentional check to her personal demands. Within the operating framework of the play, there is only one way that Brome can explain her motive as her demands become more excessive—she becomes mad. In the play's ethical terms, she falls a victim of the equivalent of Greek *hybris*. So overpowering do her own misconceived and egomaniacal needs become, that she can no longer even manage to be tactful. In her frenzied attempts to force the King to her ends—revenge, murder to remove imagined threats to her security in the state—she speaks the truth about the King. As the play draws to a climax, she enters, calling for the King: "Where's this King? This King of Clouts."[14] Petruchio glosses this in an aside, "F·····l effect of Pride!" as she continues, "This *shadow* of a King" (italics mine). To underscore the climactic importance of what she is doing and saying, Brome has her point to portraits of the King's royal ancestors as she accuses him of being as insubstantial and lifeless as they. Rising even higher in her desperate violence of frustrated temper, she orders him about hysterically, "A cobweb," she calls him, and concludes her show of unreason with this outrageous syllogism,

> If thou beest King, thou yet art both that King
> That owes me love and life, and so my subject.
>
> (IV, vii, 95–97)

This is the most extreme run of her power over the King, who slowly begins to emerge from his dotage and to see this frantic female for what she really is.

When the Concubine enters, berating the doting King as a "shadow," the action line and the imagistic pattern of the play climax simultaneously. The elaborate, if conventional, equation of the King with the sun, sun with light, light with reason, reason with the head, and with the King as head of the body politic (and hence obliged to be a fountain of reason), is completed. This pattern, which is exactly the same one Shakespeare uses (most explicitly in *Richard II* and less explicitly nearly every place he discusses the attributes and duties of the good magistrate), may be briefly documented from the beginning to the end of Brome's play. What, in effect, Alinda has said in calling the

---

[14] This echoes Hamlet's references to Claudius as "A King of shreds and patches!" in the "closet" scene (*Hamlet*, III, iv, 102). There, too, the point is of the sharp disparity between apparent and real substance.

King a "shadow" is that he is the opposite of what he should be and hence a counterfeit.[15] He has gone so far in the confusion of appearance and reality that he has divested himself of substance.[16] Her use of the term is an instance of dramatic irony, for she means by it that he is false since he does not use his power solely to her advantage; whereas, in a larger sense she has spoken the descriptive truth with such force that it helps him become undeceived and hence able to reject her.

The Queen and Concubine opens with a short scene between two courtiers, which is like a little "poetic induction." In it (in the manner of Shakespeare's late plays) several themes are brushed over that will gradually assume importance as the play unfolds. The scene sets up a basic contrast between clouds and the sun, joy and fear. It contrasts winter and spring, desolation and flowers, and, finally and most importantly, it introduces the central notion of "new life." All this is neatly formulized in the first eight lines of the play, and is meant to apply to the return of the King from his wars. This return is merely a way of getting the action started and does not properly bear on the subsequent and real action of the play. Nevertheless, the thematic chords have been struck and they reverberate again and again as the action proceeds. The way in which these contrasts are developed to relate to the main action of the play is beautifully illustrated in epitome from a contemporary poem on marriage,

> Love comforteth, like sun-shine after rain:
> But lust's effect is tempest after sun.
> Love's golden spring doth ever fresh remain;
> Lust's winter comes, ere summer half be done.[17]

The King's lust will introduce disturbing tempest and obscuring mist into the sunny atmosphere of love and fellowship. This wintry freez-

[15] The use of the word "shadow" to mean counterfeit is widespread in the sixteenth and early seventeenth century. A good example is furnished by Robert Ashley's *Of Honour*, ed. by Virgil Heltzel (San Marino, 1947). He is speaking of the difficulty in distinguishing true from false honor: "here is men are much deceaved whilest many do follow a shadow or counterfeit of vertue in steed of vertue yt self and imbrace a vice clothed in vertues apparrell" (p. 41).

[16] The equation of shadow–to deception–to abdication of proper function is well illustrated in a contemporary discussion of friendship. "Friendship (sayth the *Stagyrian*) is *one soule* which ruleoth *two hearts*; and *one heart* which dwelleth in *two bodies*. Hearts then must not be ruled by shadowes. Congies, Cringes, Curtsies and Formalities may delude, and imparadize an unexperience'd Novice: These, I say, may transport our youngling, who never knew what dissembling meant: nor could ever yet distinguish betwixt fruite and shade, Essence and Semblance: but those, who are experimentally vers'd in the World, easily decline from such Snares" (Richard Brathwaite, *A Survey of History* [London, 1638], p. 203).

[17] Alexander Niccholes, *A Discourse of Marriage and Wiving*, (1615) in *Harleian Miscellany*, III, 273.

ing, disrupting obscuration must await the return of spring, or the renewal of sunshine, or the regeneration of love. The "second birth" is to be understood on a number of levels, all of which are variant metaphors for repentance and consequent clear-vision and love.

Just as in *King Lear* seemingly trivial confusions are symbolic indications of larger spiritual or moral flaws. The large moral formula of the play might be stated this way : "Only the good and pure of heart can see past the deceptive show of things. If you cannot see past the deceptive show of things, you are (by definition) deceived, and the deception was brought on by your own errors and vice. Therefore, the way to see truly and to escape the toils of self-deception is *to repent* and forego vice." The extensions of this are innumerable, but in this play and in Elizabethan drama generally there are certain standard factors treated. One is that the court, with its preoccupations with rank, ceremony, and clothing, is a place that trades in "show," so to speak, systematizing self-deception; therefore the artist is compelled to condemn the court in favor of the simplicities and directness of the country. Further, and slightly more subtly, court language may be the veil of hypocrisy, so that flattery is using language to deceive in exactly the same sense as dressing to appear as something you are not is a mode of flattering the sense of others even as you deceive them.

Therefore, in *The Queen and Concubine*, the obvious security of the very fulsome and transparent flatterer, Horatio, is (among other things) a good way to criticize the clear-sightedness of the King, who tolerates him. Eulalia, the banished Queen, never makes the mistake of confusing the appearance of something with its real nature, its title with its substance. A central piece of action in the play demonstrates this neatly while suggesting several other things. After the Queen has made herself useful to the rustics as their curate (in the basic sense of that term), the rustics want to worship her (i.e., attributes to her as a visible person what she accomplishes as the agent of an unseen power). Again, later, Brome has the rustics refer to her five times in thirty lines as "holy woman"—twice in concerted shouts by a strange crowd (IV, ii and iii, 85–86). The Queen refuses this title, as well as "Holiness," or "sacred sovereign," and the point is made that " 'Tis then the Greatness of The Person dignifies the Titles, not it the Person" (IV, iii, 87).[18]

---

[18] This is part of the standard pattern of moral commonplaces which the play organizes and gives new life. It is the "virtue-is-the-true-nobility" theme, which is clearly included in

The Queen's superiority to the normal human tendency to confuse reality and appearance is given very dramatic portrayal by Brome immediately following the material just discussed. *The Queen and Concubine* can be considered a rewriting of the central theme of *The Tempest*. There are many reasons for this: The Queen is pursued to her rustic seclusion by assassins who are the same couple that perjured themselves to get her convicted of adultery earlier. They approach her disguised as "poor Pilgrims," seeking her as "the holy woman." The Queen immediately sees through their evil affectation of sheep's clothing and denounces them for "treacherous counterfeits" (IV, iv, 89). The two are partially paralyzed and conveyed to temporary imprisonment, because the Queen says, "their time's not come for cure yet" (*ibid.*). The parallel with *The Tempest* is obvious. Eulalia is equivalent to Prospero when she uses "Magic-cum Providential power" to protect herself and to cure the vice in those threatening her. Both characters play the special role of teacher and inciter of repentance in others. Both are actively engaged in the ultimate moral science of distinguishing appearance from reality.

It is now clear that the imagistic pattern of the play is very coherent and that the major value judgments of the play are derived from it as an index. That is to say, the King is evil insofar as he allows his reason to be obscured (the sun to be beclouded); he is a shadow or a tyrant or a counterfeit if his private lusts displace his love and public sense. The Queen acts throughout the play as a repository of virtue and as a nearly allegorical embodiment of patience and wisdom. Her role is to redeem by example and counsel. She represents the sun-filled side of the action just as Alinda, the Concubine, represents the lust-ridden, ambitious, shadowy side of it. Alinda is completely taken in by the vain appearances of the court. She came originally from the country and was corrupted by the systematized, glorious deceptions of the court.

The remaining developments of the image pattern can be traced through the King's gradual return to reason as the play approaches its end. Immediately after the raging Concubine has berated the King and stomped from the stage, the King, in a modified soliloquy, falls

---

the idea that seeing clearly is evidence of purity of heart and the corollary (that members of the nobility and of royalty must see clearly, i.e., act virtuously, or the commonwealth will be corrupted, just as habitual vice corrupts the individual heart). Muriel C. Bradbrook treats this idea as what she calls the "governing idea" of Shakespeare's *All's Well That Ends Well*. Cf. her "Virtue is the True Nobility," *Review of English Studies*, I (N.S.: 1950), 289–301.

into meditation. In this show of passion of the Concubine, he has seen his own self-deception reflected. He has an inkling of the dire effects it has had on others. He begins to change. He calls on "Just Heaven" to "Afford me light to see I am misled" (IV, vii, 98). Brome then interjects a scene which is initiated by the shouts of a violent mob crying, "Kill him, kill him" (IV, viii, 99). The audience cannot know the object of the mob's fury and is probably briefly titillated with the notion that the King is meant. As it turns out, the scene is a thematic one showing the undisciplined disorder that is resulting from the King's dotage, or suspension of reason. Actually, the mob's will is directed against the King's general, Petruchio. This metaphorical reflection of the King's mental disorder in the disorder of the state he rules is basic in the play and is a technique of analogous action on different planes, familiar to readers of *King Lear* and *Macbeth*.

This piece of mob action comes to nothing in itself, though it acts (like nearly everything else in the remainder of the play) as a stimulus to the King's returning mental balance. The King, distressed by the disturbed state of his kingdom which he now recognizes for the first time, falls to prayer:

> Great Power, that knowest
> The subtletie of hearts, shew me some *light*
> Through these Cymmerian *mists* of doubts and fears,
> In which I am *perplex'd* even to distraction:
> *Shew* me, *shew* me yet the *face* of glorious *Truth*;
> where I may read
> If I have *err'd* which way I was *misled*.
> (IV, viii, 103 [italics mine])

Rather movingly, the King here equates misty darkness with error and sin and blindness and asks for light. Immediately the news is brought to him of the Concubine's raging madness. She is completely bereft of reason. This is followed closely by an ambassador from the province called "The Paradise of Love," who testifies to the renewed loyalty of the province to the King. The action here is not meant to be *realistic*. The renewal of the bond is a symbolic reminder of the King's return to reason. This is clearly indicated at the end of this short scene when the King is asked, "you see your way," and he answers,

> Yes, Yes, I *know* now what to do,
> And mean to put it presently in Act . . .

How full of *April-changes* is our life?
Now a fit *shoure* of sad distilling *Rain*,
And by and by the *Sun* breaks forth again.
(IV, ix, 106–7 [italics mine])

In the imagistic terms of the play, the sun shining again is another way of saying the King is once again himself.[19]

All the characters are brought together for the final action in the play. The King, whose return to reason has been advertised imagistically, has still not *done* anything to manifest his new view of things. He and the Concubine go on a Royal Progress to visit the country province where the exiled Queen is living. This long awaited dramatic confrontation of the two women is moderated by a fairy tale device. The King, whose change of heart is not generally known, has granted the unsuspecting Concubine's request for the fulfilment of three wishes by saying, "What I have promis'd to my lawful Queen, I will perform"[20] (V, iv, 113). Before the Concubine makes her three requests, the old Queen expresses directly the moral polarities of the situation.

Let your Demands be for *the common good*.
Nor for your own respects; *self love* my hurt you:
Beware Ambition, Envie, and Revenge.
(*Ibid.* [italics mine])

In keeping with the original fable he is dramatizing, Brome then has the Concubine make three cruel and inhuman requests, whereupon

---

[19] In Shakespeare's *Henry IV*, Part I, Prince Hal is related to the sun image in exactly the same way:

herein will I imitate the *sun*
Who doth permit the base contagious *clouds*
To smother up his beauty from the world,
That when he please again *to be himself*,
Being wanted, he may be wonder'd at
By breaking through the *foul* and *ugly mists*
Of *vapours* that did seem to strangle him.
(I, ii, 203–9 [italics mine])

The image is also picked up again in the next scene of *The Queen and Concubine* where Lodovicio, the loyal counsellor to the banished Queen, describes the improved state of things at court by saying merely, "Madam, the Sun shines fairly" (V, i, 108). See Marlowe's *Edward II* (I, iv, 340–41) for an exactly analogous image cluster.

[20] It must be understood that the Concubine has considered herself, and has been addressed as, Queen ever since the doting King ceremonially repudiated his old Queen. I have referred to them as Queen and Concubine throughout only to avoid confusion.

the King rejects her and restores the actual Queen to her rightful place:

> *Eulalia,* take now thy wonted Seat and keep it ever.
> Thy povertie and patience have restor'd thee
> By the just Providence: while her Excesse and Pride
> Casts her before thee, to receive that Doom
> She had devis'd 'gainst thy immortal Goodness.
>
> (V, iv, 114)

If Brome were doing nothing more than giving stage life to Greene's original story, the play should end here. Since, however, Brome has the larger aim of the re-education of his erring characters through the inspired agency of the Queen, there is still more action. The evil ones who conspired against the Queen (agents of the moral corruption in the court) are brought before the Queen for judgment. The worst of them, Flavello, the Concubine's minion, asks for death. The Queen answers.

> I cannot give thee death: nor will my prayers
> Be prevalent for thy *cure* poor sinful man!
> Till rhou [sic] layst ope the *cause* of thy *disease*;
> (Thy hainous *sin*) by fair and free *confession.*
>
> (V, vii, 121 [italics mine])

When Flavello freely confesses both his misdeeds and his sorrow for them, he is freely forgiven: "you do well to seem so penitent: I do forgive you" (*ibid.*, p. 122). The play has in a sense "prosed" the moral of *The Tempest.* The characters, controlled by the providentially inspired magical gifts of healing and teaching, have been cured of the disease of their sins by penitence (i.e., by speaking and seeing the truth about themselves). They have been led to "heart's sorrow and a clear life ensuing." [21]

The King, now reunited with his virtuous Queen, feels buoyed up by this access of virtue and, looking about him, sees this country province, this "Paradise of Love," freshly for the first time:

> *Eulalia,* thou art happy, and didst rise
> Not fall from Court into this Paradise.
> Nor can it move my admiration much,
> *Thy vertue wrought the change* [italics mine], and made it such,
>
> (V, viii, 123)

Just as the disordered tumult of the mob had reflected (on the political level) the troubled condition of the King's mind, so now the restored reason of the King permits him to see that virtue has created harmony, peace and order in that part of the kingdom where love permitted its operation.

The culminating act of salvation still remains. The Queen, having converted (V, ix, 125) all other evil-doers, now pleads for the mad Concubine, her worst abuser. The Concubine is brought on the stage veiled. The stage directions then call for "*a new Song, Eulalia unvailes Alinda.*" The Queen says as she does this, "Bless'd Heaven! she lives and wakes I hope in health," and the girl's father, Sforza, adds, "If she awakes to vertue, she is welcome" (*ibid.*, p. 127). The equivalents here are patent: ambition–deception–blindness–disease–madness–sleep–dreams–unreality–death. She is reawaking to life out of the deception which was death-like. As her head clears, she testifies,

> How have I wandred in the way of Error!
> Till I was worn into an Arie vapour.
> Then warp'd into a cloud: and thence distill'd
> Into the earth to find a new creation.
> 'Tis found: and I am found in better state,
> Then I was in, before I lost my Dutie.
> For in *this second Birth* [italics mine]: I find a knowledge
> How to preserve it.
>
> (V, ix, 128)

The "second birth" rounds out the theme of "new life" which was struck in the poetic induction of the play. The central theme of penitence and the restoration of vision is clear and pervasive in the play. *The Queen and Concubine* is about reeducation and regeneration just as is *The Tempest*. The regeneration comes when each character realizes that he is not "for himself," but part of a commonwealth; when each character repudiates his self-seeking and honestly confesses his vices; when each character rejects the illusory attractions of wealth, prestige, and ceremonial tokens of place.

What has in the past been read carelessly as another mediocre example of the post-Fletcherian Romance is, if not a better play than this implies, clearly a more interesting one. Brome cleverly adapted the superficial devices of a Fletcherian initial situation and thereby made his older, homelier, and intrinsically superior product marketable on the Caroline stage. He also (apparently intentionally) misled later, hasty readers who mistook the appearance for the substance.

The thematic pattern of *The Queen and Concubine* reveals two equally important facts about Brome: he was capable of seeing things in the interlocked, analogical pattern of Shakespeare even though his limited poetic power made him far less skillful in handling this richly complex mode; and the play can be seen as a serious attempt to present a general ethic, one conservative and dignified. In a meaningful sense, *The Queen and Concubine* can be called Brome's humble *De Doctrina*. I would argue further that this reading of the play makes it easier to criticize with control plays of intermediate symbolic nature from *The Tempest* to *The Cocktail Party*.

VII

COURT DRAMA AND COMMONSENSE

It was not enough that Brome as a playwright holding traditional views should use comedy as a moderating and regulative factor on social conduct. In the years leading up to the rebellion, disruptive forces were working in all walks of English life. In the area of most concern to Brome—the drama—many innovations were being introduced by those who were, from his point of view, the least qualified to do so. It is directly analogous to his belief in the hierarchically ordered state which expected each to labor in his own status, that he should resent the amateur meddling in his craft. The normal distrust the skilled professional feels for the dilettante, particularly when the idle diversions of the latter threaten his livelihood, was reinforced for Brome by his basic assumptions about society.

In *The Love-sick Court* Brome finds it necessary to direct his satiric talent not towards the foibles and social follies of actual people in the society around him, but toward the silly distortions of human motive and conduct becoming conventionalized in the new courtier drama. Here we find the same keen eye for absurdity and pretension operating on literary subject matter—his vigorous techniques of deflation at their heartiest.

The Love-sick Court is of uncertain date. Fleay is guessing when he dates it 1629.[1] This is too early. Harbage places the play tentatively in 1640.[2] This seems too late. The play, I believe, belongs to the period of the middle thirties when numerous plays dealing with the fads of platonic love, self-denial, renunciation, and ideal friendship were being written.[3] It is a burlesque of excessive posturing in the role of

---

[1] *Biographical Chronicle*, I, 36.

[2] *Cavalier Drama*, p. 158, where he says of the play, "both its story and treatment suggest influences not in effect until after the courtier playwrights had appeared upon the scene." See his date list p. 269.

[3] It is difficult to date the onset of "court platonizing." Ben Jonson is richly aware of it in *The New Inn* in 1629; perhaps the play's failure is because he anticipated his audience too

friend and lover and hence depends for its satiric effects on a background of immediately current and overindulged theatrical affectations.

The burlesque intentions of *The Love-sick Court* have not been
recognized by previous students: Thorndike categorizes it as being "in
the Fletcherian manner" and adds that it "borrows directly from
The Two Noble Kinsmen."[4] More importantly, Harbage, after commenting on Brome's distaste for this sort of play, says,

> Once, however, he weakened and paid the new fashion the tribute of imita-
> tion . . . In the heroic vein of the rival friends and the ethical confusion of the
> Princess, all of whom the author tries valiantly to endow with the new-fangled
> sensibility, we discern the leaning toward courtly romance, even though
> Brome moves with ludicrous awkwardness amidst the emotional subtleties of
> his theme.[5]

This assumes that Brome made a poor attempt at a form beyond his
reach; it accuses him of pretensions which are out of character; it
makes him look humorless and unself-critical. This seems inherently
improbable, and orthodox opinion seems to miss the point altogether.
This chapter will demonstrate by analysis of the structure, tone, and
producing context what Brome's intentions were.

The play has a double plot. The setting is Thessaly. The primary
plot recounts the simple story of twin brothers, Philargus and Philocles,
who are in love with the same Princess Eudina. Eudina is the daughter
of the King of Thessaly who has, after the death of Endina's mother,
married the mother of the twins. The plot postulate is that Eudina
must be married by an early date in order to guarantee the succession.
The commons petition and pressure the court into taking action.
The last important factor in setting up the plot is the use of the ambitious Stratocles, "a Politician," to expedite the desirability of the

---

much and they were not ready for the ridiculing of a fashion they were just learning. In 1629
Brome notes the court custom of men acting as "servants" (or platonic lovers) to court ladies
in *The Northern Lasse* (IV, i, 69). Kathleen Lynch is overcautious when she says, "in 1634,
Platonic gallantry first became conspicuously practiced at the English Court" (*The Social
Mode of Restoration Comedy* [New York, 1926], p. 57). The customs date from as early as
1628; they become literary subject matter from Carlell's *The Deserving Favorite* (1629)
onward, but the really intense fad seems to date around 1633–37. See Harbage's *Cavalier
Drama* for a full account.

[4] *English Comedy* (New York, 1929), p. 248. Similar descriptions of the play as an unsuc-
cessful attempt to imitate the courtier style are to be found in Thomas M. Parrott and
Robert H. Ball, *A Short View of Elizabethan Drama* (New York, 1943), p. 174 and in
Swinburne's essay on Brome in the *Fortnightly Review*, LI (1892), 506.

[5] *Cavalier Drama*, pp. 158–59.

early choice of a husband.[6] He is a suitor for Eudina's hand himself and he has used all his power with the rabble to press his own claim, so that he can achieve the throne. Therefore the essence of the plot is a Princess obliged for state reasons to choose a husband from among three suitors. The special development is the "rival friend" theme. Philargus and Philocles are so devoted to each other that neither will press his own claim. Eudina, the perplexed Princess, loves them both equally, so that her deliberate personal choice cannot resolve the impasse. The action of the play is then an examination of the power of the dilemma over the two brothers and, of course, its ultimate and satisfactory resolution.

A subplot closely parallels the main action and is, in a sense, as Lawrence Mills has pointed out,[7] a burlesque of the main plot. Each brother has a servant who is in love with Doris, waiting maid to Eudina. The role of third lover in the subplot is filled by Geron, a foolish scholar and son to Garrula, the court midwife and confidante of the mother of the twins. The serving men on the superficial and obvious level of action ape their masters' conduct. They are determined to act as "true friends" though rivals.

One last element must be added to make the plot pattern clear. The twins, unable to resolve their problem, go off to the Delphic oracle to ask who shall marry the Princess. The oracle answers darkly and with multiple contradictions. The developing action is, as in *The Winter's Tale*, a resolution of these contradictions so that the oracle's "ridelling language" is ultimately rendered clear and comprehensible. In the subplot the role of Garrula, the Queen's companion and court midwife, parallels that of the oracle. She in her silly, garrulous way constantly hints to the audience "I know what I know," and that consequently she can by speaking resolve the dilemma. The fact that her meandering garrulity is the very opposite to the terse and cryptic message from the oracle (though accomplishing the same thing, i.e., effectively obscuring the truth) is only part of the burlesque humor of the play. The plot then is a double contest for a wife among two sets of three suitors and one woman, with an oracle, real and burlesque, relating to both plots.

[6] Stratocles is very much like Seleucus in Thomas Killigrew's *Claricilla* (c. 1636). They are both scheming, villainous politicians who, enjoying temporarily the position of favorite of the King, seek to win the Princess and hence the throne by guile. Could the popularity of this figure in the plays of the 1630s relate in any way to the potent figure of Strafford?

[7] *One Soul in Bodies Twain, Friendship in Tudor Literature and Stuart Drama* (Bloomington, Indiana, 1937), p. 352.

The playwright's problem in designing the stage action for the fable is to create as many situations as possible in which the twin brothers will be under pressure to act and yet will not. In carrying out this task Brome devotes the first act to exposition and most of the last to a standard resolution in which the two brothers are found not to be brothers at all, so that only one is eligible to marry Eudina after all, the other having been discovered to be Eudina's brother. The resolution is routine and unoriginal. The conventional mistaken identity is handled with minimum professional skill and is no better and no worse than a dozen versions of the same device in the hands of Brome's contemporaries. The point of the play lies elsewhere.

While it was not unusual in tragicomedy for Fletcher and his followers to use comic plots which vary sharply in tone from the main plot, it was unusual to find a very close thematic correlation between the two.[8] Even where the playwright had worked out a close parallel in action between the two plots, it was unusual that he should use the minor plot to undercut the plausibility of the main plot—to destroy its temporarily convincing solemnity of tone and even worse to minimize the importance of the issues central to the main action. The drama of love and honor, of idealized chastity, friendship, and self-renunciation was in nearly every sense escape drama. It depended for its effects on acceptance of its own interior ethics as suitable criteria for judgment. It depended on maintaining a sufficient distance between stage action and real life lest the seeming magnitude of the abstract issues being argued with impassioned rhetoric on the stage be reduced to the factitious dimensions they rightly occupied by comparison with everyday issues. Dramatists practicing this form did not try to arouse commonsense from the slumber induced by the remote, dreamlike, but swift and absorbing action of their plays. If a playwright took great care to create excitement and romance around issues which were really distant and unreal he would not deliberately break into the action and remind his audience that these issues, so absorbing as to seem immediate and important, were indeed distant and unreal. If these plays without roots in the soil of normal psychological probability were easily

---

[8] Eugene M. Waith in *The Pattern of Tragicomedy in Beaumont and Fletcher* (New Haven, 1952) would seem to offer a counter argument when, speaking of the structure of *King and No King*, he says, "As in most of the Beaumont and Fletcher plays, the central situation is surrounded by secondary situations to which it is formally related" (pp. 34–35). However, as his further argument makes clear, this arrangement was mainly contrapuntal or a tonally lowered parallel not, as in Brome, a steady and destructive editorial commentary on the very validity of the play's main action.

blasted by transplanting them into a setting they were never meant to exist in—that of current actuality—then a playwright would be more than foolish continually to invite cross-reference from the stage to real life. The popularity of plays built on the remote and fantastic does indicate an audience anxious to be pleasantly deceived and to be transported, an audience not anxious to question the plausible against the standards of probability. If the audience could disregard the subplot's satiric and destructive commentary on the quality of motive and conduct in the main plot, it is unlikely that it could ignore derogatory criticism by minor characters within the main plot itself.

Brome disliked postures current in the cavalier mode of his time. The evidence is considerable and all points in one direction. He had, like most able comic writers, an alert eye for the absurd. The code of unself-sparing friendship was carried to *absurd extremes* in the coterie drama of Lodovick Carlell, Thomas Killigrew, Sir John Suckling, Jasper Mayne, and William Davenant.[9] It is the absurdity of the Hellenistic romances of Heliodorus, Longus, and Achilles Tatius—the tedious and unrelieved absurdity of the *romans de longue haleine* transferred to the English stage. For all its superficial similarity to the Elizabethan friendship plays in the pattern of *The Two Gentlemen of Verona*, it is an un-English and suspect thing. It was solemn and naïvely unconscious of its own chilly and formal quality. It was ostentatious and inept. Even in the absence of rich internal evidence that Brome could not take these friendship plays seriously in their currently inflated

---

[9] It is possible to cull numerous examples of the fatuous rhetoric inspired by the ideal friendship theme. Here is one that, while representative enough, demonstrates better than most the bathos constantly within the reach of those dramatists. It is from L. Carlell's *The Fool Would be a Favourit* (ed. by Allardyce Nicoll, London, 1926). Philanthus and Agenor make one of several exchanges of vows:

> *Phil.:* Sir, you, in this assurance of your friendship,
> And her love, transport me with a double joy,
> Not to be exprest in words. I should fall down,
> And worship such a god-like friend, that thus
> Bestowes his favours on a desertlesse person,
> Made onley worthy by his love.
> *Age:* Still you forget our friendship, heaping your thanks
> And praise on me, a burthen my weak deserving
> Cannot bear without much shame; let it suffice,
> My love makes me a servant to your wishes;
> If they do take effect, 'tis your own merits,
> Whom the gods cannot refuse, that's the cause of it.
> My friendship onely a willing instrument,
> Strives to bring their divine wills to passe.
> But Oh! friend.   (II, i, 18)

See V, i, 81 for an even more extravagant example.

form, we should be suspicious of his apparent acceptance of them.[10]

A number of sequences in *The Love-sick Court* are directed toward the ineffectiveness of precious language or overlearned language to forward the action or the elaboration of theme as good dramatic dialogue should. Such direct satire would depend upon the solid entrenchment of preciosity in the fashion of the stage. Brome ridicules "the precieuse 'horreur du mot propre.'"[11] He continually attacks, through the dialogue of courtiers, the court dramatists' inability to say simple things simply.[12]

The title of the play is itself an invitation to burlesque. The play is not, as the fashions of the time would normally dictate, called "The Noble Twins," or "The Brothers Duel," or "Philargus and Philocles," but *The Love-sick Court*. Knowing the excessive emphasis placed upon love through the influence of Queen Henrietta Maria and her fascination with D'Urfé's *Astrée* and the "platonizing " code of the Hotel de Rambouillet, this title is a fairly direct cut.[13] It is not to imply that Brome intended *directly* to satirize the court of his own reigning monarch; he set the scene in Thessaly and the main plot action is conventionally romantic and harmless. What is suggested is that initially

[10] Lawrence Mills, who includes *The Love-sick Court* in his survey of the exploitation of the "friendship" theme in drama, points it out as a particularly inflated instance of a generally exaggerated category of plays. Writing of Peter Hausted's *The Rivall Friends* (1632) he says, "The play is amusing, and the certain satire in it might lead one to suspect that Hausted is burlesquing the extravagant handling of the friendship theme in other plays (such as *The Love-sick Court*) were it not that in his 'Preface' Hausted defends the play seriously" (*One Soul in Bodies Twain*, pp. 356–57).

[11] Kathleen M. Lynch, *The Social Mode of Restoration Comedy*, p. 69.

[12] Miss Lynch asserts that contemporary playwrights did not engage much in literary parody of the precious style. "It is not surprising that the influences of contemporary préciosité manifested themselves but slightly in the realistic comedies composed during the reign of Charles I. Any sustained satire of the new vogue would have been foolhardy enough, at a time when its chivalric passions were fanned by majesty itself" (*ibid.*, p. 94). The inference that should be drawn here is that direct stylistic parody to be dramatically effective would have to be linked with a larger more flexible parody of the elements of action, structure, and ethics for which the inflated language was the medium.

[13] Cf. Jefferson B. Fletcher's, "The Précieuses at the Court of Charles I," *Journal of Comparative Literature*, I (1903), 120–53; Alfred Harbage, *Cavalier Drama* (1936), pp. 7–28, a chapter called "The Court Invades the Drama"; Clifford Leech's essay "Love as a Dramatic Theme," in *Shakespeare's Tragedies and Other Studies in Seventeenth Century Drama* (1950), pp. 182–99; Kathleen M. Lynch's two chapters on Court Influence on Drama in the Reign of Charles I, in *The Social Mode of Restoration Comedy* (1926), pp. 43–106; George F. Sensabaugh's two articles, "Love, Ethics in the Platonic Court Drama 1625–1642," *Huntington Library Quarterly*, I (1937–38), 277–304; and "Platonic Love and the Puritan Rebellion," *Studies in Philology*, XXXVII (1940), 457–81; *The Plays and Poems of William Cartwright*, ed. by Gwyne Blakemore Evans (Madison, 1951), pp. 22–27 *passim*.

the title relates nearly enough to the condition of a platonically oriented court to suggest burlesque or satire.[14]

In his prologue Brome says, "Sometimes at poor mens boards the curious finde 'Mongst homely fare, some unexpected dish.' " There is a hint here that the play may take an unusual tack.

Doris, the free-spoken waiting-maid, strikes this chord early in the play when she receives a love letter from the pedant Geron and a visit from Placilla, sister of the twins.

> What a sick Court is here? Shee's love-struck too.

> The Princess she's love-sick for two; and her
> Despair of gaining either's her consumption.
> But what think I of their loves, when mine own
> Is trouble enough?[15]

(II, i, 107)

Later in the same scene after Doris has been receiving inquiries after the health of the Princess from the servants of her suitors, she replies in some exasperation,

> *Dor.* She was well when I left her,
> But subject to much passion: She is well
> And ill, and well again all in three minutes.
> Great Ladies may be so. But if I should
> Be sick and well, and sick again and well
> Again as oft as she; the world would say
> I had it—— And had been a courtier, to some purpose,
> *Var.* [illus. servant to Philocles] They would say
>   the Handmaid had been handled
> Would they?
> *Dor.* Like enough, but great ones must not be
>   talk'd on so.[16]

(II, i, 109–10)

[14] Sensabaugh's articles closely identify the codes developed in the court plays with the actual practice of the members of the court surrounding Henrietta Maria, "because of its dark ethics and Catholic members, the Queen's cult of love seems to have fanned in some measure the flame of the coming rebellion. Crystallizing court manners and morals by establishing standards of conduct and speech, it brought into sharp relief what might have escaped notice had not the Queen openly nurtured 'Platonic' affections. Court drama, in turn, codifying cult standards of hollow compliment, worship of beauty, and promiscuity in marriage and love, brought into sharper relief court behaviour" ("Platonic Love and the Puritan Rebellion," *Studies in Philology*, XXXVII, 481).

[15] References are from the first edition of the play: *Five New Plays* (London, 1659).

[16] Note the following about Henrietta Maria's influence on the English court. "What the English needed as a cooling-card was a prescription of platonic love in their regimen, and this

A little later Doris is speculating on her own chances of rising in court through marrying the servant of the successful suitor for the Princess' hand.

> His [Philargus's] follower *Tersulus* loves me past *Varillus*,
> And may as much advance me. But I love not
> Him, And the love of honour above husbands
> Has been so common among Ladies, that
> The fashions stale and ougly.

(II, i, 112)

As the subplot progresses the two servingmen suitors are brought together to discuss the conduct of their love competition which parallels that of their masters.

> *Var.* We should love one another, brother *Tersulus*,
> More inwardly, and be in friendship true
> As our Lords are. Prithee let their example
> Piece up all difference betwixt us.

Tersulus, who is also a tailor, takes exception to the phrase "piece up" as a slur on him and a brief argument follows. Then

> *Var.* But come, Lords followers are their
>   Apes in most things,
> Why should not we be as friendly Rivals, now
> In *Doris* Love, as are our Lords in the
> Princess *Eudinas*. We will take up a fashion.

(IV, i, 134–36)

Doris, realizing they are both neglecting their masters, urges them to attend to their duties.

> *Var.* I came but since to call
> My brother *Tersulus* [He means, "But I just got here."]
> *Dor.* Your brother *Tersulus*?
> *Ter.* As deeply vow'd in friendship as our Lords are.
> *Var.* It is with us as tis with them: we both
> Are brothers, friends; yet Rivals in your love.
> Can you now, as the Princess is to them,
> Be equally affected to us both?

---

she set out to give them . . . at the very outset of her campaign her cherished Henry Jermyn so far forgot his duty and allegiance as to seduce Eleanor Villiers . . . her husband i.e., Charles I, being more strait-laced, angrily banished the culprit from court, she interceded with him prettily, and the sentence was speedily recalled" (Arthur H. Nethercott, *Sir Wm. D'Avenant* [Chicago, 1938], p. 116, from *Strafforde's Letters*, I, 175 [January 9, 1633/34].)

Doris, who is portrayed as matter-of-fact, is rightly suspicious.

> *Dor.* Do you stay me to abuse me.
> *Var.* Nay, dear *Doris*
> We love our Lords? and as you love the Princess,
> Who loves them, love you us. You are *Eudina*,
> I *Philocles*, and he *Philargus* is.
> *Dor.* Are the men mad.
> *Ter.* Suppose so Gentle *Doris*.

Varillus continues the direct point by point drawing of the analogies of their situation to the main plot naming names in direct burlesque.

> *Var.* The King commands you to make present choice
> Of one of us, or else ambitious *Stratocles*
> (That's *Geron*) must enjoy you. Now sweet Princess
> Be speedy in your choice. The Kingdoms good
> Depends upon it. And in your Election
> O make *Philargus* blest: He best deserves you.
>
> (IV, i, 136–37)

It should be noted that Varillus has represented himself in the burlesque as Philocles, but like his master he argues for his "brother" not himself. Tersulus takes up the same strain.

> *Ter.* Admired friend, and brother *Philocles*,
> Your courtesie ore-comes me: I must sue,
> Though my heart akes the while as much for you.

Doris is amused and pleased but still rather impatient with them.

> *Dor.* This is fine fooling——
> Good Barber *Philocles*, and Taylor *Philargus*,
> You shall not need to trim up his Affection,
> Nor you to stich up his with your forc'd courtesies.
> I know, in this, each wooes but for himself,
> And my Affection runs as even betwixt you
> As nothing but your sizors, or your sheares
> Had parted.
>
> (IV, i, 137)

Though it is not unusual to have a comic subplot in a serious love-friendship play, it is unusual to have a direct and explicit parallel drawn with the obvious intention of debasing the stature and ridiculing the motives of the principals of the main plot.

There is evidence in the play of another sort of satire—the very

ridiculousness of the principals' conduct. There are repeated instances
when each twin argues the cause of the other rather than his own. A
typical example of this is quoted from Philargus:

> let me beseech
> The favour that I seek and would obtain,
> Equal with heavenly bliss, to shine on *Philocles*.
>
> (II, i, 115)

The Princess is so impressed by his unselfishness that she shrieks,

> In wooing for him [you] have won me to your self,
> I am your own. (*She kisses him.*)

Just then Philocles enters, sees them, and faints, calling out weakly as
he sinks, "O, you are partial." They hover anxiously over him bathing
his temples and speculating on the cause. The Princess attributes it to
jealousy aroused by her attention to Philargus. But Philocles, recover-
ing, says (perhaps from the floor),

> It is no jealousy
> Onely a fear *Philargus* had broke friendship:
> So, my souls better part exited, left
> The other languishing.
>
> (*Ibid.*, p. 116)

Then follows a heartwarming reconciliation between the two brothers,
much mutual interchange of compliment and further idolatrous commendation of the divine Eudina. Now Philocles, recovered in strength,
takes up his task,

> I for *Philargus* should your love obtain.
> The Gods deal after as they please with me,
> My sute is that you take *Philargus*.
>
> (*Ibid.*, p. 117)

Eudina, who is nothing if not impressionable, is swept away.

> *Philocles* you have made a double conquest
> You have got the victory of me
> Which was before assigned unto *Philargus*.
> Your fortune thus embraces you. (*She kisses him.*)
>
> (*Ibid.*)

Of course the impasse is quickly reestablished, but this scene with its
swoonings, spirited reversals, florid language is its own burlesque. If one
is still in doubt about the intended tone, there is more convincing evidence to come.

Stratocles, the ambitious politician and third suitor, is impatiently pressing his own claim to the hand of the Princess as a means to gain the throne. His servant Matho conceives the scheme of sending challenges to both the twins pretending that each is challenging the other. The challenges are identical and, in part, read

> Brother Philocles [or Philargus], we are the laughing stock of the Nation; and injurious both to the King, our Country, the divine Eudina, and our selves, by our childish love.   (III, iii, 134)

Of course Matho is a villain and would not be expected to put the most charitable construction on the conduct of the twins, but the playwright is in control of the terms he chooses and Brome chose to remind the audience that the lovers are "the laughing stock of the Nation," and that some may consider their conduct "childish."

The twins arrive at "the north vale of Tempe" to fight their duel and here the acting burlesque, considering the build-up provided by Brome, becomes unmistakable. The two brothers decide independently "to be sacrific'd for expiation" of the others "discontent." The stage directions, which are unusually full and explicit,[17] best describe what ensues, "They espie one another draw, and pass at each other, instantly both spread their arms to receive the wound" (IV, ii, 141). Each questions the other, puzzled by his conduct, and they argue for prior right to self-sacrifice.

> *Philoc.* I came to make experiment of none
>   But what consists in suffring.
> *Philar.* That's my part.
> *Philoc.* My self
>   If you deny me that last friendly office.
> *Philar.* Brother you dally with me. Therefore I conjure you
>   By faire Eudina let your anger loose . . .
> *Philoc.* By the same Beauty
>   (Then which no greater subject of an oath)
>   I swear to be your nuptialls sacrifice,
>   Be you the Priest. I'le suffer without noise
>   *In my displayed bowels you shall read*
>   *An augury of bliss unto you both* [italics mine].
>   (*Ibid.*, p. 142)

---

[17] It could be maintained additionally that the very fullness of the stage directions is a further indication that Brome wanted no misunderstanding of just the sort of ridiculous stage business he desired at this point.

This is high comedy, but they are not done yet. Each is unwilling to be outdone in nobility by the other. But Philocles takes the initiative as we find in the stage directions: "He offers to kill himself, *Philargus* closes with him. They struggle, and both fall down, still striving to hold each others sword, &c" (IV, ii, 142). They are simultaneously uttering complimentary remarks. It does not take much visual imagination to see how ludicrous this could be made in the acting.

The important part of the action concludes here and is picked up again at the beginning of the last act. The twins have been missed at court and their deaths have been rumored. Disanius, presented throughout as a wise and loyal old counselor, is sent to find them. They are still arguing who will be allowed to renounce the Princess. "Brother, and friend, I'm deaf to all deswasion./ I charge you be Eudina's love." And "That resolution's mine," etc. (V, i, 151). They continue to argue thus even after the arrival of Disanius. The old counselor's patience is finally exhausted. He plays what is in effect the role of author *raisonneur*:

> Come, let me tell you, your courtesie is foolish,
> And you unworthy to have such a fortune
> Hang like a pregnant cloud over your heads
> Ready to be dissolv'd in showres upon you,
> While your own madness conjures up a wind
> To blow't away.
>
> (V, i, 152–53)

They still persist, though more briefly and with a suggestion of embarrassment; so Disanius continues,

> I could even swadle 'em both for a brace of Babyes.
> Your folly makes me mad:
>
> (*Ibid.*, p. 153)

and again as they perversely continue their resistance to reason,

> What frost has ceiz'd their blood, & brains, which neither
> Beauty nor dignity can thaw?
>
> (*Ibid.*, p. 153)

No matter what Disanius says, however, the two brothers continue their contest in renunciation. Finally, in desperation, the counselor asks them to draw lots, one saying "love" and the other "friendship."

> Love and friendship Gentleman.
> Love shall abide at home, and friendship walk,
> *According to the custom of the world* [italics mine].
>
> (*Ibid.*, p. 154)

The last line, appealing to a reasonable man's construction of the situation, is too pointed to be missed. They draw lots but are unwilling to act upon the result without long discussion. As they exchange reams of noble sentiment the old counselor punctuates the interchanges with laconic remarks.

> *Philoc.* With this embrace my brother, and my last
> Of present ceremony, I now wish you
> In th'arms of your *Eudina*—
> And may my better part of soul, which now
> I leave in trust with you, by you be breath'd
> Into her breast; that she may lively find
> She has my love in yours; and that in you
> She has us both.
> *Dis.* So, so, enough. H'ye done yet?
> *Philoc.* How is it with you brother?
> *Philarg.* [weakly] As it is
> With souls that leave the world in peace.
> *Dis.* For shame
> *Leave womanish ceremony.*
>
> (*Ibid.*, p. 155 [italics mine])

Fortunately, since there is no reason to expect a breaking off of this too enjoyable parting, one of the servants has slipped a sleeping powder into the loving cup the brothers drink before parting, and the apparent death of Philargus results. This gives opportunity for further heroics by Philocles. While poor old Disanius is busily trying to revive Philargus and giving directions for the procurement of aid, he has to interrupt himself (again referring to extensive stage directions) as Philocles "offers to kill himself. Dis.[anius] snatcheth his sword away." and "Philocles offers again to kill himself" (*ibid.*, p. 157)—with what we are not told.

The effect of this conduct after the scolding just administered by Disanius is enough to confirm the accumulated inferences of folly, childishness, and womanish conduct.

A summary of the burlesque elements so far surveyed: There is structural burlesque in the subplot directly paralleling the main action.

These parallels are explicitly pointed out to the audience to insure that the intended effect is not lost. The exaggeratedly noble sentiments and action of the principals, so typical of the plays burlesqued, are pushed over the line into the absurd in the duelling scene and its aftermath. A minor character of the main plot, Disanius (whom we have every reason to accept as a good, honest character), has censured and ridiculed the conduct of the twin brothers at what would be a climactic point in a serious attempt at this type of play.

There is further internal evidence of a secondary order. Brome has not restricted himself to a burlesque of unnatural action and unreal motive, but has interpolated criticism of the inflated and undramatic language in which these plays are characteristically written. Throughout his career Brome had grumbled about the use of uncolloquial and ostentatious language in drama. In the prologue of an early play he had warned his audience that he was not one of "Those Poet-Bownces that write English Greeke."[18] Later he had his prologue-speaker say of court fashions, "But for the Compliments, the Trips, and Dances, Our Poet can't abide um, and he sweares, They're all but cheats."[19] References to pompous, insincere usage are laced through his plays, but nowhere does he give so much space to criticism of courtier language as in *The Love-sick Court*.

In a subplot scene early in the play (II, i), a succession of servants approach the waiting-maid, Doris, to enquire after the health of the Princess. They speak pompously and are referred to by Doris as "My great Lords Howdies." The least sympathetic, Matho, servant to the evil Stratocles, enters first. Doris mimics him.

> *Ma.* May I prevail then, to impart the duty
> I have in charge, unto the Ladies daughter?
> *Dor.* That is the Mistriss whom I wait upon,
> Though now at remote distance: She attends
> Her Mother at this instant, and her Mother
> The Princess in much privacy. If I
> May be thought worthy to receive the knowledge
> Of what you have in trust unto the Princess
> It shall be orderly convey'd unto her Grace.
>
> (II, i, 107)

---

[18] *The Novella* (acted 1632), published in *Five New Plays* (London, 1653).

[19] *A Mad Couple Well Match'd*, (probably acted 1639) published in *Five New Plays* (London, 1653).

Matho reels off his memorized formal message of solicitude ending that his master "prayes to be advertis'd/In what condition of health she fares." Doris replies,

> Sir, you have lost much time: you might have said
> How does the Princess.
>
> > (*Ibid.*, p. 108)

Matho, still unruffled, continues in his court vein, "Yet let her know My Lords obsequious care for her recovery." Doris sarcastically retorts,

> I'le *tell* my Mistriss, who shall *certifie*
> Unto my Lady, who shall *intimate*
> Unto the Princess what you have *left* in trust
> With me, her Graces hand-maid thrice remov'd.
>
> > (*Ibid.* [italics mine])

The scene continues in this vein with each messenger speaking progressively more simply. Brome manages to indicate his rising approval of the three speakers (it is the first appearance for the subplot characters) by having all of them suitors to Doris, who comments on them as they approach. Thereby the illusion that their language is being increasingly commended as it simplifies itself is conveyed. Finally the favored, Verillus, inquires merely, "How fares her highness" (*ibid.*, p. 109).

Criticism of the inflated language of courtier drama is not confined to the subplot. When Philargus is granted his first major audience with the Princess he essays the fashionable compliment after he has been welcomed most simply by her.

> *Philar.* Princely Madam,
> > That language from your gracious lips is powerful
> > To save him from the grave, that onely lives
> > By your free favours.
> *Eud.* Nay, my dear *Philargus*
> > I thought me nearer to you, then that you
> > Should rove [*sic*] at me with Courtship.
> >
> > > (II, i, 113–14)

She explains to him that Stratocles, the villainous politician and courtier, conducts his suit in such language; so Philargus responds

> therefore Madam, by your fair command,
> [I resolve] To avoid all Court-circumlocutions.
>
> > (*Ibid.*, p. 114)

One of the principal comic scenes in the play relates directly to this problem. In the subplot Geron, tutor to the twins and son to Garrula, the Queen's midwife, occupies the role corresponding to Stratocles in the main plot. That is, he is the third and least favored suitor who tries to secure his suit by the application of pressure. He is a "tag-line" character of a kind rather frequent in Brome. He cannot speak without the phrase "So *Whilome* said . . ." he is "all for Apothegmes" (I, ii, 102). His whole role is devised in ridicule of heavy, learned analogy and false-wit. His mother, Garrula, knows that the Queen is not the mother of one of the twins and therefore holds power over the Queen. Garrula pressures the Queen into favoring her son's suit with Doris. An interview is granted. Geron prosecutes his suit in fly-blown courtly phrases.

> *Ovid* by his *Corynna* sweet, said o—
> She comes, she comes. My joyes do overflow.
> (III, i, 122)

Doris dutifully listens but is completely at sea,

> He cloaths his words
> In furres and hoods, so, that I cannot find
> The naked meaning of his business,
> (*Ibid.*, p. 123)

Geron still stumbles learnedly along, finally frightening Doris. "It is some horrid thing/That you desire, and are asham'd to speak it" (*ibid.*, p. 123). The Queen, gentle, patient, and commonsensical, has to assume command, saying to Geron,

> *Geron*, you speak too learnedly, as if
> You woo'd a Muse: And *Doris* understands not,
> (*Ibid.*, p. 124)

Again in this scene the point of the whole dialogue is the ineffectuality of unnatural language in pursuing normal goals. There is a further rich comic reference in the frightened inference drawn by Doris (and obliquely seconded by the dramatist) that the end of courtship can only be obscured, not altered, by elegant circumlocution. Suckling himself had described the "Platonic" court fashion of endless love talk as designed merely "to enhance the price of kisses."

Brome employs a third means of ridiculing the language practices of the courtier romantic dramas. These dramas virtually abandon the laws of the medium. The simple principle that the function of dia-

logue is to advance the action, develop the theme, or to illuminate
motive is utterly overthrown. One of the principal students of this
courtier drama has described its dialogue well.

> Drama lapses and action comes to full stop while the characters weave their
> fine spun disquisitions . . . often we might think we were reading pages from
> a conduct book in dialogue. The discourses of the characters are not exclusively,
> or even principally, about platonic love; all phases of love are treated, of
> courtship, of jealousy, of honor—but all artificially and within a pitifully
> narrow range.[20]

Brome's burlesque of this kind of anti-dramatic dialogue can be
well illustrated from the play. He creates a situation in which this
practice is ludicrously exposed through the fatuous long-windedness of
the twins. At the climax of his action, he follows the scene of the foolish duel between the twins with a court scene where the King decides
that the time for his daughter's marriage is upon them. He will not
wait. The choice must be made. The King speaks to the point:

> The time for my *Eudina's* match draws near,
> And I no longer will attend on fortune . . .
>
> (IV, iii, 150)

In the following scene Disanius, dispatched from the court, hurries in
telling the twin brothers,

> The King expects your quick return, and will not
> Let pass this peremptory day, set down
> For matching of his daughter; to preserve
> Life, State, or Kingdom.
>
> (V, i, 152)

The cause is urgent and the time for quick action upon them. What do
the brothers do? They continue their debate on the properties of love
and friendship which goes like this:

> *Philar.* Can a bliss
> Be purchas'd with your absence? No: 'Twil fortune
> Equally in fruition as in want.
> Were it a Kingdom onely, we could part it
> Without the quarrel of the *Thebean* brothers,
> Or, were it heaven itself, *Castor* and *Pollux*
> Should be our imitation. But *Eudina*
> Is only indivisible.

[20] Alfred Harbage, *Cavalier Drama*, p. 37.

Philoc. Add to it this,
  Their sentence is erroneous, that deny
  Partition to the soul: For ours do witness,
  Friendship can give her a division,
  And make reciprocal community
  Of all her faculties. But still *Eudyna*
  Is indivisible.
      (*Ibid.*, pp. 151–52)

Disanius expostulates and berates them and they agree to draw lots. After the lots are drawn, they are still moved irresistibly to talk their fortunes away. Philocles draws the losing lot and graciously surrenders his right but Philargus is puzzled.

  But how can you forgo that equal interest
  You have with me in *Thessaly*, and *Eudina*.
      (*Ibid.*, p. 154)

Disanius exasperatedly interjects

  Why should that trouble you? You see he does
  Forgo't; and is a going. Would he were gone once.
      (*Ibid.*, p. 154)

But Philargus stubbornly refuses to be satisfied with such an empirical reply. "Can love allow't," he asks. Philocles, true to the code, has a ready similitude.

  Variety of objects
  Like Nails abandon one another. So
  May I, by novelties of Travail, lose
  The thought of Love; and chearfully return
  Both hers and yours in a more just relation.
      (*Ibid.*, p. 154)

They have sufficient sentimental momentum to keep this up for some time, but the point is clear. Brome has Disanius on stage with them, urging them to hurry, for his sole function is to get them back to court quickly. By using Disanius as a commentator, the ludicrous action-impeding quality of their theorizing is forcibly established in the minds of the audience. It is an efficient exposure device with Disanius here, as elsewhere, serving as an author-tool in directing the critical response desired from the audience.

Finally, in marshaling the evidence that this play, far from being in Harbage's phrase, Brome's "tribute of imitation" to the new cavalier fashion, is rather a detailed and thoughtful burlesque of this very fashion, a few words should be said about the attitude toward women. It is a commonplace that love in the conventions of Shakespeare's age could easily slip over into idolatry. If one adores a woman for her own sake he is guilty of idolatry.[21] It is equally true, as many critics have pointed out, that there was an increasing tendency in the seventeenth century to exalt woman, particularly at the court of Charles I. The platonic love cult made man subject to woman and continually used religious imagery to express its feelings for feminine beauty.[22] There

[21] It is not necessary to go to religious tracts, commentaries, or sermons for a concise statement of this. Bacon in his essay "Of Love" sums up the traditional attitude neatly, "It is a poor saying of Epicurus, *Satis magnum Alter Alteri Theatrum sumus*, As if Man, made for the contemplation of Heaven and all Noble Objects, should do nothing but kneel before a little Idoll, and make himselfe subject, though not of the Mouth (as beasts are), yet of the Eye, which was given him for higher Purposes. It is a strange Thing to note the Excesse of this Passion, And how it braves the Nature and value of things, by this, that the speaking in a perpetual hyperbole is comely in nothing but in love" (*Bacon's Essays*, ed. by A. S. West [Cambridge University Press, 1908], pp. 26–27). A "perpetual hyperbole" is, incidentally, a fine descriptive phrase for the sort of play Brome was burlesquing. One other citation will be useful. In a preface to a play of approximately the same date as *The Love-sick Court*, Peter Hausted is trying to explain how he could have portrayed a woman-hater before ladies whom he should have labored to please: "how shall we hereafter dare to bring upon the Stage a *Bawd*, an *Vsurer*, an *Intemperate* man, a *Traytour*, or one that commits *Idolatry* to his *Mistris* (which is as good a sinne as most of these) if onely to *personate* be to *approue*?" (*The Rivall Friends*, 1632).

[22] Out of a wealth of instances a few chosen from various dramatists will illustrate the kinds of excess they were given to. T. Killigrew is probably the worst offender. In *Claricilla* (*c.* 1636) Melintus, the hero and worshiper of Claricilla, dislikes the idea of killing the villain Seleucus (note again the continual religious imagery) because, "I am asham'd to think this necessity forceth me to offer one so lame in honour, and in passion blinde, to the power I worship [i.e., Claricilla]; for the imperfect are not fit for sacrifice" (*ibid.*, III, vi, 28). In *The Princess* (*c.* 1636) he perhaps carries it as far as it can go, where Virgilius, the hero, is pleading with Cicilia, the Princess who wrongly imagines he has killed her father. The plea is shockingly like a religious mystic's prayer, "Oh, Divinist, stop not your mercy, but let it fall here; your eyes are full of pity; let that precious dew drop upon my thirsty heart, and save me, ere despair hath licked all my life thence; Turn not away, but look upon me as I appear in repentence, in the whitenesse of my tears, in their Innocency, in my Souls love to *Cicilia*, strewed upon the Earth in submission" (IV, vii, 46). Cf. also similar religious transference in the same play, I, iv, 14–15; II, ii, 22; IV, ii, 31, *et passim*. There are other plays in which idolatrous affections are rationalized or dissected; e.g., in Robert Mead's *The Combat of Love and Friendship* (*c.* 1638) Lysander, the hero, makes a normally inflated profession of his devotion and is answered by his Mistress, "Sir, that Devotion which adores the Image/May chance perswade It self, that through that Image/It worships the true Diety: but yet/Must Excuse others that do still suspect it/As very like Idolatrie, if not It,/ . . . Sir, take heed least your Idolatrous love,/Passe not so truly through the fictitious object,/As still remain there" (I, i, 7 [1654 quarto]). Thomas Randolph in *The Jealous Lovers* (1632) has his hero berate himself for one ill thought of his beloved, "Away foul sin.—Tis Atheisme to suspect/A devil lodg'd in such divinity" (I, iii, 6–7 [1643 edition]). It would seem that the cult was already literary material as early as 1629 and that by around 1636, it was beginning to wane. It is impossible to be exact. There is no question, however, as to the prevalence of the fad, the religious images it used, and the absurdities it was guilty of. Brome had an ample target.

is an effeminacy of attitude through the literature of the Cavalier period just as there is in the music, painting, poetry, and novel at the French court of Louis XIII. The simplest way for a man of anti-new-fangled sympathies to explain this bent (and to express his objections to it) is to illustrate how this veneration of women is virtual idolatry.[23] Brome put speeches in the mouths of the twin brothers which are so explicitly idolatrous that they require no comment. In the overall context of the play, they are additional evidence of his disapproval of the mode and his condemnation of the "love-debate" fad. A few instances from the play will suffice to make this clear.

Philargus argues the case with himself showing that he understands clearly what orthodox morality requires.

> So glorious is that love [i.e., of woman], so necessary.
> But, where it rules and is predominant,
> It tiranizeth; *Reason* is imprison'd;
> The *will* confined; and the *memory*
> (The treasury of notions) clean exhausted;
> And all the sences slavishly chain'd up
> *To act th'injunctions* of insulting love,
> *Pearch'd on the beauty of a woman.* Thou
> Masculine love, known by the name of friendship
> Art peaceful and morigerous: But that
> Of woman, is imperious and cruel.
> Why should I then lose *Philocles* for *Eudina?* Ent. Eudina
> Why? Can I look on her, and ask a Reason? . . . *reading a letter*
> O *the divinity of woman!* sure
> *There is no heaven without 'em.*
>
>   (II, i, 113 [italics mine])

The beginning of the speech repeats in clear almost syllogistic form the argument against surrendering one's reason to the evidence of the senses (in this instance the perceived beauty of woman). The argument is properly posed and he is drawing the right conclusion when Eudina appears and he, perceiving her beauty, throws over all reasoning deliberately and extols the *divinity* of woman—literally equates

---

[23] Brome elsewhere expresses his contempt for courtier idolizing of women. In *The Novella* (1632), Piso, the *raisonneur* of the play, scorns love affectations, "I thinke with scorne upon such poore expressions,/And am above the art of *Amorists*,/That Cringe and creepe by weake degrees of Love;/To Kisse the hand, the Cheek, the Lip, then cry/O Divine touch!" (III, i). In the same play, in a sequence comparing national modes of courtship he has the "French cavalier" laud his hoped-for mistress in standard inflated rhetoric and receive the reply, "Good sir beware idolatry." He continues to flatter her, whereupon she pretends that his language is insultingly low for a courtier. He is upset and says, "No Courtier Lady?" (III, i).

her with God.[24] Let us not misunderstand what is involved here. Brome is not asking of the audience a monkish condemnation of his hero, but he is trying to make it as clear as possible in the theological terms of his time that Philargus has willfully and knowingly rejected the firm counsel of his own informed reason, and he has given as his excuse the divine power of feminine beauty. In the context of the play this is merely another reminder that this is a foolish love and foolish conduct may be expected.

Philargus admits in the presence of Eudina that his own powers of choice are enslaved. He pleads when asked by his mother, the Queen, why he tarries when she has asked him to accompany her.

> I may not stir,
> When she [i.e. Eudina], whose power above me countermands
> The precepts of the Gods requires my stay.
>
> (II, i, 116)

Philocles tries to match this (again notice the religious imagery),

> To say I love you, Madam, with a zeal
> That dares to meet the tryal of Martyrdom,
> And suffer't for your sake, might get a name,
> A glorious and an immortal Crown:
>
> (*Ibid.*)

When Eudina expresses a preference, Philargus typically replies,

> The Gods have spoke it in you; it is their
> Divine injunction; Madam, I obey it.
>
> (III, iii, 130)

and Philocles swears his oath:

> By the same Beauty
> (Then which no greater subject of an oath)
> I swear to be your nuptialls sacrifice,
> Be you the Priest.
>
> (IV, ii, 142)

The use of religious imagery relating their love for the beautiful Eudina more and more closely to veneration and adoration, the regular

---

[24] The most profound demonstration of this process in the literature of the era is Shakespeare's *Troilus and Cressida* where the outcome of the play turns on the self-conscious rejection of soundly reasoned conventional moral judgments. Cf. especially Hector's argument (II, ii, 53–193) and Troilus's pivotal speech, "Oh that I thought it could be in a woman" (III, ii, 165–77).

attribution of divinity to her, the willing surrender of themselves to her choice and rule weaves a texture of idolatry. This is a minor strand of the play but the direction in which it moves converges with that of the other evidence.

The evidence of Brome's intention has gradually piled up in the course of analysis of the text. A recapitulation of the contributing elements will reinforce the original claim that the play has been mis-read by previous students, and that it is a burlesque, not an imitation of the prevailing Caroline fashion of proto-Heroic drama. Brome's intentions are apparent in the burlesque subplot, in the censure of the wise counsellor Disanius, in the detailed stage directions, in the satire on courtier speech and in the identification of the love of the twins with an idolatrous confusion of values. The play is clearly a detailed and well thought-out burlesque of the pretentious, woman-worshiping, undramatic, and overwritten plays of the courtier dramatists. Their values, dramaturgical skill, and control of language are all questioned and satirized. The previous opinion, that the play was a capitulation on Brome's part to a set of fashionable conventions he everywhere else objects to must be rejected. The play, understood as a burlesque, is altogether consistent with Brome's practice and with his reiterated beliefs. It is also better drama when seen for what it is. It furnishes more evidence that in the theater, as in society, he is a clever, good-humored but unrelenting conservative. The play stands as a capable instance of criticism as mimesis, or, put more modestly, it reminds us again that effective parody and thoughtful burlesque are complex critical acts creating as they destroy.

VIII

USURY AND BROTHERHOOD

In addition to his advocacy of good sense and respect for tradition in the theater, Brome developed conservative social theories in his plays. In *Covent Garden Weeded* (1633) Brome argued for an ethic of restricted paternalistic state interference in a society rapidly being polarized into militant and mutally intolerant factions. His carefully projected belief in the ordered society, with specific social responsibilities attaching to one's status, informs *The Queen and Concubine* (1635?). Economics, as a separate, specialized discipline in the sense it is understood today, was only coming into existence in the seventeenth century; this development is itself another symptom of the breakdown of the cohesive, fully interrelated society in which Brome believed. Generally, in the older view economic activity, and hence discussions of that subject matter, were merely a facet of the larger problem of social ethics. So it is in Brome who sees the usurer not in terms of a necessary money source for a rising capitalist economy but as a type of social vice, and offender against reason, love, and humanity. *The English Moor* (1637) and *The Damoiselle* (1638) develop the same usury theme in quite different ways and will furnish the subject matter of this chapter.

Usury was a major economic and social question in England for many centuries.[1] The problem was argued about with special intensity during the sixteenth and seventeenth centuries under the pressure of the Reformation, the expanding commerce of the growing nation states and the increased circulation of money following the discovery of new lands. By the latter half of the seventeenth century the traditional opposition against usury had been completely undermined by the new mercantilist economy and the new devotion to private interests and the cash-nexus.[2]

[1] See Benjamin H. Nelson, *The Idea of Usury* (Princeton, 1949).
[2] The best treatment of this transitional phase is Richard H. Tawney's long, lucid introduction to his 1925 edition of Thomas Wilson's *A Discourse upon Usury, 1572*. Ernst

With the historical record we can see that religious leaders, conservative moralists, and most literary men continued to oppose their "stale arguments" to this trend long after such means ceased to be of any avail. They did not, however, know the future. Happily, they could not foresee their coming defeat; so they continued their opposition in the readiest, most comprehensible terms they had available.

A good many years after the triumph of an economy which made money bear money, Jeremy Bentham, who gloried in this outcome, wrote in his *Defense of Usury*,

> It is the business of the dramatist to study and to conform to, the humors and passions of those on the pleasing of whom he depends for his success. . . . Now I question whether, among all the instances in which a borrower and a lender of money have been brought together upon the stage, from the days of Thespis to the present, there ever was one, in which the former was not recommended . . . and the other, the man of Thrift, consigned to infamy.[3]

If Bentham's logic is correct, one has to assume that prior to 1642 an overwhelming majority of the audience joined with the playwrights in an unqualified opposition to usury. It is obvious that the attitude toward the money economy is different in eighteenth-century drama from what it had been in the seventeenth. It became increasingly necessary to add other vices to that of taking of high interest on money to make the usurer into a suitably detestable stage villain until finally, in the melodrama of the nineteenth century, the usurer was metamorphosed into the foreclosure of mortgages who tried to disrupt an otherwise happy prospect for young lovers. The point is that the abstract vice lost its edge and had to be bolstered up for stage presentations by gratuitous and arbitrary additions of other vices which were not necessarily associated with it at the outset of the modern period.

The usurer was a man who did not conform to the informing ideals of the static medieval society—a society based on notions of common

---

Troeltsch, *The Social Teaching of the Christian Churches* (London, 1931), 2 volumes, is invaluable as background for any study of this problem: see particularly I, 312–28, and II, 461–500.

   [3] Quoted by A. B. Stonex, "The Usurer in Elizabethan Drama," *Publication of the Modern Language Association*, XXXI (1916), 190. See also his "Money Lending and Money Lenders in England during the 16th and 17th Centuries," *Schelling Anniversary Papers* (New York, 1923), pp. 263–85. Celeste T. Wright in two articles, "Some Conventions regarding the Usurer in Elizabethan Literature," *Studies in Philology*, XXXI (1934), 176–97; and "The Usurer's Sin in Elizabethan Literature," *Studies in Philology*, XXXV (1938), 178–84, makes a fully annotated study of the characteristic traits assigned to the stage usurer up to 1642.

purpose and brotherhood.[4] He expected to gain returns for no personal services rendered. He demanded rights for serving no beneficial function. He was for himself in a society that professed to live by a code of mutual effort.[5] His whole code ran against the notion that money (like other mutable treasures) was for use and not to be enjoyed or valued as a thing in itself. These things are well known but they should be repeated, so that it becomes evident why the usurer was the logical figure to single out as a scapegoat, if you will, or as a point of maximum irritation and disease in the dying body of medieval social thought.[6]

In the drama then the usurer was a favorite type.[7] One critic cites forty-five plays ranging in date from the late morality, *Respublica* (1553), to Brome's *The Damoiselle* (1638), in which he appears with more than an incidental part.[8] Stonex derives him from medieval descriptions of avarice which approximate closely "the physical appearance, the dress, and the personal habits of the usurer."[9] It is further argued that once the conventions were established, the usurer did not change as an object visualized in the minds of the people who wrote about it.

In belletristic literature between 1540 and 1640, we find crystallized conventions about the moral question of usury. The enormous changes in business life and in economic thought made no perceptible dent in this stubborn traditional doctrine.[10]

[4] Bishop Jewell, the most eloquent of religious leaders in his opposition to usury, says, "What are the fruits of usury? 1. It dissolueth the knot and fellowship of mankind. 2. It hardeneth mans heart. 3. It maketh men vnnaturall, and bereaueth them of charity, and loue to their dearest friends" (quoted by John Blaxton, in *The English Usurer* [1634], p. 16).

[5] "Christians must serue one another in loue, and not themselues alone in selfe-loue: both which principles are directly contrary to the very trade of the Vsurer; for he makes sure for himselfe to haue a part onely and infalliably in the profit, and therefore serues himselfe alone, and not also his brother." Mr. Wheatly, a churchman, quoted by Blaxton, *The English Usurer*, p. 39.

[6] Cf. Nelson, *The Idea of Usury*, pp. 1–27 *et passim*, for his description of the transition from the medieval "Universal Brotherhood" to the modern (Calvinistic) "Universal Otherhood;" and R. H. Tawney, *The Acquisitive Society* (London, 1920) particularly the second chapter, "Rights and Functions." Cf. also Lionel C. Knights, *Drama and Society in the Age of Jonson* (London, 1937), pp. 1–95 and pp. 200–27.

[7] There is interesting direct testimony in Peter Hausted's "Preface to the Reader" in the 1632 edition of his play *The Rivall Friends*. Defending his practice in presenting a woman-hater type before an audience including many ladies, Hausted to make his point conveniently lists some of the principal current comedy types, "how shall we hereafter dare to bring upon the Stage a *Bawd*, an *Vsurer*, an *Intemperate* man, a *Traytour*, or one that commits *Idolatry* to his *Mistris*, (which is as great a sinne as most of these) if only to *personate* be to *approue*? ... when we act a *vice* it is not because we *allow* of it, but rather labour to *extirpe* it by shewing the odiousnesse of it to the world."

[8] A. B. Stonex, *Publication of the Modern Language Association*, XXXI (1916), p. 191, *n*. 3. Stonex says that he found seventy-one plays concerned with usury, in twenty-six of which "the usurer is an unimportant character or his usuriousness is incidental or even doubtful."

[9] *Ibid.*, pp. 192–93.

[10] Celeste T. Wright, *Studies in Philology*, XXXV (1938), 178.

If the traditional doctrine would not be "dented" by change it was ultimately burst into pieces by the irresistable pressure of the new opportunities for wealth. The conservative playwrights, not being bred in a twentieth-century environment which only now begins to realize the corruption wrought in the human spirit by uncontrolled exercise of the profit-seeking drives, could not see their opposition as anything but proper, even necessary. So long as the medieval Christian system of moral sanctions remained intact in the minds of literary men, their traditional opposition to usury was formed by these sanctions and their arguments prescribed by them. The playwright's moral function was to refer present conduct back to that system, for thereby the monstrousness of the usurer's activities were more eloquently and meaningfully condemned than by any novel arguments he could provide. As a playwright his function was to present the vice in as unfavorable a light as he could, which usually meant embodying it in a character unattractive, destructive, and unserviceable to society. If he did this he had dispatched his function as a conservator of decency and justice.[11] The playwrights did not usually fail in this respect. But there is another way in which they did fail even while seeming to hold out against the pressure of the new economy.

The failure may be detected in the gradual encroachment of sentimentality and sheer farce upon their presentation of the usurer. When the playwright rolled out all the old (and rightful) objections to usury and sent them forth to battle, there were dual temptations. The first and less dangerous was to make the character of the usurer farcical, i.e., make him merely eccentric and ridiculous for personal reasons rather than reprehensible and comic for his failures to comprehend the relative values of things. The other danger, and the one that vitiated many efforts to effectively satirize the usurer on the stage, was that from a sense of the inadequacy of his traditionally conceived opposition to halt the trend, or from a deeply felt wish that he might destroy the threat, the playwright sentimentalized the fable and the figure. He made the usurer into a monster who suddenly repented, usually through an appeal to his human sentiments by which tribal harmony was quickly restored. So long as this practice was followed the dramatic presentation of the usurer could serve no social purpose. The audience could fore-

---

[11] Bishop King speaking on the necessity of striking out against usury says, "If vsury bee too stiffe to bee moued, yet we must free our soules, and if it were possible we would also free them that are wrapt in their snares" (quoted by John Blaxton, *The English Usurer*, p. 50).

gather and temporarily join in the fictitious belief that by such sentimental methods as this the threats of the new economy symbolized by
the usurer could be met and overcome. To contrast the closing scenes
of *The Merchant of Venice* or *Volpone* with some of the later plays
demonstrates clearly the failure in contact with reality such a sentimental evasion of issues entails.[12]

Just as the figure of the devil, as imaged in the mind, may not in itself change much over long stretches of time even while men's *attitudes*
toward that figure may become more fearful, skeptical, off-hand or
scornful, so the figure of the usurer might remain conventional in form
and detail but take on a different specific gravity in continual usage
during changing times.

Brome was the last of a long line—which includes nearly every
major Elizabethan dramatist—to treat the usurer as a major character.[13] In two of his plays written very close together, *The English
Moor* (1637) and *The Damoiselle* (1638), satire of usury plays a major
part. There was at about this time a spate of plays which placed the
usurer (or closely related economic extortionist) at or near the center of

---

[12] Sentimentality, when it is an informing influence during a whole artistic period, is
inevitably sustained by some philosophical assumptions, or, to put it less formally, it reflects
agreed assumptions about the nature and *meaning* of social life. In the two principal studies
toward an understanding of the use of sentimentalism in English literature (particularly in
the drama) we find the following working definitions: "Confidence in the goodness of average
human nature is the mainspring of sentimentalism" (Ernest Bernbaum, *The Drama of
Sensibility* [Boston, 1915] p. 2); and "Sentimentalism . . . I take to be merely facile, and
usually shallow, illogical emotion" (Joseph Wood Krutch, *Comedy and Conscience after the
Restoration* [New York, 1924], p. 192).

Bernbaum's discussion is more carefully developed theoretically, but both authors do a
very inadequate job of appraising the role of sentimentalism in pre-Restoration drama: see
Bernbaum, pp. 27–48; Krutch, pp. 1–23. I look on sentimentalism primarily as an improvised
attempt to fill the ethical vacuum left at the dissolution of the structure of sanctions felt and
referred to in a sacramental universe. It is an ego-oriented system cultivating private rather
than public reactions. Beginning in desperation it culminates in a kind of pseudo-toleration of
greed and malpractice invoking twin standards of rationalization: (1) I have no right to judge;
and (2) to mean well or to seem to mean well is the equivalent of doing well. It displaces the
critical intellect. Comedy, as a critical instrument with an appeal beyond the transient
demands of an audience seeking entertainment, is dramatically opposed in spirit and theory to
sentimentalism. A study of this aspect of English comedy based on a rigorous conception of
what an audience seeks from the drama could illuminate the historical evolution of the drama
from the Restoration through the nineteenth century. The new dispensation of power after
the Restoration and throughout most of the eighteenth and nineteenth centuries was able
completely to "fog over" the mirror dramatists held up to nature. Sentimentalism is the
death of critical realism—is opposed to it in nearly every sense. A new study of this phase of
English drama is badly needed.

[13] None of the special students of the usurer convention has noted that Sir John Frugal,
in Massinger's *The City Madam* (1632), is quite sympathetically portrayed though he is
qualified on all other counts.

the action.[14] Both of Brome's plays have rather elaborate intrigue plots but the burden of the plays, that which makes them distinctive, is the exposure of usurious motives. The intrigues are so designed as to deal with and discommode the usurer.

The earlier play, *The English Moor, or the Mock Marriage*, is sentimental and gives less space to the old man, Quicksands, described in the Dramatis Personae as "an old Vsurer," than the character Vermine has in *The Damoiselle*. There is, however, in the treatment of Quicksands, a number of revealing particulars which gives an insight into the use of the convention on the Caroline stage.

Brome's *The English Moor* (though not the more serious *Damoiselle*) is sentimental, because Brome himself has not really grounded the issues. He is dealing with a problem of social concern—the depredations wrought by the economic self-seekers in the community. But the treatment is artificial, contrived, and misleadingly easy. Brome tampers with psychological probabilities in order to flatter and relieve his audience. The play is designed to ridicule the old usurer Quicksands as an agreeable means of retaliation against the social forces he represents.

Old Quicksands is a usurer but is only indirectly exploited as such. Brome takes advantage of the accumulated dislike of the usurer-type (and the consequent repertoire of theatrical labels to indicate this type) in order to escape the need for a careful characterization. In short, he can appeal to available prejudices through stereotype hints and suggestions. The audience registers the hints, and their own associations complete the characterization. They do part of the author's work for him.

Quicksands is described as "The bottomless devourer of young Gentleman . . . By three-score i' the hundred" (I, i, 3); "the grave patron of Arch-cosonage" (I, ii, 6); "that unworthy *Quicksands* (Devil take him)" (*ibid.*, p. 9); by Millicent who sings a song about a Lady who "lov'd a swine"[15] (I, iii, 13); and as "That villain, old in mischief

---

[14] The plays run from Jonson's *The Magnetic Lady* (1632) to these two plays of Brome's and include Massinger's *The City Madam* (1632), Marmion's *A Fine Companion* (1633), Cartwright's *The Ordinary* (1635), and Shirley's *The Constant Maid* (1636?), as well as two earlier plays first published in 1633: Massinger's *A New Way to Pay Old Debts* and Rowley's *A Match at Midnight*. Add to this John Blaxton's *The English Usurer* (1634), which is a kind of commonplace book of quotations from all the divines who have spoken against usury in the previous hundred years. The concentration of so many plays on a similar theme into such a short period is rather impressive.

[15] Turner points out that the swine was a conventional emblem for the usurer. This epithet is used again in III, ii, 43. The frontispiece to John Blaxton's *The English Usurer*

(Hell take him)" who is liable to maltreat his young wife and "either work her death By poyson, or some other cruelty" (II, i, 24); "that *Babilonian* Tyrant Quicksands" who is too stingy to buy more than "a penny pot of Muscadine"[16] on his wedding day (III, ii, 42); and "the old *Jew*" and "this Rascal" (III, iii, 45 and 46). This might be described as the method of "medley-portraiture" with nearly every character adding a stroke or two. The important thing is that Quicksands as portrayed on the stage does not justfy at all the severity of the terms used to describe him. The kind of criticism that limits its vision to recurrent employment of conventional materials has to be expanded to encompass the total disposition of such materials within a particular play and the gradually different ends to which conventional means are applied.

The fact that Quicksands is a usurer is mainly a means of shorthand characterization. About all such shorthand character notations tell us is that we are not meant to receive him sympathetically. As the play progresses other disagreeable facts about him are adduced to secure the justice of his final chastisement. The simple, dominating, and (in traditional terms) inhuman attachment to gain that delineates a Shylock is no longer sufficient. By the time all the spirited younger characters have used up a busy plot tormenting and tricking the old man we find him quite transformed, for Quicksands, who started as the conventional type of the usurer, has actually been trapped, evaluated, and condemned in other terms—as an ungenerous master, as a lustful and adulterate beast—rightly punished as the father of an idiot bastard. This lust we find in the summing up is "an old vice grown in him from his youth."

The English Moor yields a double caution, then, in the study of type-characters or exploitation of theme through character. The portrayal escapes mechanical interpretation. Brome rather cleverly exploits the stereotype prejudices towards the usurer to get his play underway, but

---

(1634), is a drawing of a usurer paralleled by a rooting pig. They are paired together by a "posie" (cartoon strip style) saying "Mine is the Vsurer's desire./To roote in the earth, wallow in Mire."

[16] Critics have been known to object to the seemingly sloppy practice of equating misers with usurers in plays. The convention is sound. Quoting from Aquinas (*Summa*, II, ii, 118, 4) O'Brien explains "avarice . . . he defines as 'superfluus amor habendi divitias.' Avarice might be committed in two ways—by harbouring an undue desire of acquiring wealth, or by an undue reluctance to part with it–'primo autem super-abundant in retinendo . . . secundo as avaritem partinet superabundare in accipiendo' " (George A. T. O'Brien, *An Essay on Medieval Economic Teaching* [London, 1920], p. 74).

he finds them inadequate (without more careful thought on his own part) for drawing the cumulative emotional response he requires. He therefore adds on other vices essentially irrelevant to the original type conceived in a narrow sense. The action of the play is conducted in terms other than the condemnation of the usurer's social or economic viciousness. The play suggests that although a playwright could expect the usurer to be unsympathetically received, the economic vice by itself was not sufficient to render a man villainous in the eyes of his audience unless extended analysis were undertaken.

That a critical comedy of the same period could exploit the usurer-type in very different fashion is evident in Brome's *The Damoiselle*. Although it has some superficial similarities to *The English Moor*, it is much more thoughtful and better constructed. Brome works out a set of parallels, some ironic, around the central theme of the proper attitude toward goods. He weaves the play together very tightly by analyzing the consequences of the fear of *loss* as well as the consequences of the greed for gain. He reexamines the bonds of human relations in his attempt to reanimate the crucial concept of brotherhood the validity of which the usurer ultimately challenges by his practice. Though the play is called a comedy, it is what the twentieth century would call simply a drama.

As traditional Christian ideas about usury began to break down there was much wordplay and equivocation in discussions of it. There were morally dubious concessions to the realities of the new economics. There were laborious and strained arguments to justify the inevitable. These concessions were made in particulars but did not reach the heart of the doctrine that the best traditionalists continued to cling to. Here is the way the best historian of usury describes it:

However one might be inclined to assess the ethical character of their writings, one must acknowledge one decisive fact: not even the most accommodating of the casuists presumed at any time in the medieval period to call in question *the historic assumption that the taking of usury was antithetical to the spirit of brotherhood*. The proliferation of casuistry may have taxed the credulity of conscience, but both conscience and casuistry *clung tenaciously to the myth, if not the reality, of universal brotherhood* [italics mine].[17]

Though Nelson is commenting here on the sixteenth-century canonists and their seventeenth-century probabilist descendants in professional

[17] Benjamin N. Nelson, *The Idea of Usury*, pp. 26–27.

apologetics, the passage is illuminatingly useful when applied to the English dramatists of the first half of the seventeenth century. Gradually, in them, the extensive meanings of the traditional opposition to usury were pared away or equivocated. But the clear-eyed among them did not sacrifice the informing principle—the idea of brotherhood. This is one point. The other merely extends this into the future. Nelson's thesis in his excellent study is succinctly stated.

In short, Western morality after Calvin reaffirmed the vocabulary of universalism, refused to concede that God could authorize or equity allow us to treat the Other differently from the Brother, assimilated the Brother to the Other, and eventuated in the Universal Otherhood. In modern capitalism, all are "brothers" in being equally "others."[18]

This stresses the way in which the doctrine of brotherhood was effectively cut off from its real meaning. Unable and unwilling to reject outright the formal morality of Christian brotherhood with its bonds of mutual responsibility and charity, the intellectual conscience of the early modern era gradually translated the content of the traditional morality into new terms, deeply opposed in spirit to brotherhood but with its inclusiveness and form. Such specious, self-interested exactions are commonplaces of the historical process whereby the mind gains what the conscience is unwilling to grant. It is important to remember in the study of the drama that such stealthy translations are best accomplished without reference to concrete human relations. Drama by its nature must observe concrete human relations, or it must embody the issues motivating a period in the concrete terms of actors acting. In *The Damoiselle* Brome essays to put the issue of usury squarely in terms of brotherhood, that is, in terms of father–son, father–daughter, man-to-man relationships and to make clear that goods cannot rightly take priority over the bonds of love. The figure of Vermine, the usurer, stands squarely in the middle of the play and all the action is in some way related—thematically or otherwwise—to his reeducation.

The play opens with Vermine on stage making a usurious transaction. The recipient of the money is Sir Humphrey Dryground, an old Knight who acts throughout the play as the organizing force in the reeducation of Vermine. The first scene pitches the key for the play and in its constant reiteration of matters of money, property, and

[18] Benjamin N. Nelson, *The Idea of Usury*, p. xxi.

goods defines the image-pattern of the language. The very first lines of the play are:

Ver. You have your Money; full a thousand pound, *Sir Humfrey Dry-*
ground.
Dry. And you have my Mortgage.   (I, i)

Vermine feels compelled to deliver a pat little speech admonishing Dryground not to waste his money. They argue, Vermine saying, "You spirited men call Money Dirt and Mud. I say it is the Eele," and Dryground retorts, "And you the Mud that foster it."

They are bitter and Dryground finally reflects,

> This is the Usurers Scripture;
> And all they pretend Salvation by:
> To give good admonition with their Money;
> Though, in their hearts they wish the quick subversions
> Of all they deal with. This is all they plead
> Against the curses of oppressed soules:
> Did not I warne you? Did not I say, take heed?
> And so, and so forth. I must thank you Sir.[19]
>
>   (I, i)

Then follows an interchange between them which lays out the shape of the subsequent action.

Vermine asks what the borrowed money is going to be used for. Dryground replies and in so doing restresses Vermine's character.

> my Project is in the behalfe
> Of the poor Gentleman, you overthrew
> By the strong hand of Law, Bribes, and oppression;
> *Brookall:* Do you know him Sir? Whose state you suck'd;
> That wrought him to a poverty that cryes
> Your sinfull Covetise up to the heighth;
> And renders you the Monster of our time,
> For avarice and cruelty.
>
>   (I, i)

By this speech Dryground accomplishes two primary things. He introduces Brookall, the main passive figure in the play, and he associates Vermine's success as an extortionist with the corruption of the law—

---

[19] This perversion of friendship is singled out by John Blaxton when he says, "the vsurer lendeth like a friend, but he couenanteth like an enemy, for he claspeth the borrower with such bands, that euer after he diminisheth, as fast as the vsurer encreaseth" (*The English Usurer*, p. 49).

the symbol of economic order and authority—thereby broadening the base of the social criticism in the play. Brome uses various means to emphasize this *complicity* in guilt.

It is then necessary for plot purposes that Vermine retort, "*Brookall* had a Sister, whom you vitiated/In your wild heat of blood, and then deny'd Her promis'd Marriage" (I, i). Dryground responds honestly to this *tu quoque* evasion of responsibility, but he makes a legitimate moral distinction that is fundamental to the subsequent action of the play. He says he is sorry for his sin of youthful passion and means to expiate it if possible, whereas Vermine's coldly calculated destruction and "Inhumane cruelty is inexpiable: Unlesse . . . thou tak'st a speedy course/To give him threefold restitution . . . regaine a Christian reputation,/Till age shall lead thee to a quiet Grave." Vermine replies, "You have your Money" (I, i).

The plot follows Dryground's ingenious policies of restitution. He seeks to relieve Brookall and Brookall's son, and to find the daughter of his youthful illicit union with Brookall's sister. He reforms the corrupted son of Vermine; frees Vermine's daughter from her father's jealous control and sponsors her marriage to young Brookall. He unifies the efforts of all the characters towards the conversion of Vermine to decency and generosity, both by his example and by his skill as tactician. He controls the plot in the same way that Duke Vincentio controls *Measure for Measure*—nearly every character is morally reoriented through his agency.

Valentine, Dryground's son, has just married the daughter of an old Justice, Bumpsey, without the latter's knowledge. This group of characters is introduced in argument over the marriage settlement. Valentine has no money but is heir to his father's title. The two parties in the argument represent, respectively, the new country gentry on the way up the social scale (in Bumpsey), and the older landed nobility being deprived of its holdings by the lawyer–usurer combine of the new economy. That this was Brome's deliberate intention is made amply clear by a long harangue from Bumpsey, a garrulous but not meanspirited character, on his now disrupted chances to have married his daughter to a man with land and money. When Dryground objects that this suitor was "Perhaps no Gentleman," Dempsey interrupts with,

> Yet honourable, Land-Lordship's reall honour,
> Though in a Trades-man Son: when your faire Titles

Are but the shadowes of your Ancestry;
And you walk in 'em, when your Land is gone:
Like the pale Ghosts of dead Nobilitie.

(I, ii)

Becoming positively eloquent he swings into a long recital on the land:[20]

where's the Land you once were Lord of? Ha!
The goodly Cornfields, Medows, Woods, and Pastures
That must maintain the House, the Gownes, the Coach,
With all by complements of Horses, Hawks and Hounds.

(*Ibid.*)

And so after many such lines he charges Dryground with bad husbandry of his substance contrasted to Bumpsey's own wealth, "Which I have got by thrifty Industry" (I, ii). The antitheses is simple and editorialized but clear. Valentine responds that his father-in-law should keep all his money, "And as you finde my regular life deserve/Your future favour, so extend your bounty" (I, i). Bumpsey refines on this by agreeing to split his money with the following aim,

Now marke; if you increase,
Or keep that halfe, then, doubtlesse, I shall do,
As well with tother for you: If you diminish
Or waste all, ile do the like with my part.

(I, i)

He ends his proposition with a solemn, biblical warning, "But (heark you) do you remember 'gainst the evening?" (I, i).

This scene shows how explicitly the play is couched in terms of money and property—a degree of emphasis exceptional even for this period. It also develops one of several father–children relationships that contrast sharply with Vermine's attitude toward his children. Whereas Bumpsey's attitude toward his money, and through it toward his children, is merely humorous, Vermine's parallel outlook is serious and vicious.

Vermine is early presented with his marriageable daughter in a most effective scene. He asks her what is evidently a routine question.

---

[20] Reminiscent of Middleton's prose poems on the land by city new-rich in *A Trick to Catch the Old One* and *Michaelmas Term.*

> Note my care
> Pil'd up for thee in massy sums of wealth;
> Too weighty for thy weak consideration
> To guesse from whence it came, or how together
> So layd in mountainous heaps.
>
> (I, i)

His daughter, then, in a tone of mock-naïvete, ironically exposes his craft by returning the Calvinistic cant prevalent in contemporary justifications of the new economy. She says all economic matters are strange to her

> But my duty
> Perswades me twas your thrift, and that great blessing
> That gives increase to honest Industry,
> Drawne on it by your prayers and upright life,
> That wrought these heaps together.
>
> (I, i)

The effectiveness of this irony is made further apparent when Vermine's professed motive for amassing wealth, his care for his children, is brought out for examination. Vermine flatters his daughter that she is the only child he cares for, her brother being "an utter stranger . . . a Wolfe That teares my very bowells out." His daughter in an aside interpolates, that is, "Your money." Vermine gloats over his son's imprisonment for debt and swears that if his friends bail him out he would "force him to a tryall for his life" to recover "two hundred Peices" from him (*ibid.*). Such are Vermine's relations with his son. As one might expect, Vermine wants to force his daughter to marry a foolish country knight whom she later privately describes

> he got his Wealth by, casuall Matches;
> Of forty, fifty, and sometimes a hundred
> For one. When bounteous Fortune (seldome failing
> Men of his Brain) cast all into his mouth,
> The Gudgeon gap'd for. And how slight a thing
> It is, for such base Worldlings to be rich?
> That study nothing but to scrape and save.
> That have no Faith, but in their ready money,
> Nor love to Worldly pleasures above those
> Poor Coblers use.
>
> (I, i)

Obviously the kind of man her father would choose, and it is equally clear that her condemnation of the suitor is implicit criticism of her usurious father. She expresses privately her defiance of her father.

Here Dryground enters in as the manipulator of the lives of other characters. He bails Vermine's son Wat from jail and sends him to aid his sister to escape. Wat persuades his sister to flee with him by saying of their father

> He loves a stranger better then's owne Childe:
> And that mans money, better then that man,
> The Devill 'bove all
>
> (I, i)

Such then is the love of Vermine's children for him.

Since the shaping of the play depends on Dryground's management of the other characters, it will be necessary to outline his scheme. He borrowed money from Vermine and with it did three main things. He bailed out Wat, Vermine's corrupted son, and by employing him set about redeeming him. He rented a tavern as a base where, disguised as a merry host, he could hide out Vermine's daughter and raise money for other purposes. He sent his son with money to relieve Brookall, the man whose sister he had victimized. Since Brookall's bitter experience has rendered him touchy, Dryground has to provide Valentine with strategems to persaude him to take the money. It is unnecessary to relate the many embellishments Brome gives the plot. The point is that Dryground's activities (again, like Shakespeare's Vincentio) reach into all the subplots and orient all the characters. It is revealed at the end that Dryground's beneficent activities have reached even further than we realized, since he has tricked Vermine out of his daughter at the same time he is making restitution to his injured friend Brookall by aiding his son to a love-marriage with her.

Parent–children relations are obviously important in the play. Brome carries the theme into further parallels and combines their use with other thematically relevant materials. The mutual devotion of the elder and younger Brookall is exemplary and needs no comment. The devotion of a daughter to mother is heavily, even sentimentally, exploited. The daughter is a beggar girl; in reality Dryground's bastard by Brookall's sister though this is not immediately apparent. She is willing to beg to support her mother. Brome uses her neatly to add weight to the picture he presents of Vermine's unregenerate nature. When Vermine is seeking intelligence of his escaped daughter, he walks by the law courts. The beggar girl approaches him asking for alms. In a long set sequence he not only refuses but curses her despite her advice "make not Thy money such an Idoll".[21] (II, i). The effective staging of this scene would score indelibly against Vermine in the minds of the audience.[22] This is particularly true since Brome sandwiches it between Brookall (now reduced to destitution) directly accusing Vermine of destroying him, and Brookall's imprecations against the corrupt law that had abetted Vermine's evil schemes.[23] The stage medium is exploited by having mutes dressed as lawyers cross and recross the stage in pairs—only stopping once to try to hire the destitute Brookall to perjure himself in a suit (the association of Vermine's and his lawyers' methods is clear). The dramaturgy of this scene is complicated and mature, combining purely thematic materials with action doubly and trebly serviceable to the plot structure.

Brome follows up this sequence on the perversion of values by devising a scene in which Brookall can, seemingly by the way and indirectly, state the traditionally proper attitude toward goods, that they are the gifts or loans of Fortune. Thinking his son is dead, Brookall is made to say, not piously but as if he wanted to forestall routine consolations:

> Nature sent us
> All naked hither; and all the Goods we had
> We onely took on Credit with the World
> And that the best of men are but meer borrowers:
>
> (II, i)

[21] Bishop Downam, "The Vsurer sinneth by Idolatrie. For seeing the roote of vsury is couetousnesse (which is the roote of all euill) it cannot bee denied; but that every Vsurer is couetous, and euery couetous man is an idolater *Eph.* 5.5. And a Seruant of *Mammon, Mat.* 6.24. And therefore no true Seruant of the Lord, now you must remember, that for couetous persons and idolaters, there is no inheritance in Heauen" (Blaxton, *The English Usurer*, p. 26).

[22] The purpose of this scene is more specific than the modern reader might realize, since Vermine's sin is unnatural greed for money its opposite virtue would be almsgiving which is defined by Aquinas as "an act of charity through the medium of money" (*Summa*, II, ii, 32, 1). Cf. O'Brien (*Medieval Economic Teaching*), p. 80, who quotes Aquinas further, "There is a time when we sin mortally if we omit to give alms—on the part of the recipient when we see that his need is evident and urgent, and that he is not likely to be succoured otherwise—on the part of the giver when he has superfluous goods" (*Summa*, II, ii, 32, 5 ad. 3). Cf. O'Brien, *Medieval Economic Teaching*, p. 83.

[23] Brookall's speech contrasting the present law, "More false and mercilesse then Dice or Strumpets; That hast into thy Hydra-throated mawe Gulp'd up my lives supportance," with "That Law, once called sacred, and ordain'd For safety and reliefe to innocence, Should live to be accus'd in her succession, And now be stil'd Supportresse of oppression; Ruine of families" (II, i, 408) recalls Middleton, and further stretches the plane of applicability of the play. The corruption of the order that makes the law partner to the activities of a Vermine is the "Ruine of families" in more senses than one.

Brome, by this means, achieves direct contrast to the cash-nexus morality of the prior scenes without employing the undramatic direct piety that disfigures Massinger's plays.

Dryground continues his role of reeducator by so manipulating Vermine's reprobate son that Wat accepts him as a father. Wat, after joining forces with Dryground, falls in love with the Damoiselle, not knowing that she is in reality a man. Wat, thinking that Dryground is using the inn as a brothel and that the Damoiselle, his alleged daughter, is a genteel whore, desires her fervently. Dryground uses this base motive as a control over Wat. Wat reacts favorably and honors Dryground as a substitute for his own father, "that Old Wretch, my Father," telling Dryground "Had I been Your Son now, how I could honour'd you! Though I had kept a Precept by't "(III, i). Dryground, while not directly encouraging this misconception, goes along letting Wat and various town gallants believe that he is indeed a pander for his own daughter. There is much incidental comment such as "Can there be such Fathers?" (III, i), and "canst thou be so base to sell thy Childe To Lust and Imprudence?" (*ibid.*), and on the infamy of one "To betray his Childe" (*ibid*). All this contributes to the thick texture of parent–child relationship on which the play builds.[24]

The other gallants find, before Wat does, that the Damoiselle is virtuous and, thinking that Wat is a pimp who has coerced her into this unflattering role, punish his impudence by kicking and ducking him. He sees his folly, and Dryground, who has built up the situation to make him appear a pimp, says that he has cured him homeopathically by urging

> him past his Nature.
> He was so free in's Villany, that I
> Giving the Spurs, ran him beyond his speed;
> Quite off his legs, and glad to be led home.
>
> (V, i)

Directly related to the study of father–son relations is the theme of goods and the loss of property elaborated through the play. Vermine, the usurer, has lost his daughter; Brookall's son has diappeared; Dryground has lost his "wife" and daughter. Their various attitudes to-

---

[24] In fact Dryground (disguised as inn-keeper) avows that he will give his daughter as the prize in a lottery. This is a false proposition, but the ironic parallel between this and the practice of fathers like Vermine who auctioned off their daughters to the highest bidder would probably have been clear to a Caroline audience.

ward their personal loss present substantial clues to their characters. We have already seen Vermine's attitude towards his children. His fear is exclusively that his daughter will marry a beggar and that he will lose money by it. Brookall takes his loss hard but with dignity. Brome provides a neat internal parody of the improper attitude toward loss through the foolish country knight, Sir Amphilus, the miser chosen by Vermine for his daughter's hand. His sole role in the play is to wander around bemoaning the loss of his horse, mistress, and dog, all three of which he levels to one value. He speaks in jingling rhyme. A sample:

> Three Losses I have had; gone, past all help.
> My Mare, my Mistresse, And (which grieves me most of all) my Whelp.
> (III, ii)

His commonsensical servant interpolates gruff reminders like this,

> I pray beare it as well as you may:
> And set not your heart too much upon transportable things.
> (III, ii)

Amphilus's role makes no sense except thematically. He accomplishes nothing and influences no one. He contributes as a thematic foil to the building of Brome's dramatic point.

Brome returns in the fourth act to the area near the law courts— again the lawyers cross and recross silently in the background. Brookall, rugged and destitute, still seeking justice, addresses the audience direct as Vermine approaches: "See the *Vermine* That hath devoured me living" (IV, i). This sets the scene and the key for the collective frontal assault on Vermine by the sympathetic agents of Dryground. Valentine, Dryground's son, leads the attack.

> Can all thy Gold redeem thy good opinion,
> To thine owne Son? And though thou wouldst no [*sic*] give
> to save his life,
> A Hangmans Fee . . .
> Yet may this Son survive thee; and hourely he
> Unto thy last houre, thine Affiliction be. . . .
> Hadst thou a vertuous Childe (as here and there,
> Some Mothers win a soule) it would be taken
> Dead or alive from thee . . .
> that's thy Daughters case. . . .
>
> What corrupt Lawyer, or usurious Citizen,
> Oppressing Landlord, or unrighteous Judge,

But leaves the World with horror? and their wealth,
(By rapine forc'd from the oppressed Poor)
To Heires, that (having turnd their Sires to th' Devil)
Turne . . . Prodigals . . .
All wanting either wit, or will, to save
Their fatall Portions from the Gulfe of Law . . .
    and Luxury,

                                        (IV, i)

Brookall swells the chorus,

His tainted wealth
Got by corruption, kept by niggardise,
Must flye as ill, through Luxury and Riot:
I add, that they who get it so, shall leave it,
To run at the like waste, through their succession
Even to the World's end: tis not one age,
Though spent in prayers, can expiate the wrong
Such an estate was gotten by, though the estate
Be, to a doyt, spent with it: But it shall
Fly like a fatall scourge, through hand to hand;
Through Age to Age. . . .
mingled with the curses
Of hunger-bitten Labourers; whose very sweat
Thou robst them of. . . .
Whose marrow thou hast suck'd; and from whose bowels,
The nourishment was crushed that fed thee, and
That ravenous Wolfe, thy conscience. . . .
untill, at last,
All hands, affrighted with the touch of it [Vermine's tainted wealth]
Shall let it fall to earth; where it shall sinke
And run into a veyne of Ore, shall reach . . .
To Hell. And they, that shall, hereafter, dig it,
Hundreds of Ages hence, must all compound
With the grand Lord o'th Soyle, the Devill, for't.

                                        (IV, i)

The long quotations[25] should serve to clarify several points. The
violence and heat of the speeches indicate that the usurer was a scape-

---

[25] I have collapsed several consecutive long speeches. In the play these angry attacks take
several times as many lines. They are violent and instinct with hatred. This speech should be
compared to Bishop Jewell's address to the usurer, "How darest thou looke vpon thy Children? Thou makest the wrath of GOD fall downe from Heuen vpon them. Thy iniquity shall
be punished in them to the third and fourth Generation. This thou knowest. How darest

goat. All the resentment directed toward the corrupt combination of the law and the holders of fluid wealth—against money itself—is heaped upon his symbolic head. The usurer's maleficence is seen primarily in terms of its destructive influence on human relations—the progressive moral corruption of the generations as they succeed one another. The cash-nexus is seen truly, if with wild anger, as inimical to human ties.[26] To peg home his point, Brome duplicates the earlier begging scene and again Vermine refuses to give alms to the beggar girl.

The plot now rolls swiftly toward its conclusion. Valentine finally persuades the upright Brookall to take the needed money Dryground has sent him, but not until Brookall has demonstrated motives diametrically opposed to those of Vermine. Valentine, who has delivered the money, comments admiringly on Brookall's extreme scrupulousness,

> Was ever given Gold so weigh'd and try'd?
> What Lawyer, Nay what Judge would be so scrupulous?
> No want corrupts good Conscience: Nor excess
> Allaies in bad, the thirst of Gov'tousness.
>
> (IV, ii)

Dryground's beneficent role of educator and reworker of consciences is set clearly by his ability to arrest the terrible destructive cycle of vice passed down through the generations. In these terms his deliberate policy of reforming the usurer's son and helping the usurer's daughter to a marriage of love (the question asked is, "Was Love your chiefe Instructor to this Marriage?" [V, i]) as well as direct reformation of Vermine himself becomes meaningful. When in the end all have achieved a proper attitude and consequently their desserts—families have been united—follies purged, Dryground simply says, "This binds us all into a Brother-hood" and creates "the Heart of Friendship, not the Face" (V, i). It is not a routine conclusion. Within the limits of his powers, Brome has vindicated human relationships against unnatural attachment to goods only. He has constructed a

---

thou looke vp into Heauen? Thou has no dwelling there: . . . Because thou robbest the poore; deceiuest the simple, and eatest vp the Widowes Houses: therefore shall the Children bee naked, and begge their bread: therefore shalt thou and thy riches perish together" (Blaxton, *The English Usurer*, p. 19).

[26] It is here that Brome approaches most closely to the Jonson of the late plays of *The Magnetic Lady* and *The Staple of News*, particularly in his tendency to make money evil as a thing in itself.

dramatic fable to explore parallel aspects of a complex theme. The diagnosis is traditional but carefully directed so that the play has an essential thematic integrity which translates a problem of great contemporary concern into the medium of drama. By showing that usury literally subverts the family and the hierarchy of loyalties which makes for the good community Brome resurrects the ideal of brotherhood, the very heart of the anti-usury tradition.

IX

SUCKLING'S NEW STRAIN OF WIT

Brome's next to last play, *The Court Beggar* (1640), is sometimes
thought to be another conventional intrigue comedy from the decadent years of the Elizabethan drama. Actually, however, it shows
how the stage may be used to register a sharp political protest through
detailed personal satire of specific public figures. Our absorption in this
proceeding is intensified by our independent interest in Brome's satiric
victims, Sir John Suckling and Sir William Davenant.

The destructive fun Brome makes of these two is related to the
"second war of the theaters" being waged between the courtiers and
the professional dramatists, as well as to the rising anti-Cavalier sentiment which was one of the unapprehended tremors of the coming
rebellion. Harbage has described Brome as the spokesman for this anti-
Cavalier faction which, as a group, had to resent the fact that the
amateur court dramatists were giving their plays away and also wooing
the jaded Caroline audiences away from professional competitors by
the expensive novelty of elaborate scenery and costume.[1]

Brome sarcastically attacked these encroachments in the prologue to
his popular 1638 comedy, *The Antipodes*:

> Opinion, which our Author cannot court,
> (For the deare daintinesse of it) has, of late,
> From the old way of Playes possest a Sort
> Only to run to those, that carry state
> In Scene magnificent and language high;
> And Cloathes worth all the rest, except the Action,
> And such are only good those Leaders cry;
> And into that beleefs draw on a Faction,
> That must despise all sportive, merry Wit,
> Because some such great Play had none in it.[2]

[1] Alfred Harbage, *Cavalier Drama* (New York, 1936), p. 154.
[2] Quoted from *The Antipodes* (London, 1640).

The "deare daintinesse of it" expresses his distaste for the essential femininity of these plays; "those Leaders" and "a Faction" suggest he has something fairly specific in mind. In the same year he wrote a scoffing poem on the sumptuously mounted, 1638 folio edition of Suckling's heroic play, *Aglaura*, where he jibed,

> This great voluminous Pamphlet may be said
> To be like one that hath more haire than head.[3]

There had been a whole procession of similar courtier attempts, stretching back at least to Wat Montague's hopeless pastoral of 1633, *The Shepheard's Paradise*, yet Brome singled out Suckling's play for attack. It is a fair assumption that Suckling's impudent handling of the aged and dying Jonson in *A Session of the Poets* the prior year provoked Brome.

Even without this special provocation, it is not surprising to find Brome directly satirizing Suckling a few years later in *The Court Beggar*, since Suckling epitomized just those Cavalier qualities which Brome reprehended. This reprehension was extended to the professional dramatist, Sir William Davenant, who increasingly identified himself with Suckling and the court circle while he pushed forward his considerable ambitions for a professional theater under his own management. This made him an especially dangerous opponent of Brome's interests, an opponent to be feared as well as scoffed at.[4] Davenant had secured on March 26, 1639 (less than a year before the composition of *The Court Beggar*) a royal patent to erect a theater in Fleet Street. Despite considerable influence with powerful court figures, Davenant was forced to give up this plan for reasons we can only infer. Bentley suggests that "His agreement to forgo the privileges of his patent was probably due to protests of the housekeepers of other London theaters."[5] Whether or not this is so, it is probable that when Davenant renounced his rights to the patent on October 2, 1639, it was with the conviction that he could manage by intrigue to secure the managership of one of the going London playhouses. His aspirations

---

[3] The poem, "Upon *Aglaura* printed in Folio," appears in the front matter to *The Weeding of the Covent-Garden* in *Five New Plays* (London, 1659).

[4] Cf. Alfred Harbage, *Sir William Davenant* (Philadelphia, 1935), pp. 61–71; and Arthur H. Nethercot, *Sir William D'Avenant* (Chicago, 1938), pp. 148–81.

[5] Gerald E. Bentley, *J. and C*, II, p. 421. Bentley's conjecture is strengthened by the Heton papers (see *ibid.*, p. 684). Dated September 14, 1639, these papers show Heton trying to protect his investment in the Salisbury Court theater. He complains of "one that hath gott a grant from the King, for the building of a new playhouse wch was intended to be in Fleet Street wch noe man can judge that a fellow of or Company, and a wellwisher to those that owe the house would ev'r be an actor in."

to put on elaborate spectacles limited his choice to three theaters; the Blackfrairs, the Cockpit, or Salisbury Court.

The King's company at the Blackfriars was too powerful to be taken over. Heton's 1639 petition for clear title to sole and uncontestable governorship at Salisbury Court was evidently, among other things, a successful attempt to insure himself against Davenant's intrigue. William Beeston's Cockpit theater remained. Beeston, as the opportunistic Davenant could note, had a knack for embroiling himself in difficulties with the authorities which (sponsored by Davenant's intrigue or not) he conveniently did on May 4, 1640, when he was arrested for acting an unlicensed play which gave offense by too intimately referring to the political activities of the King, having to do with "the passages of the K's journey into the Northe, and was complaynd of by his M.tye." [6] For this offense he was committed to the Marshalsea. Less than two months later, on June 27, 1640, Davenant was the beneficiary of a letter from the Lord Chamberlain empowering him "to take into his Gou'nmt & care" Beeston's company which the Lord Chamberlain enjoins to "obey the sayd Mr. Dauenant & follow his Orders and dirrecions as they will answere the contrary." [7] This firmly magisterial pronouncement to the company appears to have been aimed at a preexistent antagonism to Davenant of which the Lord Chamberlain and, a forteriori, Davenant were aware. There are excellent grounds for believing that Beeston's friend and house playwright, Richard Brome, was the center of this resistance to Davenant. With this opposition in mind, and with a reminder of the community of interest Davenant had built up with the court circle of Suckling, Endymion Porter, and Henry Jermyn,[8] we can examine *The Court Beggar*.

The prologue to the play is the most straightforward and harsh of Brome's numerous attacks on the Cavalier interlopers into the professional theater, "those whose forwardnesse Make's them your Creatures thought" and who "write Lesse for your pleasure than their own delight." [9] Brome states his own feeling quite simply:

---

[6] Joseph Q. Adams, *Dramatic Records*, p. 66.
[7] *Malone Society Collection* (London, 1913), II, 395.
[8] For information on the subject of Davenant's friendship with these courtiers, see Nethercot, *Sir William D'Avenant*, pp. 93–96, 130–31, and 144–46; and Harbage, *Sir William Davenant*, pp. 61–71.
[9] From the prologue of *The Court Beggar* in *Five New Plays* (London, 1653). All subsequent quotations of the play are from this text.

> For of late day's (he know's not how) y'are grown,
> Deeply in love with a new strayne of wit
> Which he condemns, at least disliketh it,
> And solemnely protests you are to blame
> If at his hands you doe expect the same.

Having set forth in general terms how he feels, he proceeds to specify more particularly what he dislikes:

> no gaudy Sceane
> Shall give instructions, what his plot doth meane;
> No handsome Love toy shall your time beguile
> Forcing your pitty to a sigh or smile.

Again warning the audience to "spare To vex the Poet full of age and care," he proceeds to a censure of those courtiers who "To purchase fame give money with their Play," even saying that if they do not like what he is doing in this play "may he be a Sceane of Mirth in their next Comedye." This invitation to satirize him seems to be an indirect confession of his own intentions.

The play is set in London. It opens with the conventional device of an elderly father, Sir Andrew Mendicant, trying to force his daughter into an unwelcome match to recoup his failing estate. It closes, like all others of this type, with the daughter's successful evasion of her father's plan, her marriage to the young man of her choice, and the suitable chastisement of Sir Andrew for his presumptuous folly. The plot is highly conventional and is full of the standard intrigue and rapid reversals which are the "theatrical alphabet" of the Caroline dramatist, but a closer examination shows what special satiric content this intrigue envelope contains.

The court beggar, Sir Andrew Mendicant, is a country gentleman who, having sold his lands in the familiar Caroline fashion, is forced to hang around the court lobbying through favorites for his own rather quixotic interests. He is "begging" monopolies "by Mediators tongues . . . who Reape the crop of all, And leave you but the Gleanings" (I, i). This is what his outraged daughter, Charissa, tells him when he proposes that she permit herself to be used as a counter in this game by marrying the court favorite, Sir Ferdinando (Suckling). This combination of monopolists, projectors, and self-interested court favorites who used the too uncritical regard of Charles I as a shield for their profiteering constituted a major social problem in the years leading up to the revolution. Putting down monopolies stood first on the Committee of Grievance's list of abuses when the Short Parliament opened in the spring of 1640.[10] This event is almost coincident in time with the production of Brome's satire.

The Court Beggar is, then, a comically conceived petition for responsible government through a serious and timely attack on a major social vice, favoritism. What is more directly our concern is that Brome indicts a particular favorite, Sir John Suckling, and his associate, Sir William Davenant.

Brome does not waste any time getting after Suckling. In the first scene of the first act, Sir Andrew describes the favorite to Charissa:

> The hopes that I have for thee in the hopefull,
> Exquisite Cavalier, Courtier and Souldier,
> Schollar, (and what not!) brave Sir *Ferdinando*:
> There's a Man rising in the favour Royall.
>
> (I, i)

Shortly afterwards the servant, Gabriel, brings news that Sir Ferdinando has gone mad:

> Starke staring mad; as mad
> As you can thinke a Courtier must be
> That is more mad than all the rest.
>
> (*Ibid.*)

Brome puts this fabricated instance of madness to an interesting satiric use. When Sir Andrew asks the cause of the madness, in a passage important for the interpretation of the play Gabriel recounts the opinions of the several consulting doctors:

> 1 One finds he was ambitious of Court favour,
>   And guesses he was cross'd in some great suite;
> 2 Another takes him as he was a Souldier,
>   And losing cost and travaile in the warre
>   Must lose his wits for that. A third collects
> 3 He was a Poet that drunk too deepe of *Helicon*,
>   And turned his braine in clyming of *Parnassus*:
> 4 A fourth considering that he was a Gamster
>   Long and much favour'd, and uprais'd by fortune
>   To mountaynous heapes of Gold, conjectures, that

Some late unlucky hand or chance at play
Hath with his money swept his wit away.
(*Ibid.*)

After an incredulous interruption by Sir Andrew, Gabriel adds the opinion of the last doctor, who,

5 Has known this noble patient to have beene
An extreame Amorist, desperately devoted
Unto the service of some threescore Ladies,
And honord every one the most in costly presents,
Banquets and Verses; and thinks the disdaine
Of one or all of them have turnd his braine.
(*Ibid.*)

Early in the play we are thus furnished with detailed information about Sir Ferdinando. He is a Cavalier; he is ambitious; he is a poet; he gambles and has been highly successful at it previously; he is an amorist on the grand scale and he has been a soldier at some personal expense. We find out a little later that he is also a dandy.

Several of these attributes could be found combined in a number of court figures although the combination of youth, poet, lover, and courtier would narrow the selection considerably for the years 1639 and 1640. And when we add to the more conventional qualities allusions to unusual success as a gambler our suspicions are not only aroused but pointed. It is common knowledge that Suckling was a gambler. John Aubrey wrote, "He was the greatest gallant of his time, and the greatest gamester, both for bowling and cards, so that no shopkeeper would trust him for 6d."[11] Later he adds (this time, interestingly enough, on the testimony of William Beeston, Brome's friend and colleague at the Cockpit when *The Court Beggar* was written) "He sent his cards to all gameing places in the country, which were marked with private markes of his: he gott 20,000 *li* by this way."[12] George Garrard, writing to Thomas Wentworth then Lord Deputy for Ireland, tells him of a recent quarrel between Suckling and John Digby. He prefaces this by saying, "Sir *John Sutling*, a young Man, Son to him that was Comptroller, famous for nothing before but that he was a great Gamester."[13] We will return to Suckling's card playing later, but it is

---

[11] *Brief Lives*, ed. by A. Clark (Oxford, 1898), II, 240–41.
[12] *Ibid.*, p. 245.
[13] *Strafforde's Letters*, ed. by W. Knowler, I, 336.

clear that if one wished to single out a courtier gambler in 1639 or 1640 Suckling, by contemporary testimony, would have been a natural choice.

The "extreame Amorist" opinion of the fifth doctor is supported by a speech later in the play when Charissa's true love, Frederick, tells Sir Ferdinando (confined during his madness):

> You are mist abroad sir,
> And chiefly by the Ladies, who now want
> The Court-ships, Banquets, and the costly presents
> In which you wonted to abound to 'em.
>
> (IV, iii)

In Aubrey's short account of Suckling we find the following:

> he [Suckling] made a magnificent entertainment in London . . . for a great number of ladies of quality, all beauties and young, which cost him . . . hundreds of poundes, where all the rarities that this part of the world could afford, and the last service of all was silke stockings and garters, and I thinke also gloves.[14]

This episode in Suckling's life was sufficiently memorable to be recounted to Aubrey, and it is just the sort of ostentatious and extravagant behavior which would appeal to the satirist. Brome's highly circumstantial reference to Sir Ferdinando's service to "some threescore Ladies . . . honord every one with the most in costly presents, Banquets and Verses," is impressively close to Aubrey's account.

Brome, after bringing in the various doctor's opinions for satiric purposes, seizes upon the last opinion—that Sir Ferdinando is mad for love of a particular lady—to further the plot. This lady is discovered to be Lady Strangelove, a haughty *grande dame* who has a salon and a devoted court following. Herbert Berry points out in his excellent unpublished study of Suckling that, "with the well-known bluestocking Elizabeth Grey, Countess of Kent, Suckling enjoyed some sort of intellectual association which may have existed in 1639 and probably before. The Earl and Countess of Kent kept two households which were gathering places for literary people; one was in Whitefriars in London." [15] The play is very circumstantial and much of the action then takes place in Lady Strangelove's house where a circle of wits

---

14 Clark, *Brief Lives*, II, 242.
15 A Life of Sir John Suckling. Unpublished University of Nebraska thesis (Lincoln, 1953), pp. 242–43.

gather. Sir Ferdinando is brought there on the doctor's advice that only her presence can cure his madness.

All this exposition takes time and it is not until the third act that we see Sir Ferdinando on the stage. The entrance is impressive. He is brought in, the stage directions say, "in a chaire bound and hooded." His first speech is important:

> Am I then taken prisoner in the North?
> Wounded, disarm'd and bound? I shall be ransom'd.
> To which of your rebelliously usurp'd
> Castles ha' you brought me? you sir *Presbiter*,
> That better can *pugnare* then *orare*,
> And so abjure all duty and allegiance.
>   (III, i)

Sir Andrew explains, "Hee takes you for a Northerne Pastor Mr. Doctor." Sir Ferdinando then continues alternately threatening and pleading with his supposed captors: "use me well; and like a souldier," "And use my horse well too, and let my horse and armor Be decently preserv'd," assuring them he "shall soone be sent for, or fetch'd off With ruine of your country 'bout your eares" (III, i). The doctor tries to console him, telling him to be merry, whereupon Sir Ferdinando answers,

> Merry! why not? come lets ha' cards; and you and I to cribbidge
> For an od hundred pound, I meane not Scotch
> But sterling English pieces, where's your money?
> All gone in Ammunition and charge money.
>   (III, i)

Whipping around, Sir Ferdinando notices Sir Andrew and, wishing him included in the fun, urges a game of cards (Gleeke). He finds the "Covenanter" stakes of his hosts too meager so he cries,

> Away with cards. Bring dice, set all at hazard
> And though I lose all, I have yet a project
> That at the end o' th' war, and the great sitting
> Shall fetch all in agen. But O my Muse!
> How dare I so neglect thy inspirations?
> Give me Pen, Inke and Paper.
>   (III, i)

The scene continues as he waxes hotly eloquent about his loves and how he can deify them in his verse.

The military references are obviously to the First Bishops' War of 1639 in which Suckling served with a beautifully uniformed troop of one hundred horsemen of his own equipping.[16] (A little later in this scene, when servants come to quiet his ravings, Sir Ferdinando shouts, "Have I no troupe? Give me my horse and armes, and come a hundred" [III, i].) Suckling was unfortunate enough to have been the most noticeable coward among a wretched band at Berwick in that campaign, and this aroused scornful comment among his uncharitable contemporaries. Sir John Mennis, the doggerel satirist who was at Berwick with Suckling, gives a quotably circumstantial account:

> Sir *John* got him an ambling nag,
> To *Scotland* for to ride a,
> With a hundred horse more, all his own he swore
> To guard him on every side a.

> No errant knight ever went to fight
> With halfe so gay a bravado,
> Had you seen but his look you'ld have sworn on a book
> Hee'ld have conquer'd a whole armado. . . .

> For when the Scots army came within sight,
> And all men prepar'd to fight a,
> He ran to his tent, they ask'd what he meant,
> He swore he must needs goe shite a.

> The colonell sent for him back agen
> To quarter him in the van a,
> But Sir *John* did swear he came not there,
> To be kill'd the very first man a.

> To cure his fear he was sent to the rere,
> Some ten miles back, and more a,
> Where he did play at tre trip for hay,
> And nere saw the enemy more a.

> But now there is peace, he's return'd to increase
> His money, which lately he spent a,
> But his lost honour must still lye in the dust,
> At *Barwick* away it went a.[17]

---

[16] Clark, *Brief Lives*, II, 241–42.

[17] "Upon Sir John Sucklings most Warlike Preparations for the Scotish Warre," in *Facetiae, Musarum Deliciae* (London, 1817), I, 81–83 (originally published in 1656). For a parallel account told from the Presbyter's side, see *Vox Borealis: or, The Northern Discoverie* (1641), in the *Harleian Miscellany*, III, 235–36. Berry adds, "his colorful participation in the First Bishops' War caused . . . a blizzard of satire . . . . At least four poems were written . . . and in at least three tracts ridicule was undertaken in prose."

Brome, with his references to Scots, Convenanters, Presbyters, and usurped castles, has made apparent to the least perceptive the northern setting of this imaginary episode. With Sir Ferdinando's eagerness to gamble in any form he has reminded his audience again of Suckling's "gamester" passion. He becomes even more explicit with his reference to "cribbidge" for Aubrey tells us, "Sir John Suckling . . . invented the game of cribbidge."[18] Then, with a quick shift to Sir Ferdinando's devotion to his poetic muse, Brome added the phase of Suckling's activities by which we know him best—the coterie love poet.

> Nor will I write, nor will I emulate
> *Ovid's* smoth vaine, or *Petraks* buskined stile.
> Nor *Laura*, nor *Corinna* did deserve
> To have their prayers written in such Verse
> As i'le bestow on her that I adore.
>   (III, i)

That Suckling (though not uniquely) rejected the methods of Ovid and Petrarch in amatory verse, and that he succeeded in finding a personal idiom after some attempts at imitation of Donne, is evident to any student of Caroline verse.

So far Brome has concerned himself largely with Suckling as a self-absorbed lover, a poet, a would-be soldier, a gambler, and a ladies' man. His final attack is sharper and more fundamental. It should be remembered that Suckling was in 1640 still a very young man—only 26—and that approximately five years before he had been described to the Early of Strafford as "famous for nothing before but that he was a great Gamester."[19] He had risen quickly and on November 20, 1638, he was sworn a gentleman of the Privy Chamber Extraordinary.[20] He reached a position of too much prominence for his valor to bear in the Royal Expedition to the North in the First Bishops' War. The miserable showing of the English troops at Berwick constituted a national disgrace, and the feeling that the fiasco was owing to incompetent leadership was natural and prevalent in the atmosphere of court in 1639–40.[21] There were still many factions pressing their special

---

18 Clark, *Brief Lives*, II, 245.
19 On November 10, 1634. See Clark, *Brief Lives*, II, 242.
20 *Malone Society Collection*, II, 338.
21 Cf. Gardiner, *History of England*, IX, 36–37; John W. Allen, *English Political Thought, 1603–1665* (London, 1938), I, pp. 359–63; Cicely V. Wedgwood, *Strafford* (London, 1935), pp. 220–24; Godfrey Davies, *The Early Stuarts, 1603–1660* (Oxford, 1949), pp. 87–88.

interests and the terrifying pressure of events that would weld the Royalist sympathizers into a practically seamless unity was not yet fully felt.

In the fourth act of *The Court Beggar*, Brome has the question of Sir Ferdinando's right to his present eminence at court discussed. Frederick, the man Charissa loves and intends to marry, is planning with Gabriel, Sir Andrew's servant, a counter-intrigue to displace Sir Ferdinando. Sir Ferdinando has just attempted forcibly to seduce Lady Strangelove in whose house he has been placed in hopes of curing his "madness" by proximity to her.[22]

> *Gab.* Yet this is he
> That did aspire to be a glorious Courtier.
> *Fre.* Courtier? A meere vain glorious imposture;
> Pretending favour, having nothing lesse.
> Witnesse his want of Merit. Merit only
> It is that smoothes the brow of Majesty,
> And takes the comfort of those precious beauties
> Which shine from grace Divine . . .[23]
> (IV, i)

The discussion of Sir Ferdinando's merits continues in this same vein.

It is discovered also that Sir Ferdinando's doctor was an accomplice in the feigned madness and had recommended the staying in Lady Strangelove's house to give Sir Ferdinando a chance to attempt her rape. The doctor is disposed of in a crudely uproarious "mock-gelding" scene. The ulterior purpose of this scene is to enable Federick to adopt the doctor's clothing and enter the room of the "mad" Ferdinando. There Frederick talks bluntly:

---

[22] This reputed attempt at rape while a guest and with the assistance of another can be closely correlated to a very discreditable passage in Suckling's life in which Suckling forcibly kept the daughter of Sir Henry Willoughby in private conference under her father's roof in his attempt to wring an agreement of marriage from her. His conduct was offensive enough to require a letter of protest from Sir Henry to the King. Assisted by a friend and "vnder the title of yor Matyes sacred name," he took her for "some howers" and with a "hye hand keeping me her father from coming in" until by "vndue suggestions they had wrested from my daughter somewhat that by noe meanes they would suffer me to be acquainted with all" (Berry, *A Life of Sir John Suckling*, p. 443; from the *MSS. of the Marquis of Bath*).

[23] Ferdinando is early given ironic praise for his great merits and service. In the attempt to cajole him out of his madness, Sir Raphael, an egregious flatterer, tells him: "The Wisdome, Justice, Magnanimity,/And temperance of court you are exactly/Fram'd and compos'd of" (IV, i). When Sir Ferdinando's silliness, cowardice, and emotional instability are contrasted to these absurd claims, the satire has become pretty bitter.

They say y'are mad;
Mad with conceit of being a favorite
Before your time, that is, before you had merit
More than a tumour of vaine-glory in you . . .

(IV, iii)

Frederick gives him a further tongue-lashing and then, dropping his doctor's disguise, accuses him of selfishly and wantonly using his position at court to win Charissa away from him. An argument follows in which Frederick tries to force Sir Ferdinando to fight like a man. Sir Ferdinando does not act very courageously, even offering money to dissuade Frederick. Finally, there is this brief exchange:

> *Fre.* Now are you pleas'd, or dare you now to fight sir?
> *Ferd.* I neither will nor dare fight in this cause.
> *Fre.* This is a daring Courtier!

(IV, iii)

Earlier we saw that Suckling was accused of cowardice at Berwick —accusations that would have been fresh in the minds of Londoners in 1639–40. It is also true that there was another episode in Suckling's life which he found it hard to live down. It is mentioned by several contemporaries. Aubrey's account, though not completely accurate in detail is succinct and underscores the impression it made upon his contemporaries.

Sir John, with some 2 or 3 of his party assaults Sir John Digby goeing into a play-house, Sir J. D. had only his lacquey with him, but he flew on them like a tigre, and made them run. 'Twas pitty that this accident brought the blemish of cowardise to such an ingeniose young sparke.[24]

This taint of cowardice is confirmed by another letter: "Here at home Sir John Suckling, in place of repairing his honor, hath lost his reputation for ever."[25] The whole episode is described in some detail by George Garrard in a letter to the Earl of Strafford where he explained that the original quarrel was over the daughter of Sir Henry Willoughby whose hand Suckling hoped to obtain through court influence in disregard of John Digby's prior claim on her affections. Suckling

---

[24] Clark, *Brief Lives*, II, 241.
[25] *The Private Correspondence of Lady Jane Cornwallis; 1613–1644*, ed. by R. G. Braybooke (London, 1842), p. 197 and quoted by Bentley, *J. and C.*, I, 42, *n.* 3, where the date of the letter is correctly given as November 21, 1634.

bragged that he would win her, whereupon Digby, with encouragement from the girl herself, confronted Suckling and

> asked him, whether he had any such Promise from her as he gave out, in that
> he [Suckling] said he would not satisfy him. Mr. *Digby* then falls upon him
> with a Cudgel, which being a Yard long, he beat out upon him almost to an
> handful, he never offering to draw his Sword.[26]

There is a definite parallel between this and the dramatized incident
in the play where the girl's favorite, Frederick, resenting the unfair
use of court influence in the attempt to gain her hand, challenges the
courtier rival to fight only to have him refuse in a cowardly way.[27] It
is not suggested, however, that this is an attempt at exact point for
point portrayal. Plot demands would not permit this, and the aura of
cowardice could be suggested without exact evocation of the original
episode. This is especially believable if we remember that Suckling's
conduct at Berwick would be just the sort of thing to induce his unsympathetic contemporaries to recall this prior incident. We might
keep in mind, too, that the second phase of the quarrel, Suckling's re-
taliatory attack on Digby, took place at the Blackfriars at a time when
Brome (having just finished writing *The Late Lancashire Witches* for
the King's men) may still have been working with that company. We
can be certain that he would have heard much of the episode.

Brome had prepared for this episode in the subplot. The subplot
centers on three *types* of young men who frequent the salon of Lady
Strangelove. They are named City-Wit, Swayn-Wit, and Court-Wit.
The first is a foolish backbiter and a notable coward. In a long scene
his two companions cross-examine him on the proposition "What is
the cause to fight for?" Court-Wit states quite clearly, "You may
safely say for Religion, King or Country" (III, i). But City-Wit, by
specious logic, justifies his refusal to fight for any of these honorable
causes. (This scene confirms the sharp and central topicality of the play
since one of the primary reasons for the crumbling power of Charles I
at this time was the downright refusal of the "city" to support his
campaign against the Scots with either funds or men even when
invasion of England was threatened.[28] They did refuse to fight for

---

[26] Knowler, *Strafforde's Letters*, II, 337.
[27] Frederick tells Sir Ferdinando that Charissa was his until Ferdinando "Diverted her weake Father from the Match/To my eternall losse . . . ./like a Gentleman, i'le call ypon you/ Give me the swords" (IV, iii).
[28] See Gardiner, *History of England*, IX, 39–40, 130, and 174.

"Religion, King or Country.") City-Wit is then subjected to insults of his mother and father, buffets and kicks by his companions who are trying to find what can arouse him. Nothing does until they mention his wench, whereupon Court-Wit summarizes their findings:

> a man, whom neither Lie, Kick, Battoune, scandall, Friends, or Parents, the wrongs of Countrey, King or Religion can move, that will yet, fight for his wench

(III, i)

This set scene immediately precedes that of Sir Ferdinando's cowardly behavior. So we see that even the miserable City-Wit will fight for his wench—a thing the "glorious Courtier" Ferdinando refuses to do.

There are then numerous external reasons as well as considerable internal evidence for believing that Brome was satirizing Sir John Suckling as Sir Ferdinando in *The Court Beggar*. To recapitulate: Suckling was distinguished in a relatively small court circle as an aspiring soldier, as a successful, compulsive gambler, as a spectacular ladies' man, as an ambitious and successful favorite without accomplishment to justify his advancement, as a love poet, and as a notable coward. These are exactly the qualities Brome ascribes to Ferdinando. When we add that the two most discreditable episodes in Suckling's life—his refusal to fight a duel when beaten like a lackey and his flight at Berwick—are duplicated recognizably in the play, the probability of Sir Ferdinando being Suckling is made virtually certain.

It was stated earlier that Sir William Davenant was a friend and associate of Suckling and that he, too, had been previously singled out for satiric comment by Brome in the prologue to *The Damoiselle*. It is demonstrable that Brome extended his personal satire in *The Court Beggar* by mocking Davenant and his theatrical aspirations in the character of Court-Wit. Court-Wit, as a figure in the subplot, has little to do with the action. He is described by Lady Strangelove, whose salon he adorns, as "my speciall favorite" (III, i). He is more or less constantly in the company of his country and city counterparts; he talks projects with Sir Andrew; he chafes City-Wit for cowardice and Swayn-Wit for rudeness; and, finally, he writes a "Revells" for Lady Strangelove.

The first hint that Davenant may be under fire comes early in the play when Sir Andrew Mendicant, the court beggar, is listening to the ideas of his projector companions. One of them has devised

A new project
For buylding a new Theatre or Play-house
Upon the *Thames* on Barges or flat boats
(I, i)

On March 26, 1639, Davenant received a royal patent to build a grand new theater, but renounced his right on October 2 of the same year, probably because of the opposition of powerful theatrical factions. In the renunciation he agreed not to "frame, erect, new build or set up upon any other parcel of ground lying in or near the cities, or suburbs of the cities, of London or Westminster any theatre or playhouse."[29] If we assume that the audiences in the Caroline private theaters were becoming increasingly initiate groups, then satire of a quite subtle turn is feasible. It is conceivable that Brome was making a sly joke regarding Davenant's reliability when he implied that though he agreed not to build a theater on any *ground* in London he had not said he would not build it on the water. But even if this is not so, the reference to a grandiose theatrical building project was most likely aimed at Davenant.

Court-Wit makes his first appearance on the stage when he brings his city and country friends to meet Lady Strangelove. She is arranging an entertainment or masque for which she will need their services. Sir Andrew Mendicant joins them and asks Court-Wit about his projects:

Cou. Sir my affection leanes much to Poetry, especially the *Drammatick.*
Men. Writing of strange Playes?
Cou. I am glad I speake sir, to your understanding. And my project is that no
 Playes may be admitted to the Stage, but of their making who Professe
 or indeavour to live by the quality: That no Courtiers, Divines, Students
 at Law, Lawyers-clerks, Tradesmen or Prentises be allow'd to write
 'em, nor the Works of any lay-Poet whatsoever to be receav'd to the
 Stage, though freely given unto the Actors, nay though any such Poet
 should give a summe of money with his Play, as with an Apprentice,
 unless the Author doe also become bound that it shall doe true and
 faithfull service for a whole Terme.
Men. Here's a trim businesse towards, and as idle as the Players going to Law
 with their Poets.
Cou. I have another sir, to procure a Patent for my self to have the onely
 priviledge to give instructions to all the actors in the City (especially

[29] See J. Q. Adams, *Shakespearean Playhouses* (Boston, 1917), p. 430.

the younger sort) the better to enable them to speake their parts emphatically and to the life.

(II, i)

The satire here is of two different sorts. The first is for Court-Wit to
say something that Brome believes in (that drama should be written
by professionals)—only to have it classified as similar to the outlandish
projects already suggested to Sir Andrew and therefore equally absurd.
The problem he is trying to solve is getting his straight-forward opinions into the comedy without impeding the action or spoiling the tone.
He does this by making Court-Wit (as a portrayal of Davenant) request something that Brome himself desired as strongly as Davenant
emphatically did not. The second project of Court-Wit's is satire of a
different, more direct kind. Davenant wanted a company, and more
particularly it becomes clear he wanted Beeston's company. All Brome
has done here is to make Court-Wit express his intention in the slightly
exaggerated idiom of the monopoly seeker for "all the actors in the
City."

Through the central section of the play Court-Wit's function is to
act as a foil to City-Wit and his follies, and as a complaisant aid (he is
described in the *dramatis personae* as "a Complementer") to his patroness, Lady Strangelove. It is in the last act that Court-Wit comes in for
further specific satire. First of all he is described as being "pepper'd so
full of the watsha callums, that his spittle would poyson a Dog or a
Rat" (IV, i), an allusion unintegrated with the action of the play and,
most probably, a "plant" regarding Davenant's notorious bout with
syphilis. Aubrey, with admirable brevity, recorded the facts for posterity: "He gott a terrible Clap of a black handsome wench that lay
in Axe-yard, Westminster . . . which cost him his nose, with which
mischance many witts were too cruelly bold".[30] Once suspect that
Brome was making fun of this misfortune of Davenant's and an earlier
reference in the play becomes clear. Brome introduces some Rabe-
laisian humor at the expense of Court-Wit. After the mock-gelding of
Sir Ferdinando's doctor, Lady Strangelove asks Court-Wit to stand
guard over the doctor. The ruckus has caused the terrified doctor to
befoul himself,[31] and when City-Wit complains that he and Swayn-

---

[30] Clark, *Brief Lives*, I, 205–6.

[31] The doctor has been frightened so badly that Swayn-Wit, who is boorish and crude,
says, "The Devill fright him next for a spurging Skitterbrooke" (IV, ii). Spurging is "To
empty or relieve the bowels by evacuation," *Oxford English Dictionary*, IX, i, 712). A skitterbrooke is "One who befouls his breeches; a coward" (*ibid.*, p. 154). We recall that this is
what Suckling is supposed to have done at Berwick.

Wit have been cut off from the fun by not being asked to remain,
Swayn-Wit says, "No matter. I list not be no nearer him: no more
would my cozen had he my nose" (IV, ii). The point is that Court-Wit
cannot smell anything. Such a remark loses absolutely all point unless
Court-Wit is being played as Davenant either with facial makeup or
with the special voice quality or twang that characterizes a noseless
man.[32]

The play's concluding masque or revels were written and directed
by Court-Wit at the request of his patroness. When Lady Strangelove
orders the entertainment prepared quickly, Court-Wit tells her he has
"cast the designe for't already Madam. My inventions are all flame and
spirit."(V, ii).[33] Having made this claim with just that quiet modesty
which Brome evidently loved in Davenant, Court-Wit is made to
stand on the stage writing, "sometimes scratching his head, as pumping
his Muse," according to the stage directions, saying "Umh" as all
around him the others dance jigs and scurry about in extempore re-
hearsal (V, ii). After this mad nonsense whirls along a for a few min-
utes, the following dialogue takes place between Court-Wit and City-
Wit;

Cit. Ha' you done the speeches Mr. *Court-wit?*
Cou. I have already from the forked top of high Parnassus fetcht 'em.
Cit. And shall my wife and *Billi* boy speake 'em?
Cou. As i'le instruct you.
Cit. You write admirably I confesse; but you have an ill tone to instruct in;
    I'le read to 'em my selfe, you give your words no grace.

(V, ii)

This is doubly suggestive. If Davenant had a peculiar twang or un-
pleasing tone from his lack of a nose, the player doing the part could
imitate this defect to fine effect. Furthermore, if Davenant was working to gain Beeston's place as governor or instructor of the members of
Beeston's company who were doing the play, this burlesque of his in-
capacity would be most telling even though, as events proved, it was
inadequate to prevent his appointment.

Seen from this standpoint, Brome's reference to William Beeston
in the epilogue gains in meaning. After mocking at the Cavalier
dramatists for peddling other men's wit, Brome says:

---

[32] Two allusions are made in the play to the voice quality of Court-Wit (II, i; V, ii).
[33] This sequence may well have drawn on Davenant's very recent successes as a royal
masque writer. Cf. Nethercot, *Sir William D'Avenant*, pp. 175–81.

this small Poet vents none but his own, and his by whose care and directions
this Stage is govern'd, who has for many yeares both in his fathers dayes, and
since directed Poets to write & Players to speak till he traind up these youths
here to what they are now. I [sic] some of 'em from before they were able to
say a grace of two lines long to have more parts in their pates then would fill so
many Dryfats. And to be serious with you, if after all this, by the venemous
practice of some, who study nothing more then his destruction, he should
faile us, both Poets and Players would be at losse in Reputation.

Brome, in complimenting Beeston for his skill and experience in in-
structing actors, is doubling the criticism of Davenant's inexperience
and lack of ability as satirized in the play. There is a tone in the epilogue more earnest and forceful than Brome usually permitted himself. It is very likely that this commentary was written following
Beeston's imprisonment on May 4, 1640.[34]

In *The Court Beggar* we have seen the two main strands of Brome's
resistance to innovation and changes brought together. His generalized
distrust and censure of the new courtier with his new effeminate
values replacing the old robust Jonsonean ideals of "valour" and "public service," and his hearty disdain for amateur meddling in the sphere
of his professional craft, the theater, find identical objects in personal
satire of Suckling and Davenant, the most representative new courtier
and new dramatist respectively. Close inspection of the play has established the near certitude that Brome *did* satirize these two men; his
entire life's practice and his implicit and avowed attitudes throughout
his dramatic work make it understandable why he should have done
so.

[34] A summary of the dating evidence will strengthen this probability. The play was written
after the treaty of Berwick ending the First Bishops' War on June 18, 1639, and probably
after Beeston's play list of August 10, 1639, since *The Court Beggar* is not mentioned
(*Malone Society Collection*, II, 389–90). At the end of the Epilogue, Brome puts in a "plug"
for his own past successes: "And let me tell you he has made pretty merry Jigges that ha'
pleas'd a many. As (le'me see) th' *Antipodes*, and (oh I shall never forget) *Tom Hoyden o'
Tanton Deane* [i.e., *The Sparagus Garden*]." Both these plays were written under Brome's
contract with the Salisbury Court theater and they were entered in the Stationer's Register
on March 19, 1639/40 (o.s.) and published the same year. Since Brome was not to publish
his plays without the consent of Salisbury Court, it is not likely that he would have advertised
them from the Cockpit stage until he had established his clear title to them, that is, some
time after March, 1640. Finally, if we can assume that Brome was satirizing Davenant in
the person of Court-Wit, it seems almost impossible that he could have done so after Davenant
had taken over the governorship of the company on June 27, 1640. Therefore, I suggest that
the play was written in the winter and spring of 1639–40 and played between Beeston's
imprisonment on May 4, 1640, and the issuing of Davenant's warrant in June. It is quite
conceivable that the play and its recognized antagonism to Davenant elicited the Lord Chamberlain's order that Davenant be obeyed by the Cockpit group.

X

UTOPIAN EPILOGUE

Brome's last play, *A Joviall Crew*, though appealing and gay is not a completely joyous creation. It is a touching partial capitulation by an ageing and tired Brome to the inevitability of a new order which he could neither condone nor ignore. It shows that he, after a life of criticizing "escape," finally came to advocate a very basic variant of it.

Brome claims in his dedication to the 1652 edition of the play that it "had the luck to tumble last of all in the Epidemicall ruine of the Scene." It is a little confusing, since the title page of this carefully prepared edition states that the play was acted at "The Cock-pit in Drury Lane, in the year 1641," whereas the theaters were not closed until September, 1642. Furthermore, internal evidence suggests that the play was designed for performance in the spring of 1641. This leaves a rather long period during which Brome evidently wrote nothing new, even though he was at last working with his "most deserving Friend Mr. William Beeston" and his King and Queen's young company at the Cockpit theater. It is possible that this cessation of creative activity was a result of an old age hurried by the fall of the things he cared about. Brome asserted in his dedication of the play that it was an "Issue of my Old Age." Brome was to live on at least eleven years after the composition of this play, but this does not prove that he was not already old and tired in 1641.

Read against the backdrop of the total earlier canon and with the political and social situation of pre-rebellion England in mind, *A Joviall Crew* reads like the play of a man spent, disenchanted, and old. The play reflects—conventional opinion to the contrary—the social dislocation, malaise, and uncertainty of the last months before the theaters were posted on the growing casualty list of institutions and customs which require a stable, civilized society for their maintenance. *A Joviall Crew* is, though superficially realistic and buoyant, more profoundly escapist than the far more fantastic and remote heroic plays.

It is a minor contribution to Utopian literature, a nostalgic but not very hopeful denial of the reality of the heavily political nature of life in a society becoming rapidly more complex and impersonal. But the play does have considerable charm and theatrical variety.

Its appeal is testified to in a number of ways. It has been written about appreciatively more than any other Brome play; its stage history is the longest and most prosperous, and it has also appeared in more editions than his other plays.[1] If the play has been written about favorably, it has also been written about repetitively. It is seen as a link in the chain leading from Fletcher's *Beggar's Bush* and Middleton and Rowley's *The Spanish Gipsy* to Gay's *Beggar's Opera*. In merely theatrical terms, this is of course true, but it tells us little about *A Joviall Crew*. Speaking of the play itself, critics have usually confined themselves to a few stale remarks about its freshness: "a fresh breath of country air"; "fresh, humorous, and plausible"; "romantic, ingenious and original"; and "combining realism and romance with charming effect."[2] This is a sampling of the friendly and uninformative remarks of the critics.

This book will not undertake a full analytical treatment of the play, but I would like to express my dissent from conventional opinions of the work as lighthearted, gay, thoughtless, and full of fun. By setting up a concentrated recapitulation of the central thematic pattern of the play as reflected in the action, it can be seen that *A Joviall Crew* is virtually a social parable for the times—full of a weary disenchantment and something almost like despair for reasonable solutions of real social problems. The method is somewhat overt and direct for a work of such evident lightness of movement, but without this risk the center of the play may be missed. A full-scale analysis would run an even greater risk of crushing the relatively fragile structure under weight of concepts of primitivism, social status, and degree, and theories of freedom which are, unquestionably, elements of the play's total economy.

Brome describes in his prologue his reaction to "these sad and tragick daies" which he hopes to treat to a little mirth. But reflecting on the state of public taste in the theater, he adds,

---

[1] The mere listing of the editions of the play and of the opera derived from it given by C. E. Andrews in *Richard Brome*, p. 40, is the best testimony of the play's popularity. It lasted steadily on the stage for over one hundred years.

[2] Quotations in order from: Thomas M. Parrott and Robert H. Ball, *A Short View of the Elizabethan Drama* (New York, 1943), p. 178; A. Swinburne, "Richard Brome," *Fortnightly Review*, LI (1892), 507; Ashley Thorndike, *English Comedy* (New York, 1929), 250–51; and Andrews, *Richard Brome*, 69.

(Our Comick Writer finding that Romances
Of Lovers, through much travell and distresse,
Till, it be thought, no Power can redresse
Th' afflicted Wanderers, though stout Chevalry
Lend all his aid for their delivery;
Till, lastly, some impossibility
Concludes all strife, and makes a Comedie)
Finding (he saies) such Stories bear the sway,
Near as he could, he has compos'd a Play,
Of Fortune-tellers, Damsels, and their Squires,
Of Love and Fate.[3]

The tone of this is a good bit more complex than most play prologues, for even while capitulating by personal necessity to public taste
he, at the same time, writes an admirably concise criticism of the kind
of romantic, far-fetched, badly organized plays he had been actively
resisting throughout his career. And then, when the play is read, we
find it bears only the most superficial relationship to such plays. His
capitulation to public taste is not unequivocally sincere.

Reading the play without preconceptions, one is impressed with the
manifold reiteration of abstract concepts: freedom and responsibility or
stewardship, liberty and rule, pleasure and service, fortune and providence, law, custom, and justice. This repetition is not accidental. The
play centers on the beggars who form a community within the community—small, cohesive, autarchical, and mutually interdependent
under a patriarch (called Patrico) who rules by reasonable persuasion
not by invested power. They are,

The onely Freemen of a Common-wealth;
Free above Scot-free; that observe no Law,
Obey no Governour, use no Religion,
But what they draw from their own ancient custom,
Or constitute themselves, yet are no Rebels.
(II, i)

and

With them there is no Grievance or Perplexity;
No fear of war, or State Disturbances.
No Alteration in a Common-wealth,
Or Innovation, shakes a Thought of theirs.
(IV, i)

---

[3] All quotations from *A Joviall Crew* (London, 1652).

It takes no great effort of historical imagination to understand the specific attraction of such freedom of mind to a generation caught up in the accelerating dissension leading to Civil War.

The plot of *A Joviall Crew* calls for two daughters of an old country gentleman to run away from their father's house in order to join the beggar band. They are accompanied by their sweethearts. They leave their father's house because it is a "melancholly house," for though he is rich the house is full of "sadness" (II, i). They have some liberty there, but it is by their "Father's Rule and Government, or by his allowance" and "What's that to absolute freedom" (II, i). Once on the road they meet with Springlove, their father's "good steward," who annually strips himself of his rank and lives in poverty with the beggars. Springlove introduces them to the beggars' way of life, giving them what he calls a "Birthright into a new world" (III, i). They join the beggars and are instructed in their laws and customs based on equity and respect for individual dignity. Impressed, they join them in preparing a play to be composed by one of the beggars, "a decay'd Poet, newly fallen in among" the beggars (I, i). The poet explains his plan,

> I would present a common-wealth; *Utopia*, with all her Branches and Consistencies . . . The *Country*, the *City*, the *Court*, and the *Camp*. Epitomiz'd and personated by a *Gentleman*, a *Merchant*, a *Courtier*, and a *Souldier* . . . to our Morall I must adde two Persons, *Divinity* and *Law* . . . I would have the *Country*, the *City*, and the *Court*, be at great variance for *Superiority*. Then I would have *Divinity* and *Law* stretch their wide throats to appease and reconcile them; Then would I have the *Souldier* cudgell them all together, and overtop them all. Stay, yet I want another person . . . A *Beggar* . . . He must, at last, overcome the *Souldier*; and bring them all to *Beggars-Hall*.
>
> (IV, ii)

This isn't the play they do put on. The one they give fits in with the superficial action. Brome simply planted this to correlate with his theme. The plot described within the play is a partial sanction for reading Brome's own play as more than a mere diversion The "decayed poet's" play sketch is a neat epitome of the historical situation in England in 1641. The factions of society were falling out with each other, and efforts of law and divinity were showing a marked failure to "appease" and "reconcile" and the "Soldier's cudgell," a war, was looming as the inevitable "reconciler." Brome adds a further step—the beggar who overcomes the soldier. In the terms of the play, the beggars live in simple, unpretentious fellowship—in charity; so the "moral" can be read as meaning that only love and fellowship can ultimately restore amity, though a second more grimly ironic reading is possible. The final outcome of this sequence of dissent, factionalism, and civil struggle may be simple depletion and poverty—beggary in the more normal sense. Perhaps both are meant.

Ever since bigness has been dimly perceived as the primary fact of modern life, individuals relegated to anonymity have felt caught up in "Grievance or Perplexity," and made helpless factors, willy-nilly, in "State Disturbances" and "Alteration in a Common-wealth." Thus they sometimes see themselves victims of forms of "Innovation" that they as individuals cannot understand. Hence the temptation has been strong to revert to irresponsibility, break off into fragmentary, apolitical communities, and to go back to simplicity. If the organized community, "their father's house," is a sad house, they wish to withdraw from it. If stewardship of one's responsibilities is too confining, they wish to divest themselves of it. These movements away from formal allegiance to received social authority conventionally have had quasi-religious associations as, indeed, the beggar's group does in *A Joviall Crew*. This is not to say that Brome was consciously advocating a Mennonite or Digger movement, or that he wanted a more secular Little Gidding, but it is to emphasize that the thematic center of *A Joviall Crew* is a product of the same forces that produced and continue to produce such phenomena. The paradoxical nature of this impulse is implicit in the relation of this play to Brome's overall attitude as expressed in his plays as a whole. Believing in corporate values —in the life of the individual in the community, in brotherhood and service—he was forced, under the pressure of civil dissension and factionalism, to repudiate the very community in which he believed and to advocate allegiance to a smaller, more tractable community where the individual was not totally subsumed in larger more impersonally conceived aims. In short a community in which his conservative values would have a chance for survival. Seen in this way, *A Joviall Crew* is a meaningful culmination of Brome's career as a playwright in a theater which had a critical relation to the life of the community.

Brome's work does add up steadily to a point of view and it does possess a genuine tone that is his own. He has a consistent attitude toward the social and human materials out of which a sense of community, of decency, of sane proportion can be built. It is not too much to say that he uses his talents to translate the crucial pre-Civil War abdications and retentions of good sense into theatrical language. In doing this, he tests (and affirms the validity of) conservative values in the family, in the social heirarchy, and in the use of money as an inadequate means of establishing and maintaining public relationships between men. He carried this program through. He used his powers, first genially in *The Love-Sick Court*, and then more bitterly in *The Court Beggar*, to defend the integrity of his particular social function, the making of plays. Behind this defense, clearly enough, there is the realization that the theater is a place with a social function and that its state of health is both a symptom and a cause of the society's state of health.

Thus, Brome's work in the theater forms a kind of reduced but undistorted model of what the serious writer of critical comedy must do. He must sense, project, and test the social preoccupations of his time. His job is to keep the incessant dialogue between a society's practices and its professed aims active and public. This is precisely what Brome did. The honest immediacy with which he performed this high task is what gives a firmness and point to plays largely conventional in device and homely in language. Brome is a good minor artist, sensitive to his own limitations and with a gifted sense of social proportion. This along with his persistant good humor and his manifest liking for life and people proves, I think, T. S. Eliot right in saying that "Brome deserves to be read."

APPENDIX I

UNDIGESTED RECORDS

Birth Records

There are separate pieces of evidence which seem to converge toward a birthdate of 1590:

1. In the parish register of St. James Clerkenwell under the year 1591: "April 5 Richard s. [on] of Henry Brom." (*Register of the Parish of St. James Clerkenwell*, ed. by R. Hovenden, in *Harleian Society Publications*, Registers Series, IX [1884], 24). There are no further references to Richard Brome in this parish.

2. In a Chancery suit of 1639, testimony was given by a man who identified himself as "Richard Brome of the Prsh of St. Andrew in Holborne Esqur aged 50 yeares or thereaboutes" (Public Records Office, C24/637 #32, "Harrington vs. Leake"). The deposition is dated February 7, 1638 (i.e., 1639). It includes no further personal information about the deponent.

3. In another Chancery suit from the following year we find, "Richard Brom of the prsh of St Martin in the Feildes . . . Esqur aged 50 yeares or thereabouts" (Public Records Office, C24/638 #42, "Mortlake vs. Williams"). The deposition date is illegible, but the suit is in 15 Chas I (Easter Term).

Although there is no certainty that any of these refers to Richard Brome the playwright (there being a fair number of Bromes in Tudor and Stuart London), still the likelihood that the latter one or both of the deponents is Brome is fairly good. This would give a birth date near the conventional figure of 1590.

Marriage Records

1. In the register of St. Thomas the Apostle under 1612/13 (o.s.): "Jan . . Richarde Broome and Barbara Will" (*Harleian Society Publications*, Registers Series, VI (1881), 11). I doubt that this is our Brome, for in the register of St. Antholin Budge Row there

is the following entry for March 17, 1653/54 (o.s.); "Barbary wife to Richard Broome bur," and then in the same register for December 30, 1655: "Richard Broome bur" (*Harleian Society Publications, Registers Series*, VIII, 82, 84). The death date is too late for our Brome and it is unlikely that there were two Richard Bromes of the same evident age with wives named Barbara in Stuart London.

2. In the register of St. Dunstan's Stepney, in the year 1615: "Nov. 1 Richard Broome of Shadwell & Emm Sowe" (T. Colyer-Fergusson, *The Marriage Registers of St. Dunstan's, Stepney in the County of Middlesex*, Canterbury [1898], I, 97). The register of Shadwell is not available.

3. In the register of St. Michael Bassishaw, "Richard Broome & francis Lott wedow" dated July 8, 1616. This entry seems less likely than the others since the death of "Rychard Broome, cordwayner" is entered on September 2, 1625, for the same parish. (For the record of the marriage see G. E. Bentley, *Jacobean and Caroline Stage*, II, 389; for the burial see *Harleian Society Publications*, Registers Series, LXXII [1942], 185.) However, this death record is not conclusive since a "Mr. Broome" is listed as an inhabitant of St. Michael Bassishaw in 1638. (See *The Inhabitants of London in 1638*, ed. by T. C. Dale [London, 1931], I, 142 from Lambeth MS 272.)

4. In the register of St. Gregory by St. Paul for December 4, 1627: "Richard Broome & Joanne Dylke, L. vg" (Bentley, *Jacobean Caroline Stage*, II, 390).

5. From November 19, 1645: "Brome, Rich. & More, Anne" (*A Calendar of the Marriage License Allegations in the Registry of the Bishop of London*, ed. by R. M. Glencross, The Index Library, British Record Society, LXII [London 1937], I, 253).

Brome an Actor?

In the Lord Chamberlain's warrant books, Brome is numbered fourth in a list of the "Queene of Bohemia's Players." The record, dated June 30, 1628, reads in part as follows: "A Warraunt to sweare the Queene of Bohemia's Players Groomes of his Mates Chamber in ordinary without ffee (vizt.). Ioseph Moore, Alexander Foster, Robert Gylman, Richard Broome" (*Malone Society Collections*, III, 347). There were two more lists of this same company in the following six months, and although the names of Moore, Foster, and Gilman appear in them again Brome's does not. The company was one that evidently spent much time in the provinces and perhaps at the Red Bull (cf. Bentley, *Jacobean and Caroline Stage*, I, 190). From this warrant Alwin Thaler has argued that Brome was an actor ("Was Richard Brome an Actor?" *Modern Language Notes*, XXXVI [1921], 88–91). Thaler's argument seems very tenuous. Moore's company was in the provinces when Brome's first plays are being acted by the King's men. I can see no reason why he would have toured with an inferior company when his plays were being accepted by the best. It is hard to believe that Brome, who was vain about his professional experience, would have failed to mention his having actually acted.

APPENDIX II

CHRONOLOGY OF BROME'S PLAYS

I list here, with concise explanatory remarks, the probable order of
Brome's extant canon along with the lost plays which can be fitted in
with any probability of accuracy. I have omitted lost plays for which
we have no real information: *Wit in Madness*, *The Jewish Gentleman*,
Christianetta, and *The Apprentice's Prize*. Cf. G. E. Bentley, *Jacobean
and Caroline Stage*, III, 49–92 for authoritative comment on them.
Rather than supply full bibliographical descriptions of the quarto
texts I have made short parenthetical reference to W. W. Greg,
A Bibliography of the English Printed Drama to the Restoration, II
(London, 1951), hereafter referred to as Greg, II.

1623

1. *A Fault in Friendship*. This lost play by Brome and "Young
Johnson" is entered in Sir Henry Herbert's license book for October 2,
1623. Nothing is known of it save that it was a comedy and was
produced by the Prince's company ("one of the weaker troupes in
London at this time and seems to have been performing at the Red
Bull theatre," Bentley, *Jacobean and Caroline Stage*, III, 69). It
seems to have been a premature effort. Brome's first play to draw
attention was acted six years later and was thought by friends like
Alexander Brome to have been literally his first.

1629

2. *The Love-sick Maid*, or *The Honor of Young Ladies*. Licensed
by Sir Henry Herbert on February 9, 1628/29 (o.s.); acted at court
by King's men April 6, 1629. This play enjoyed great popular success
and is now lost.

3. *The Northern Lasse*. Acted by King's men on July 29, 1629;
published in quarto 1632 (Greg, II, item no. 463) as "it hath often

been Acted with good Applause, at the *Globe*, and *Black-Fryers*" with commendatory verses by Jonson, Dekker, and Ford. The play presents a Dekkeresque, pathetic heroine uprooted from north country and left lamenting an unwanted marriage in London. The main action and central theme concern marriage and the problem of divorce and annulment in roughly Middletonian manner. The play was very popular but was slight and immature. It has some lovely simple songs and effective provincial dialect.

1629–30 (?)

4. *The Queenes Exchange.* This atypical, imitative tragicomedy is hard to place. The title-page attribution to the King's men is contradicted by the publisher (Henry Brom) in his prefatory statement, "when 'twas written, or where acted, I know not." The play is weakly constructed and since Brome in his mature plays excells in construction, this definitely suggests an early date. It is a virtual pastiche of borrowings from Shakespeare (*Lear* and *Macbeth*), Ford (*Lover's Melancholy*), and Massinger (*The Picture*). Since the last two plays date from November, 1628, and June, 1629, respectively, and since they and Brome's *Northern Lasse* of the same effective date, treat the fashionable "love melancholy" in a way similar to that of the Northumbrian King in *The Queenes Exchange*, the latter is probably a response to this theatrical fad and perhaps a "literary" contrivance to continue his own early success. The play was published in quarto in 1657 (Greg, II, item no. 772).

1630–31 (?)

5. *The City Wit.* I suggest a date between early 1630 and December, 1631. It was probably presented by the children of the King's Revels at the Salisbury Court theater. The play has an exceptional number of boys' parts and several comic allusions to size, dignity, etc., that suggest boy actors. It is a very expertly unified comedy exposing the new orthodoxy of dishonesty in the city. It was published in *Five New Plays* (1653) (Greg, II, items no. 718–22). See Chapter IV in this book.

1632

6. *The Novella.* "Acted at the *Black-Friers*, by his Majesties Servants, *Anno*, 1632." It was still part of the King's men's repertory

in 1641 (see *Malone Society Collections*, II, iii, 398–99). The play is competent but undistinguished. The setting in Venice is unusual for Brome who seldom left England imaginatively. There is a self-conscious effort at working up Venetian local color (see R. B. Sharpe, "The Sources of Richard Brome's *The Novella*," *Studies in Philology*, XXX [1933], 69–85). The play is notable historically for quite close topical reference to wars in the Low Countries and particularly to Dutch character. It was published in *Five New Plays* (1653).

1632

7. *The Covent-Garden Weeded*. Published in *Five New Plays* (1659) (Greg, II, items no. 806–10). It is usually said to have been acted by the King's men. This may be true. It was evidently revived in 1641–42(?), perhaps by Beeston's boys at the Salisbury Court.

1633–34 (?)

8. *The Love-sick Court*. It is difficult to place exactly. The prologue indicates Brome had written several successful plays before this one and that play was evidently done by an unestablished company. I suggest Prince Charles's men in 1633 or early 1634 at the Salisbury Court. The play is a special kind of burlesque and is analyzed in Chapter VII in this book. It was published in *Five New Plays* (1659).

1634

9. *The Late Lancashire Witches*. This is Brome's one extant collaboration. He wrote it with Thomas Heywood for the King's men in summer of 1634. It is a piece of dramatic journalism built upon the exciting discovery of supposed witches in Pendle Forest, Lancashire. See A. M. Clark, *Thomas Heywood* (Oxford, 1931), pp. 120–27 for a masterful summary of the topical background about which Andrews in *Richard Brome* (p. 48) is confused and inaccurate. See also Greg, II, Item no. 494, for description of 1634 quarto.

10. *The Life and Death of Sir Martyn Skink, with the Warres of the Low Countries*. This title appears in the Stationers' Register for April 8, 1654, were it is credited to Brome and Heywood. The play is lost. I suggest it might well have been written in 1634 to match Henry Glapthorne's *Albertus Wallenstein* which seems to have been written in 1634 shortly before Wallenstein's death in that year. Brome's interest in matters Dutch was remarked in *The Novella* (1632).

1635

11. *The Sparagus Garden.* "Acted in the yeare 1635, by the then Company of Revels, at *Salisbury* Court." This we are informed of on the title page of the 1640 quarto (Greg, II, item no. 587). The play was very popular and is reported to have earned £1,000 for the company. After *Covent-Garden Weeded* it is perhaps the most thoroughly typical of Brome's plays. See Chapter IV in this book.

1635 (?)

12. *The New Academy,* or *The New Exchange.* This is usually dated 1628 on Fleay's conjectual authority (*Biographical Chronicle,* I, 38–39). It is probably the first play Brome wrote for the King's Revels company after signing his Salisbury Court contract in July, 1635. It was published in *Five New Plays* (1659). It is a proto-manners comedy resting uneasily on a base of city-comedy. It inaugurates a style that Brome stays with almost steadily after 1635. See Chapter IV in this book.

1635–36 (?)

13. *The Queen and the Concubine.* It is assigned on internal evidence (an allusion to the "Revels of his Majesty") and style to this date. I suggest specifically that it is the play promised in the prologue to *The Sparagus Garden,* "To take your graver judgments." Hence it could well have been written in the first months of 1636 before a plague closing forced the dissolution of the company in May, 1636. It is Brome's most self-conscious literary effort. It was published in *Five New Plays* (1659). See Chapter VI in this book.

1637

14. *The English Moor,* or *The Mock-Marriage.* This is Brome's first play after the long plague closing which ran nearly a year and a half (May, 1636–October, 1637). It was performed by Queen Henrietta's men in the Salisbury Court theater. For a discussion of the play see Chapter VIII in this book. It was published in *Five New Plays* (1659). There is a manuscript of the play in Lichfield Cathedral.

1638

15. *The Antipodes.* Like *The English Moor* this play was evidently composed during the plague layoff. Unlike it, it is no potboiler but is

one of Brome's most unusual plays. It was acted by Queen Henrietta's men at Salisbury Court. There was an argument about rights to the play. *The Antipodes* was published in quarto in 1640. Brome was evidently proud of this play. See Chapter IV in this book.

16. *The Damoiselle,* or *The New Ordinary.* Numerous internal allusions make a date of late summer, or autumn, 1638 likely for performance by the Queen's men at Salisbury Court. For discussion of the play see Chapter VIII in this book. It was published in *Five New Plays* (1653).

1639

17. *A Mad Couple Well Match'd.* Written for Beeston's boys at the Cockpit. The first of three extant plays which Brome (after his Salisbury Court contract difficulties) managed to give to William Beeston for production. The play has been called "the first play in the Restoration manner" by Bonamy Dobrée. It is a skillful city comedy and the most obscene of his works. Its subject is adultery, wittolry, and witty intrigue for sexual purposes. It is worth reading but requires little critical comment. It was published in *Five New Plays* (1653).

1640

18. *The Court Beggar.* Performed at the Cockpit theater by Beeston's boys. See Chapter IX in this book for a discussion of date and content which are closely related in this satirical comedy on contemporaries in court favor. It was published in *Five New Plays* (1653).

1641

19. *A Joviall Crew.* This last of Brome's plays has always been well liked. It was performed by Beeston's boys at the Cockpit. Brome describes this play in the dedication of the quarto in 1652 as an "Issue of my Old Age." It is a play about a utopia of beggars. See Chapter X in this book for a brief thematic discussion.

Brome's further preserved work includes commendatory verses contributed to the following:

Thomas Jordan, *Poeticall Varieties,* London 1637.
Shakerley Marmion, *Cupid and Psyche,* London, 1637.
Thomas Nabbes, *Microcosmus,* London, 1637.
Humphrey Mills, *A Night Search,* London, 1640.

John Tatham, *The Fancies Theatre*, London, 1640.

John Fletcher, *Monsieur Thomas*, London, 1639. (Brome edited this play for publication and contributed a prefatory letter as well as verses.)

Lachrymae Musarum, London, 1649. (As well as contributing a poem of fair length, Brome acted as editor of this collection of elegies on the death of Henry Lord Hastings. The collection includes verses by Marvell, Dryden, Herrick, Denham, Campion, and Alexander Brome.)

BIBLIOGRAPHY OF BROME CRITICISM

Adams, J. Q. "Hill's List of Early Plays in Manuscript," *Library*, XX (4th Series: 1939), 71–99.

Allen, H. F. *A Study of the Comedies of Richard Brome, especially as Representative of Dramatic Decadence*. Ann Arbor, 1912.

Andrews, C. E. "The Authorship of *The Late Lancashire Witches*," *Modern Language Notes*, XXVIII (1913), 163–66.

———— *Richard Brome: A Study of his Life and Works*. (Yale Studies in English, Vol. XLVI.) New York, 1913.

Aronstein, P. *Das Englische Renaissancedrama*. Leipzig, 1929.

Bayne, R. "Lesser Jacobean and Caroline Dramatists," *Cambridge History of English Literature*, VI (1910), 236–70.

Bentley, Gerald E. *The Jacobean and Caroline Stage*. Oxford, 1941—. Vols. I–V.

Boas, F. S. *An Introduction to Stuart Drama*. Oxford, 1946.

Cook, E. "The Plays of Richard Brome," *More Books*, XXII (1947), 285–301.

Davis, J. L. The Realistic Comedy of the "Sons of Ben," 1625–1642. Unpublished University of Michigan thesis: Ann Arbor, 1934.

———— "Richard Brome's Neglected Contribution to Comic Theory," *Studies in Philology*, XL (1943), 520–28.

Faust, E. K. R. *Richard Brome ein Beitrag zur Geschichte der Englischen Litteratur*. Halle, 1887.

Fleay, F. G. *A Biographical Chronicle of the English Drama, 1559–1642*. London, 1891. Vol. I.

Floyd, G. A Critical Edition of Brome's *A Joviall Crew*, with Introduction, Textual Notes, and Glossary. Unpublished University of Iowa thesis: Iowa City, 1943.

Greene, Robert. "Penelope's Web," *The Life and Complete Works of Robert Greene*, ed. by A. B. Grosart. London, 1881–83 (Huth Library Edition). V, 137–234.

Guardia, C. E. "Richard Brome as a Follower of Ben Jonson," *Bulletin of Louisiana State University*, XXXI (1939), 59 ff.

Halliwell, J. O. *The Poetry of Witchcraft*. London, 1853.

Harbage, Alfred. "Elizabethan-Restoration Palimpsest," *Modern Language Review*, XXXV (1940), 287–319.

Jefferson, R. H. Some Aspects of Richard Brome's Comedies of Manners;

a Re-interpretation. (Unpublished University of Wisconsin thesis: Madison, 1955.)

Koeppel, E. "Brome's *Queen and Concubine,*" *Quellen und Forschungen,* LXXXII (1897), 209–18.

Langbaine, G. *An Account of the English Dramatick Poets.* Oxford, 1691.

Martin, R. G. "Is *The Late Lancashire Witches* a Revision?" *Modern Philology,* XIII (1915), 253–65.

Miles, T. "Place-Realism in a Group of Caroline Plays," *Review of English Studies,* XVIII (1942), 428–40.

Notestein, W. *A History of Witchcraft in England from 1558 to 1718.* Washington, D.C., 1911.

Parrott, T. M., and R. H. Ball. *A Short View of the Elizabethan Drama.* New York, 1943.

Perkinson, R. H. "Topographical Comedy in the Seventeenth Century," *English Literary History,* III (1936), 270–90.

Phillips, E. *Theatrum Poetarum.* London, 1675.

Schelling, F. E. *Elizabethan Drama, 1558–1642.* Boston, 1908. Vol. II.

Sharp, R. B. "The Sources of Richard Brome's *The Novella,*" *Studies in Philology,* XXX (1933), 69–85.

Swinburne, Algernon C. "Richard Brome," *Fortnightly Review,* LI (N.S.: 1892). Reprinted in *Contemporaries of Shakespeare.* London, 1919.

Thaler, A. "Was Richard Brome an Actor?" *Modern Language Notes,* XXXVI (1921), 88–91.

Thorndike, A. H. *English Comedy.* New York, 1929.

Tieck, L. "Die Hexen in Lancashire," in *Shakspere's Vorschule.* Leipzig, 1823. I, xxxviii–xlii and 251–620.

Wagner, B. M. "Manuscript Plays of the Seventeenth Century," *Times Literary Supplement* (October 4, 1934) p. 675 (a letter about the Lichfield Cathedral Library MS of *The English Moor*).

Wallace, C. W. "Shakspere and the Blackfriars," *The Century Magazine,* LXXX (1910), 742–52.

Ward, A. W. *A History of English Dramatic Literature to the Death of Queen Anne.* London, 1899. Vol. I.

Wedgwood, C. V. "Comedy in the Reign of Charles I" (pp. 111–37), in *Studies in Social History, a Tribute to G. M. Trevelyan.* London, 1955.

Winstanley, W. *The Lives of the Most Famous English Poets.* London, 1687.

INDEX